Praise for
In Yer's Kitchen

"This is perfect for lovers of *The Spirit Catches You and You Fall Down* and *Crying in H Mart*. Mother-daughter relationships are rough country, but this author's discovery of her mother's extraordinary story in midlife offers nothing but hope. Connection is always possible."

—BETH WAREHAM,
author of *Hair Club Burning* and *The Power of No*

"After arriving here as a baby in her mother's arms and growing up American, Yia's book recounts how she reconnected with her mother and her Hmong heritage through food and cooking, as well as a newfound appreciation of her mother's simple courage and tenacity. The roots of our being are not just psychological but grow from culture, ancestry, and family lineage, and they are all the more nourishing with acknowledgment and attention."

—EDWARD ESPE BROWN,
Zen Buddhist priest, author of *The Tassajara Bread Book*

"Yia Vang's memoir reminds us of how much we can learn about our families and our cultures through cooking. Reading it, you often feel like you're right in the kitchen, which is where I always want to be! You'll walk away with a better understanding of not just Hmong cuisine but of how food can shape a whole family."

—WYLIE DUFRESNE,
James Beard Award winner,
coauthor of *wd~50: The Cookbook*

"A moving and satiating memoir rich with food, family, tradition, and most undeniably love. This book will make you hungry and feed you all at once."

—NICOLE TRESKA,
author of *Wonderland: A Tale of Hustling Hard and Breaking Even*

"*In Yer's Kitchen* serves as a cultural guide, connecting with the heart and soul of Hmong cuisine through a family's past and relationships built in kitchens across generations. Each 'recipe' feels like a love letter to Yia's culinary landscapes, preserving family, history, and memories. This memoir will leave you inspired and craving to explore your own culinary traditions."

—STEFANIE TREPPER,
chef and food writer

In Yer's Kitchen

Memoir of a Hmong Daughter

YIA VANG

soulmaker | PRESS

soulmaker | PRESS

Soulmaker Press
soulmakerpress.com

Copyright © 2025 Soulmaker Press

Cover Photo by Steven Vang

ISBN: 978-1-961064-27-0 (Paperback)
ISBN: 978-1-961064-29-4 (eBook)

Library of Congress Cataloging-in-Publication Data
Available Upon Request

Printed in the United States of America

TSUA NAM

For Mom

CONTENTS

CONTENTS

The stories and events of Mom's life are sewn together by a thin thread. There are days when she remembers them as clearly as if it were yesterday. On other days, she tells me she is losing her memory. She'd tell the same story with slight variations as details come in and out of focus. It's both age and human nature that cause us to forget and remember things differently with the passage of time.

Other times it's because I can't understand the names and words in English, so we try to piece them together with descriptions. For example, she tells me how they would cut down *nplooj nqeeb* for rooftop houses, but I have no idea what kind of tree or plant that is. Mom and I would comb through Hmong videos on YouTube to look for whatever she's referring to. On one of these searches, we came upon a documentary called *The Meo*. A few minutes into the documentary Mom unexpectedly announced, "That's our aunt and her family!" She explained the woman is Grandfather's older brother's daughter. As we continued to watch, she would point out the people she recognized. She explained that this area was where we settled after the raid in 1962 that forced Mom's village and Dad's village to cross the

Mekong River to Xaignabouli Province. We watched the documentary together. She was reliving her life. I was watching my family's history.

I piece together Mom's life, adding salt here and there to get the exact flavor that I feel she intended. I imagine what it's like to be Mom in that experience and translate the feeling the best I can. When she tells me the location of villages and mountains, they are a mystery. The names of villages, towns, and rivers are not always translated accurately, because what exists in the Hmong lexicon doesn't always match up with the Laotian or English words. It took me three years to finally locate the district in Thailand where I was born. I looked for "Mi-chi-ling" over and over until I found Mae Charim on the map and confirmed with my nephew, Chou, that we lived at Soptuang Refugee Camp. I googled the camp and found videos on YouTube with images of life there. I looked through the faces in the pictures for anyone who resembled my family members.

The Hmong language in this book is based on my dialect, Green Hmong (*Hmoob Tsuab* or *Hmoob Leeg*). If you were to Google translate the Hmong words they might not show up, as Google only translates for the White Hmong dialect, so I put the translations and meanings within the book. I included many Hmong words in here to give you a sense of the language, the culture, the time, and world that this comes from.

When a Hmong woman marries, she takes on her husband's name, becoming a part of him and his family. This is why I refer to my sisters-in-law by their titles rather than their individual names—not out of disrespect, but as a nod to our cultural tradition. Using titles acknowledges the individual's role and status. Titles also signify the responsibilities each individual holds within the family and community. The sisters-in-law hold the responsibility of the well-being of the parents. At home and during family events, all the sisters-in-law come together to ensure those gathered are well fed and nourished for the day's activities.

In the Hmong culture, stories are passed down orally, recited and retold again and again until they are committed to memory. This book follows a similar format as I tell you the story of my mother—a Hmong woman—and pieces of her life. The events in this book are based only on Mom's memories. No doubt if I were to ask another family member to recount an event, I would get a different version. The more I listen to Mom's stories and find images, videos, and text that weave together her world, the more I find pieces of myself, of Mom, and of our people—pieces that are stitched together like a story cloth taking shape in my soul.

Getting Up

Dear Reader,

When I was younger and people asked me "What is Hmong food?" I would cringe while telling them we ate freshly killed chicken at home. We would pluck and chop it and boil it into a soup with the feet and head included. I felt embarrassed by the monotonous routine of eating rice at every meal, where breakfast consists of reheated leftovers, eaten with a side of Thai chili pepper with fish sauce. There were no eggs, bacon, or pancakes, not even cereal. I didn't want to tell them that at family events we ate raw ground pork *laab* and beef stew made with gizzards, liver, intestines, and blood. The image of a shaman sacrificing a pig filled my mind. I definitely could not tell them that.

I often started my explanation with, "Well, it's not like Thai food or Vietnamese food or Chinese food. It's kinda like Laotian food but not really. It's, you know, Hmong food."

They would persist. "So, what do you eat? What are some dishes you make?"

"Rice. Pork with mustard greens soup. Chili pepper with fish sauce. Chicken soup with herbs." I kept it safe and simple.

"Herbs like basil, oregano, and thyme?"

"No, Asian medicinal herbs. I don't know what they're called in English."

And that was how I struggled my way through describing Hmong food.

In these interactions, I tried to keep as much of my heritage hidden as possible. I was ashamed of it.

At the table during mealtimes, we kids had our American dishes, and the elders stuck with their own. The elders used to tell us, "*Thaum yug laug zog, yug yuav paub mov zoo noj yog le caag,*"—When you are older, you will know the taste of good food. Meanwhile, they'd be eating sautéed bitter melon with green onion and cilantro, and *nqaj tsawg,* pork stew that included the liver and intestines, slow-cooked with a bunch of herbs and aromatics while we children stared into our bowls of hot dogs and rice with ketchup. I knew there was no way I would ever trade that for bitter melon and *nqaj tsawg.* To us, their food was from the old country. It took hours to prepare, smelled of grass and gizzards, and tasted bitter and bland at the same time.

I didn't start cooking until I was in college, and even when I did, for a long time I didn't cook Hmong food. Compared to the rich flavors of Thai and Indian food, the romantic subtleties of Italian and French dishes, and the exotic aromas of Jamaican and Ethiopian spices, my own cuisine held little interest for me. It wasn't until I was in my early forties that those hidden parts of me emerged. The food Mom implanted in my soul burst forth, inhabiting my hands, my tongue, and my nose.

I became curious about Mom's dishes. I was hungry to know how she tasted food, how she made sticky rice cakes and sugar cane syrup, or what winter squash she used for the *kua taub hau* she ate at every meal. Her *kua taub hau* acted as a palate cleanser between dishes and was a more nutritious substitute for water. I wanted to know the taste of fresh tofu made with soybeans.

She showed me how to make *nqaj qab*, chicken soup: how long to boil the chicken, how much salt and black pepper should go in it. These became the food I missed when I was away from home and the dishes I started to make to nourish my soul.

Maybe it's an age thing. Or maybe my taste buds had finally arrived, like the rice that "arrives" when it's steamed twice. But as the elders had said, I was finally waking up to the taste of good food.

Eating, for us, is more than just nourishment; it's an act steeped in meaning, a way of existing in the world. When I sat down to work on this memoir, I found that these recipes didn't start with ingredients or measurements. No, they started with memories, each dish a story I could taste—who I was with, how I learned it, where it came from. It began with the aroma that enveloped the kitchen, with Mom walking outside to her garden to gather the necessary greens and herbs, coming back with things I had grown up with but couldn't name in English. As I flipped through memories of the dishes I ate as a child and wrote out recipes, I realized that I was learning about myself, about my mother, and about my people's culture and history.

I became the food I was writing about.

So, what *is* Hmong food?

Hmong food brings us back to our true nature. It brings us home to our body.

Hmong food is the essence of the earth: simple, with nothing extra. Use everything, eat seasonally, and eat what we grow. Hmong food is not designed to tantalize the palate; it is meant to nourish and give us energy for the day. Hmong food is food from the soul, for the soul.

Hmong food restores us to our roots. It slows us down to touch and taste our food. It strips away the oil, the sauces, the heavy, dense flavors that we as a culture have piled on top of life, and takes us back to the purity of each ingredient.

When you cook Hmong food, you connect with the earth's natural cycles. Every Hmong family tends to a small patch of herbs, either in their backyard or, if space is limited, in buckets outside their front door. Using these home-grown herbs in your dishes not only links you to the soil but also to age-old traditions and the rhythm of the seasons. You feel inspired to plant a bucket of lemongrass in your yard.

When you eat Hmong food, you're consuming more than just food. You are eating the memories, the history, the courage, the strength, the resilience, and the love of a people. You can't eat Hmong food without learning something about our history and culture.

When you eat Hmong food, you become part of a lineage that passes recipes orally from grandmother to mother to daughter, connecting generations. It is a lineage whose heartbeat connects one person to the next. It is the interdependence within the community that keeps the food alive.

What began as a cookbook of Mom's recipes evolved into a memoir, one that seemed to have come from a fairy tale about a girl from a mystical land. Except that it was very real. This became a book diving into the complex, interconnected relationship between mother and daughter that can be witnessed across all cultures and throughout time. It explores the inherent challenges of these fixed identities and serves as a road map for navigating the intricate path of finding one another. This became a love story between a Hmong woman and her mother.

For my Hmong brothers and sisters, I hope it will awaken your own childhood memories and dissolve any lingering shame about who you are. It is not us who did not understand the world, nor is it us who are too "barbaric" to inhabit more civilized cultures. Rather, people do not have the refinement of heart or depth of vision to appreciate the richness of our culture. We are not meant to be boxed into a dominant culture's ideas of civilization, success, and order. We are to awaken people from their delusion and disconnection from the natural world and show them the way home.

For the non-Hmong readers, there was a time when we were connected to the earth, when life came alive with flavors and textures, simply by adding salt to a dish. The body is home, and home is the place where our soul wants to return. The Hmong way of cooking and eating is a path to rediscover that connection, reviving your senses and nourishing both body and soul.

It has been a journey for me to arrive at home. I hope the recipes and memories in this book will comfort you in your own journey home.

Lug noj mov. Come eat.

In Love with Mom

The first time I fell in love with Mom was when she shared about her trip around the world to see her eldest brother, Uncle Fang, in France in September 2008. He was terminally ill and lived out his last few days surrounded by his family at home. Uncle Fang passed away a week after Mom and Aunt Green arrived, as if he had been waiting for them to be there by his side when he crossed over.

×   ×   ×

Mom had six sisters and two brothers. She was the *ntxhais ntxawm*, "youngest daughter." Her father passed away when she was too young to form any memories of him. She was raised by her mother and her siblings, who loved her deeply.

Mom was born deep in the jungles of Luang Prabang, Laos, where the tips of the mountains disappeared into the clouds. She was born in a village that does not exist on a map. On a mountain that remains a mystery as she tells me its name and the name of the river where she fetched water. She was born at a time and place where there were no calendars, clocks, or electricity. She was born in an unknown month in an unknown year.

Mom grew up with the waning and waxing of the moon, with the cycles of the harvest seasons. One season followed another. She grew up with pots and pans as her toys, thread and needle and fabric as her writing tools and books. The acres of land where the food was grown was her playground. As soon as she was old enough, Mom walked next to her mother to the river to carry water in thick bamboo pipes strapped to her young back. Once she was capable, she joined her sisters on the farm. She tilled, planted, harvested, slashed and burned, tilled again. Cooking and sewing were her prized skills; patience and attention her most valuable assets.

Mom had no alarm clock to wake her up. Her body would naturally rise and sleep with the rhythm of each day. She stayed in flow from the moment she woke up before the rooster crowed until her eyes drooped heavily under a burning wick dipped in pork oil. In the early morning, she'd start a fire on the hearth. The fire lit up the thatched hut with bamboo walls to awaken the family. She boiled the water for the rice. With only one flame available to cook the day's meals, it was important to get an early start so that food would be ready shortly after sunrise. They ate, packed a lunch, and set out for the acres of land that needed tending. There was no rest, no checking out, no clock to tell her when to do the next thing.

Mom learned not by asking questions, but through a relationship with her surroundings. She became intimate with her environment, with the crops she planted and harvested, knowing each one by color and texture and smell and the intricate ways they told her when it was time to pick them.

This was the life Mom grew up with into her teen years, next to her mother and sisters, imitating her mother's intricate *paaj ntaub*, flower cloth embroidery, under the moonlight after a long day of harvesting, and observing her sisters in the kitchen as they prepared simple meals of mustard greens soup and rice, which she would then replicate.

The natural flow of their family life shattered when communist forces tore into Southeast Asia. Mom didn't know why we were fighting or with whom. Just that General Vang Pao was recruiting men to help him fight a war against the *Xam Lav*, Communists. She heard whispers of people called *"Meskas"* who worked with General Vang Pao. The *Meskas* were tall men with corn silk hair, and pale skin untouched by the sun. Their hands were large and clean, virgins to the soil. They wore green and brown uniforms the colors of the jungle, with long rifles slung across their backs.

"We are here to help protect your homeland," *Meskas* told us.

"We will provide you with weapons and supplies and medical care," *Meskas* insisted.

"You will have peace," *Meskas* promised. Grown men with wives and children left to protect their land, their family. Some villages dug large underground tunnels to hide fallen *Meskas* soldiers from the sky.

We had intimate knowledge of the jungle's intricate terrain. We knew the mountains, every bend and curve and river. We knew the seasons, the rain, the heat, the sun, and the moon. We were brave, fierce, strong fighters. We fought many wars. For centuries, since before the land that is now China existed, we fought for the right to live. In Laos, we were swiftly thrust once more onto the front lines of guerrilla warfare.

Months rolled into years and the men failed to return home, or returned in body bags with their rifles laid on top of them. Their sons picked up their rifles only to meet the same fate. Across the decade, the call extended to even younger recruits: thirteen-year-olds, then twelve-, then eleven- and ten-year-old boys. The death of war is etched into their eyes in faded black-and-white photos, with their rifles towering over them.

In America and the rest of the world, no one knew of the Hmong. No one knew that, in 1964, the CIA started a Secret War in the shadows of the Vietnam War by recruiting more than 36,000 men from Hmong and other minority tribes, training and supplying them with weapons for war. No one knew Hmong soldiers were cutting into the military supply lines along the Ho Chi Minh Trail to prevent the Pathet Laos (the Lao People's Liberation Army) from transporting weapons from North Vietnam to South Vietnam.

Americans were not told of the total 270 million cluster bombs being dropped into Laos every eight minutes, twenty-four hours a day for nine years. Of those bombs, an estimated 80 million did not detonate when they hit the ground. To this day, millions of undetonated bombs threaten civilians in the mountainside, particularly children playing and running through thick foliage.

Americans were not told that the government released a deadly herbicide, Agent Orange, that rained down on Laos, killing crop and vegetation but also slowly killing those who came in contact with it and leaving behind a legacy of brutal birth defects on an innocent generation.

In 1973, the United States, sensing a lost cause, pulled out of Southeast Asia. To Americans, the government was leaving a war in which it had no business fighting. But Americans did not know that the CIA was still operating in Laos. Americans did not know that the Hmong were now the primary defenders of their democracy. We didn't fight for political reasons and had no interest in worldly politics. We fought for what we have always fought for—freedom.

Americans did not hear in the news about the 30,000-plus Hmong soldiers, both men and boys, who died without receiving the recognition they deserved from a country that had promised them home, freedom, and peace. Their souls, shattered by the brutal realities of war, wandered lost and untethered through the unforgiving jungles of Laos.

Americans felt the devastation of the communist takeover in Southeast Asia, the domino effect when the Khmer Rouge captured Phnom Penh in Cambodia on April 17, 1975, immediately followed by the fall of Saigon in Vietnam on April 30, 1975, to the People's Army of Vietnam and the Viet Cong. An America that was already divided about the conflict in the first place felt the political escalation on its own home front. The turmoil was punctuated on December 2, 1975, when the Pathet Lao captured Vientiane, the capital of Laos.

But America did not know of the atrocities of the takeover by communist forces in those countries until years later. In the immediate aftermath of the Vietnam War, there was limited access to information from these countries, and the governments in power tightly controlled media and communications.

America did not know of the estimated two million Cambodians killed under the Khmer Rouge regime.

America did not know of the establishment of reeducation camps and forced labor in Vietnam.

America did not know of the persecution of political opponents and ethnic minorities in Laos.

With no more protection left, the communist Laotian government, with support from their North Vietnamese allies, issued an order aimed to exterminate the Hmong people, sparing no distinction between those who had aided the Americans and those who had not. It marked anyone of Hmong descent as a target, regardless of gender or age.

America did not know of the mass killings, executions, and reeducation camps that descended on the Hmong and other ethnic minorities. Families who escaped death in their villages often met a tragic end in the jungles, where they hid for months or years, succumbing to starvation, diseases, or ambush.

America did not know that for the next decade, a massive exodus took place, when tens of thousands of Hmong fled to Thailand in search of refuge.

America did not know that more than 50,000 Hmong were killed or drowned across the Mekong River in addition to the hundred thousand lives who met their fate at the hands of communist soldiers.

America does not know that, to this day, the Hmong in the jungles of Laos are still being unjustly persecuted, men sometimes taken from their villages never to return; villages blocked from all access to medical care, clean water, and food and left to starve, living off vegetation and wild rodents in the jungle.

Families were uprooted from their native homes and scattered across the world, like dandelion seeds carried on the whim of the wind. Uncle Fang and his family landed amidst the brick buildings and cobblestone cities of France. Uncle Xao, Aunt Bla, Aunt Green, and Aunt Ma settled in the challenging conditions of Thai refugee camps. Mom's other three sisters, Aunt Lau, Aunt Blia, and Aunt Lee, all passed away at various times in Laos.

As for Mom, now a mother and no longer a girl, after spending four years in a refugee camp in Thailand, continued her journey on August 28, 1980, aboard the wings of a metal bird with Dad and their six children in tow, me at four months old. They carried with them four precious silver bars, two bags of clothes, Mom's jewelry, and her mother's hand-sized woven basket—the only item that Mom had left to remember her by—safeguarded within a carefully handcrafted cloth Mom had made.

To America, we were unwanted refugees—people without a country. It would be another twenty to twenty-five years after the war ended before America would come to know about our sacrifice in the Secret War.

×   ×   ×

It is Hmong tradition that parents live with the eldest son, and Mom, a widow since October 1997, was living with my brother Cher in Elk Grove, California. When she returned from France, a few days after Uncle Fang's funeral, I made one of my semiannual weekend trips home from San Francisco.

There are two places where Mom can always be found: in her bedroom sewing or resting, or in the backyard gardening. On that day, she was in her room.

Everything she loves was squeezed into that bedroom. At the entrance sat the TV console with her big-screen TV and DVD/VHS player. The drawers were filled with DVDs and Hmong-dubbed Chinese and Thai movies. Growing up, I loved watching those movies, which centered around either romance or kung fu. One show required ten to fifteen disks just to tell the complete story from beginning to end.

Next to the console was an armoire from Target where she kept all her American prescription drugs and Hmong herbal remedies. The Hmong medicine, purchased from aunts and cousins, consisted of powders and bark from dried branches whose names I didn't know—all meant to treat her lungs and coughs. On top of the armoire was a round Christmas ornament the size of a fist with a picture of me and my two younger sisters, Mary and Leah, inside. We'd taken this picture two years before at our family Christmas gathering.

In the right corner of the room, next to her bed, was her white dresser filled with clothes, some of which were too big for her since she lost a lot of weight after her trip to Thailand the previous year. Having grown up with very little money, Mom saved all her clothes, whether or not she wore them. On top of the dresser sat a small, three-drawer plastic bin holding many knick-knacks, and on top of that was a framed picture of her and her older sister, Tais Tsuab, whom we call Aunt Green because her name translates to the color green. It was taken when she came to visit Mom some years before. In the picture they were both wearing Hmong clothes and carrying a traditional bamboo woven basket on their back. It was taken against a studio backdrop that simulated the tall, lush mountains and clear blue skies of Laos. I've seen similar backdrops in many Hmong family homes. These photos often left me with a feeling of nostalgia for a homeland I never knew. After all these years, I still haven't made it back to Laos or Thailand.

Her neatly made, full-size bed was covered with a light blue fleece blanket she'd had for years, refusing to let me buy her a new one. To the right of the bed sat a box she used as a nightstand to hold the power cord for charging her iPad and phone. A big Charmin logo spread across the box with the iconic smiling bear; inside the box was extra toilet paper. On the floor next to her bed was a worn black-and-white basket that Uncle Fang made when we visited in June 2002. I had taken photos of his hands weaving the black strips with the white strips into a checkered pattern. His hands were strong and steady, his eyes focused but warm. It felt surreal that Uncle Fang was no longer with us.

The afternoon light was streaming in through the blinds, and the familiar smell of the woody herbal tree-bark tea faintly danced across my nose. I'd missed the smell of her room, which was a mixture of old and new: herbal and ancient, jungles and mountains, all combined with modern furniture and technology.

"Hi, Mom," I said in English.

"Hi, *koj nyiav lug txug lov?*" You just got here?

"Yes, I did," I responded in English, putting my overnight bag down. I sat on the bed next to her, and she propped herself up on her light green pillows.

"How was your trip, Mom?" I asked, again in English after trying to scan for the question in Hmong but coming up empty. Although I understood Hmong perfectly well, forming the correct phrases was still a struggle, especially after being in a place where I spoke only English. It usually took me a day for my mind to catch up with my tongue allowing Hmong to flow effortlessly.

Mom told me about the funeral, which lasted the traditional three days, and about all her brother's kids and grandkids. She mentioned a few names that I recognized and others that I didn't. She teared up talking about how much she would miss her brother. I listened, not quite sure how to be with her in these moments of sorrow, not sure what words I could say to console her grieving heart.

When Dad died, the only thing I could think to say was, "Don't cry, we are still here to love you." Words that I had learned from watching low-budget Hmong movies. How does a seventeen-year-old, American-raised daughter console her bereaved mother in a language that's stiff on her tongue?

Now, at twenty-eight, I wrapped my arms around her once more and spoke those familiar words. My heart ached for her. Mom had always been defined by her role as "mother," and I had never fully recognized her as someone's sister. I couldn't imagine how it would feel if, one day, I were to lose one of my brothers. I sat in silence with Mom as she continued to cry.

"How was it traveling back, Mom? How did you get back?" I asked to find something else to occupy her mind.

Everyone in the family was working, and none of us were able to accompany her. On the trip over, she went with another cousin who spoke English, but on the way back, she was alone.

Her demeanor changed as she excitedly started to tell me in Hmong about coming back to the United States. "Heavens, it was such a struggle coming back! I had no one with me. I had no idea where I was supposed to go. The airport was so big. I'm stupid and don't know how to speak French. I don't know how to speak English, nor read signs. They put me in a wheelchair like someone stupid and incapable of walking, because I didn't know where to go. People must be looking at me, saying, 'Look at that old woman who doesn't know how to get to her plane.' But I just had to keep going. The airport staff took me to my plane.

"Yia, I am such a stupid person. I had no food with me. I didn't know how to buy any food or water. On the plane they gave me food. But I didn't know how to eat the food. It was so strange, and I didn't like it. I told them to give me two bottles of water. The flight was so long. I got so hungry. I was starving to death. After I drank the two water bottles, I had no more water. The bottles were so small. I looked at the buttons on the top of the plane, and I didn't know which button to push to get the flight attendant. I couldn't fall asleep. I was so thirsty. I was trying to stay awake so that I could catch the flight attendant when they came by, but it took so long for them to come. I was so tired, but I couldn't go to sleep or I would miss them. I had to bear the hunger and keep going. I told myself I just had to make it home, then I will eat, and I will sleep.

"We stopped at another airport, and I had to change planes. I didn't know where to go! The airport was so big. I followed people on my flight. I kept walking and walking. I didn't know where I was. My feet were so tired and painful but I had to keep going. I was afraid I would miss my flight. Finally, I went up to a woman wearing a uniform and gave her my ticket. She pointed to where I needed to go. But I shook my head and told her, no English, no English. Then they put me in a wheelchair again and took me to the plane. I had walked very far away. There was no way I would have known to get to my plane. I was so tired and so hungry and thirsty. I am such a stupid person. In this lifetime I would never know how to fly on my own. I was so scared I would never make it home, scared I was lost and would not see my family again. But I kept going."

I would later learn how her "I kept going" moved her through the deadly terrains of Laos all the way to California.

As Mom was telling me about her adventure, her hunger and fear, about how she had to keep going, the light in the room shifted. I was at the edge of my seat listening. I was scared for her, I laughed with her, I was sad for her, and I was hopeful for her. Most of all, I found myself falling in love with her. Who was this woman? For the first time I saw her as childlike and scared, but also as courageous and brave. Here was Mom, just five feet tall, supposedly eighty years old, with no knowledge of French and very little English, traveling halfway around the world and back by herself. In that moment, she became my hero. She wasn't just the mom I grew up with, who was mainly either criticizing or judging me; she was a woman with her own fears and feelings. A brave woman who found her way around two airports in foreign lands in the midst of grief and pain and didn't give up. As she repeated "I kept going," it became a mantra that planted itself in my body.

I pictured her traveling from Thailand to the United States with me, a baby in her arms, coming to a country where not just the language, but the world as a whole was foreign—a place with electricity and streets and cars and toilets and grocery stores. This brave, brave woman had come here with six children and no money in her pocket. All she had were the clothes on her back and a few bags holding the few precious items she and Dad were able to carry with them. I imagined her repeating those same words to herself despite the fear of an unknown future for herself and her family.

When she finished telling her story, her eyes were shining, and her face was flushed with wonderment and awe. There was no fear in her voice, just pride at having made it all the way home. She had shifted from grieving to embodying a childlike sense of adventure and discovery. Her story made me hungry to know her better. What had she been like as a child? What adventures did she go on? What boys had she liked before she married Dad? What did she and her girlfriends talk about as they crouched over their *paaj ntaub,* flower cloth embroidery? What was life like in Laos? What did she do every day? I didn't ask her those questions right away, but they became the questions that took me on a journey of discovery—of her and of myself.

My curiosity lay dormant for a few more years as life carried on and finally came into bloom, ready for me to harvest, at midnight on December 11, 2020, when I wrote my first recipe for how to make rice. The impulse came from a sudden need to taste . . . something. This deep craving rose to the tip of my tongue. The story was a memory of Mom preparing me for the work of being a future daughter-in-law, which was the theme of our relationship. The best way I knew how to capture her was through our interactions around cooking. That first recipe reawakened my hunger to know her, to know the ins and outs of her life, and to know the lineage I came from.

That following month, on January 3, 2021, after two years of not seeing my family, first from traveling and then because of the COVID-19 shutdown, I finally made it home for a visit. I went with an empty glass and new eyes to really know Mom for the first time. She had tried to show me how to cook before, but I had participated reluctantly, only to get her to stop nagging at me. This trip was the first time I became curious about the food she made and how she made it. The day I arrived, as though right on cue, she told me she was going to make *mov ncuav,* rice cakes, the following day, meaning "we" were going to be making *mov ncuav.*

Mov ncuav is a traditional treat symbolizing the arrival of the new year. In the old country, Laos, it marked the end of the rice harvest season when all the sticky rice blades had been harvested, dried, and the grain extracted. Family members in the village came together to make these traditional rice cakes. Our family maintained the tradition in the United States for a few years after we arrived. Every December during the Hmong New Year celebration, my half-brothers and uncles would gather at our house to make rice cakes.

It started with the women soaking the sticky rice grain overnight. The following morning they would steam it and, once cooked, pour the sticky rice into a big, hand-carved, wooden tub that had been rubbed with cooked egg yolk. Two men would stand on either side holding a wooden mallet and take turns pounding the rice in the tub. Steam would rise off the rice, escaping into the air and releasing a sweet, nutty aroma. When one of the men got tired, he would hand the mallet to the next man. After a while, the pounded sticky rice started to form a dough, becoming harder to pound because it would stick to the mallet. At that point, one or two of my sisters-in-law would run over and, with hands rubbed with egg yolk, grab the clump of rice dough and unstick it from the mallet in between pounding.

This would go on for quite a while until the dough was a smooth, sticky glob. Then the women came in, rubbed their hands with cooked egg yolk to keep the rice from sticking to their fingers, and grabbed small handfuls of the dough, which they plopped onto aluminum foil. They flattened the dough into a round patty and then folded the foil over the rice cake. Once all the rice cake was made, they cleaned the mallets and the tub and everyone enjoyed some *mov ncuav* dipped in maple syrup.

Making *mov ncuav* is a happy family occasion. When I was little and we made it this way, everyone was always so happy. The men would boast or brag or poke fun at one another about the strength required to pound the rice, especially once it got really sticky. My younger brothers would try, and the older men would tease them because they were clumsy at it. The women, who were waiting excitedly for the dough to be ready, joined in the teasing.

For years, we continued this family tradition every December. After Dad passed away in 1997, many of our family traditions fell away. Dad was the glue that kept all his children together. Now, with each sibling having their own family to take care of, greater distances between us, and busy schedules, we stopped making *mov ncuav* together.

"How are we making *mov ncuav*?" I asked, since it would just be the two of us.

"With the *mov ncuav* machine," she told me.

"The what? What's a *mov ncuav* machine?" I asked in disbelief, having no idea what she was talking about.

"Your sister-in-law bought this machine. She bought one for her mom and bought one for us to use."

Needless to say, I was fascinated. Sister-in-law Cher, who happened to be in the kitchen at that moment, explained to me that it was a mochi-making machine, manufactured in Japan, that pounded the steamed sticky rice for you until it turned into dough. Just about every Hmong family had one. I couldn't wait to see how it worked.

How to Make Rice Cakes

Yield: Relationship

Cook time: Until you see her

Ingredients:
Admiration
Wonder
Connection

Step 1:
Communicate to Reveal

Later that evening, after dinner was put away and the dishes cleaned, Mom took a big bowl out into the garage where the bag of sticky rice was stored and, a minute later, came back with the bowl halfway filled.

She brought it to the sink to wash, rinse, and drain a few times until the water ran clear. Then she filled the bowl of rice with water, and left it on the counter to soak overnight.

I set up the inflatable bed in Sister-in-law Cher's craft room and got ready for bed. I went into Mom's room to see what she was doing. She was lying on her bed watching a Hmong YouTube channel on her iPad. A lot of Hmong elders watched these channels, which were devoted to people telling stories, both fictional and true. Some of these channels were Hmong stations that broadcast the news with Hmong newscasters. It was a way for the elders to connect to the world and know about what was happening since so many didn't understand English. The YouTube channels also kept them company on lonely nights when they couldn't fall asleep.

I sat down next to her and watched the story with her. I waited for a good moment to ask her about her siblings. I vaguely remembered a story about an older sister who ate opium and died, but I couldn't recall the details. Mom recounted the story of her two eldest sisters and the scenario around one of their deaths.

"One day, Mom and Dad were going to an uncle's house for a family healing ceremony. Their house was a half a day's walk away and there were many people there, so it would be too much to take them. And also, no one would be with Grandma. Bla was the oldest and Lau was second. They both wanted to go and Mom and Dad wouldn't let them. They had to stay home. Bla was very stubborn and kept pushing to go. In the end, my parents relented and let her go, but Lau had to stay home with Grandma.

"Lau became very upset and heartbroken. Although still a child, she was old enough to know that opium could kill you if you ate a large enough dose. She found some opium and ate it. She made a bed in front of the door with a pile of rice blades and lay down on it. Grandma was blind and couldn't see what was happening, but she heard the rustling of the blades and called out to Lau to ask what she was doing, but Lau didn't answer. Grandma got worried and started to feel her way around the house, trying to figure out where the rustling was coming from. Then it got quiet. She called and called, but still no answer. Grandma kept feeling her way around the house and finally came upon Lau. By the time Grandma got there, however, Lau's little soul had left her body. Grandma shook her awake but no sound came. Her lifeless body just laid there. Grandma screamed and cried and cried. Finally the neighbors came to help and a cousin ran toward the road to Uncle's house to find Mom and Dad."

As Mom shared her story, I could feel her grief wash over me. She had endured so much sorrow, most of which remained hidden. She carried this burden silently for a long time. She was not one to speak openly about these things. I had never truly regarded Mom as an individual with a rich, concealed history.

There was something beautiful in her sorrow. It was so raw and open. Naked. She didn't conceal her emotions. Didn't pretend it wasn't there, and she didn't overdramatize it. Even though this event happened before she was born, she still carried her family's grief. She told it with the depth of emotion as though she were there to witness it. There was beauty in her sorrow. The way she spoke emanated an acceptance for the hardships of life without drowning in them. She spoke to communicate her reality with nothing extra.

Step 2:
Flow with the Natural Cycles

The following day, Mom rose before sunrise to start her morning routine. She began by stowing away the dishes, which had been drying both in the dishwasher and on the countertop. Then, she diligently washed the pots, pans, and the dirty dishes my nieces and nephews left out the previous night. As the sun broke wide, Mom ventured outside to tend to her beloved garden. Sometimes, there was nothing to do at all, yet she found peace simply being in the garden's company. After carefully tending to each plant during her rounds, she returned indoors to savor a comforting cup of hot soy drink and a bread roll at the dining table.

By the time I walked into the kitchen, she was washing her mug and putting it in the dishwasher to dry. Hardly any Hmong families used the dishwasher to actually wash dishes. We used it to dry the dishes we washed in the sink. Such luxuries like a dishwasher were wasteful and inefficient.

"Yia, what do you want for breakfast?" she inquired.

"I'm fine, Mom. I'm not hungry yet," I replied, as I always do when I'm home. This had become part of our morning routine.

I returned to the bathroom to shower, get dressed, and joined Mom again in the kitchen. It was time to steam the sticky rice. Mom already had the pot of water on the stove. She poured the raw rice into the bamboo steamer and, once the liquid finished draining, set the steamer over the pot and covered it with a lid.

I washed the bowl that had contained the rice and set it on the counter to dry because it was too big to go in the dishwasher. While the sticky rice was cooking, I took the opportunity to scramble two eggs for my own breakfast.

Meanwhile, Mom made her way back outside. She was always doing something. She never sat still for long. Motion was ingrained in her bones.

×   ×   ×

In Laos there was always something to do from pre-dawn until the late hours of the night. Mom never had a moment of rest. Farming was a year-round activity. The farm itself was about a two-hour walk from the village. Each Hmong village was clan based with relatives all living together. There were eighteen primary clans, each identified by a family name. Clans linked through marriage often lived in the same village or near each other. The clans were made up of members from the patriarchal side. Sons who married brought the wives into their clan, while daughters who married left home and became part of their husband's clan.

Within the village, each family unit had their own plot of land. The farm itself would take up acres of a hillside or valley. There was a house at the farm so that during the peak periods, when it was too much to walk back and forth, some members would stay at the farmhouse while others stayed at the village to tend to the house and feed the animals.

At the field, Mom's family grew rice, corn, and opium poppies along with seasonal greens, vegetables, and medicinal herbs. At the end of the hot season, the symphony of cicadas throughout the hillside was an indication that it was time to start the process of preparing the land for farming. They set a controlled fire to clear the old crops and weeds, fertilized the soil with the ashes, and then tilled the land so it was ready for planting before the rainy season came in. Corn was the first to be planted in the field, followed by rice in the rice fields. The monsoon season brought rain to water the crops and saturate the land. By the time the rice fields were planted, it was time to harvest the corn. Once they completed the corn, they harvested the rice. By then it was time to pick the second batch of corn, and then a second batch of rice. The second harvest of rice blades, which grew as tall as humans, is called *laam nplej.* In between going from cornfield to rice field, they also tended to the vegetables and herbs. Once the *laam nplej* was harvested, the season transitioned out of the rainfall into a cooler and drier climate indicating it was time to till the poppy fields in another part of the hillside.

After tilling and planting poppies, it was back to the corn and rice fields. Often, one group of people would harvest the corn while others harvested the rice, and one group might set the rice out to dry while yet another planted the opium poppies. There was no calendar to say when to plant what. They listened to nature and the sounds of different animals, felt for the moisture and heat in the air, and watched the growth patterns of the crops.

In the midst of the labor-intensive work of farming, Mom made hemp thread and fabric from hemp plants to sew her own traditional clothes so she had a New Year outfit for the celebration. She prepared yards of fabric and thread, and took them with her to the farm so she could use what little available time she had to sew her *paaj ntaub*, flower cloth embroidery.

At the end of the day, when there was no more light, there was still much to do. Mom would feed all the animals and make dinner. After dinner they would *tuav chug*, prepare the rice grain for the following day. This consisted of separating the grains from their outer husks by putting handfuls of grain into a mortar on the ground and stomping on the end of a long wooden apparatus to pound them so that the kernels came away from the husks.

Once the chores were done, Mom would light an oil lantern, using oil extracted from fried pork fat, and sew some more of her *paaj ntaub*. The men would already be asleep, but she would stay up sewing until she could no longer keep her eyes open.

There were no clocks to guide her through the night. She responded to the natural rhythm of her body. She would sleep a few hours until her internal alarm clock woke her. She would prepare corn with greens for the animals and rice and vegetables for the family. As soon as there was light, she would go outside to call the pigs, horses, chickens, and cows with their own unique call until they gathered around for their meal. Then the family would eat breakfast and set off to the farm again.

By November, once the poppies were in the ground, it was time for the new year's festivities and soul-calling ceremonies to begin. As soon as the festivities were done, some people started separating the rice grains from the plants while others began to harvest the opium for weeks to come. This would go until early spring and then it would be time to start all over again. Mom did this year after year after year.

In America, where it's not necessary to till or plant and harvest her own vegetables, Mom still planted to stay in motion with the natural cycles of life. Everywhere she went, she prepared what little land she had in the backyard to plant a simple garden. At my sister Cha's apartment, where there was no garden, she planted medicinal herbs, lemongrass, and culinary herbs in buckets in front of the house.

Whenever I tell her to stop working so hard, to stop washing dishes that are not hers, she tells me, "If there are dirty dishes, you wash them and complete that cycle so that it doesn't soak up your ambient attention." Even if her mind is tired, her body is in motion with the cycles of the day. She moves seamlessly from one thing to the next, in harmony with a natural rhythm that carries her through days, weeks, and seasons.

Step 3:
Love Is in the Details

The sticky rice steamed for about twenty-five minutes, then Mom turned off the stove. She instructed me to go to the garage with her to get the mochi machine and bring it back into the kitchen. I untied the fabric holding the box together, took out the machine to set on the counter, and plugged the power cord into the wall socket. It looked almost like a rice cooker except that it was square instead of round, and it had three buttons: off, steam, and pound. Mom took out the bowl that was inside the machine and wiped it down with a wet towel. Then she put it back in the machine, added the fanlike attachment to the center, and snapped it in place.

She took the bamboo steamer off the pot and dropped a few scoops of steamy sticky rice into the bowl until it was slightly more than half full. She put the steamer back on top of the pot to keep the rest of the rice warm. Mom came back to the machine and pressed the "pound" button. The machine jerked awake as though disturbed from slumber, making loud thudding sounds and shaking back and forth as the fanlike apparatus started to spin, pounding on the rice. Mom kept the lid off the machine to allow the rice to cool. I could see the rice being churned. This mysterious machine was amazing to watch work. It was a completely different experience from when my brothers took turns pounding a tub full of hot, steamy sticky rice with a big wooden mallet. Gone were the days of the rice-cake-making parties.

Mom put the lid on the machine. "Now keep it covered so that the rice stays hot," she told me. We left it alone to do its thing while Mom took out a roll of aluminum foil and instructed me to prepare the wrappers for the rice cakes. I took to the task, checking with her to see how big the foil should be. Her instructions to have me get the right size included "too big . . . no, too small . . . yes, like that."

Mom cracked the hard-boiled egg she cooked earlier and peeled off the shell. She split the egg and put the yoke in a small bowl. She walked over to me and handed me the egg white to eat. It was a natural gesture, one that she has done in various ways throughout our life, from giving me the drumstick when we ate boiled chicken to stripping off the pork fat and giving me the soft meat when we ate boiled pork with mustard greens.

Growing up with limited means, *Tais*, Grandma, didn't have money to buy Mom big fancy things, but she expressed her love in the details. It was a precious and subtle, yet unwavering love. One New Year celebration she sewed two textile money bag sashes to go with Mom's festival outfit. They were made of cotton lined with one-inch beads and French coins attached to the end. Mom proudly wore them like cross-body purses that would jingle as the coins hit each other. They were nothing fancy, but Mom was very happy to have them.

Like *Tais*, Mom's love is a quiet love. One that I didn't see and couldn't feel growing up. But enveloped in the aroma of sticky rice in the kitchen that day, and in the way she handed me the egg white, all the moments I hadn't been able to feel were illuminated.

Step 4:
Two Come Together to Create a Third

After ten or fifteen minutes, Mom went back to lift the lid off the mochi machine and look at the dough. It was ready. She pressed the "off" button, took the bowl out, and brought it over to the table where the aluminum foil waited.

"Take the egg yolk and rub it on the plastic tray quickly," she instructed me.

I took a piece of the yolk and did as instructed, my motion slow and lingering.

"Do it with attention and speed. Don't do it like you're scared of it! Just grab the tray and spread the yolk to all the corners. Don't hesitate!"

I went faster to complete the task and get out of the line of fire, but it was already too late.

Mom turned the bowl upside down to the tray and waited for the dough to drop. "It's stuck to the bowl. You don't want that, so pour it right away next time." Mom reached in to carefully pull the hot dough from the sides, flinching and blowing on it as she peeled it away. She turned the bowl over again, and a few seconds later, the dough finally plopped onto the tray.

With the dough taken care of, she softened her tone and said, "Just as in life, anything you do—walking, working, cleaning—you do it swiftly and with attention."

I soaked in her words.

She rubbed egg yolk on her hands to keep the dough from sticking. She carefully grabbed it from the end, twisted off a piece the size of a tennis ball, and placed it on half the aluminum foil. She flattened the dough to an oval shape about five inches wide, six inches long, and half an inch thick. Once satisfied, she folded the other half of the foil over to cover it to make a rectangle parcel. She moved the packet to the side and prepared the next one.

After watching how she did it, I rubbed my hands with egg yolk and copied her method. Mom continued to break pieces of dough and shape them into balls for me while I took on the task of stretching and flattening them on the foil. She adjusted me on the size and thickness to get it right. She finished splitting all the dough and, after seeing that I was making them correctly, took the bowl back to the machine and snapped it into place. She poured in the rest of the sticky rice, replaced the lid, and pressed the "pound" button to start the second batch. Once I'd wrapped all the balls from the first batch, she instructed me to wash the bamboo basket and pot. By the time I finished, the second batch of dough was ready.

Mom prepped the balls again while I formed them into a patty on the foil and wrapped them. We worked in silence and a natural rhythm formed between us, punctuated by the crinkling sound of the foil.

Mom formed her last ball and left it on the tray for me to finish. She eased into putting the mochi machine away while I completed the last of my patty.

A few minutes later, Mom went into the refrigerator and brought out a jar of dark syrup. "This is sugar cane syrup I made. Khoua Neng grew a lot of sugar cane this year. He gave me a big batch of it so I turned it into syrup." Khoua Neng is the eldest of my half-brothers.

He rented a piece of land in Lodi from one of our uncles to grow his own vegetables.

I could tell Mom was proud of her sugar cane syrup and asked her how she made it.

"You peel the rind off the sugar cane. You smash it to break it and soften it. Then you put it in a big pot with water filled almost to the top. You boil the sugar cane for hours until all the sugar is dissolved into the water. You strain the liquid into another pot and throw away all the stalks. Then you boil the liquid until all the water has evaporated and what is left is the thick dark syrup at the bottom."

Mom poured some syrup into a dipping bowl. She opened one of the *mov ncuav* that we'd just folded and handed it to me. I broke off a piece of the still-warm patty and dipped it into the syrup. The golden brown syrup clung to the patty and dripped back into the bowl as I held it up to admire it. I popped it into my mouth. The splash of sweetness was subtle, light, and smooth, followed by a distinct earthy, sugar-cane taste. This was better than any maple syrup or honey I'd ever tasted. As I chewed, the two distinct flavors of floral sweetness from the syrup balanced with the natural nuttiness of the *mov ncuav* lingered in my mouth.

"Mmm, so good," I said.

Mom nodded her approval, her pride soaking into her demeanor much like that single raindrop nourishing the ground. She was never one to boast about herself, but I could feel her beaming inside.

Being here with Mom and eating her food had me exhale for what seemed like the first time in weeks. I hadn't realized how much I missed her food and care and love. I paused for a moment to let that last bite play out its subtle note on my tongue before I swallowed. I took another piece, dipped it in syrup, and put it in my mouth. The flavor of the second bite was stronger, building another layer of sweetness on top of the first. Twice more I dipped, chewed, and savored until I'd finished the whole patty.

Childhood memories of watching my half-brothers take turns pounding the sticky rice were embedded in every bite. I could even taste the oaky note of the wooden tub on the *mov ncuav* despite the fact this one hadn't gone anywhere near wood.

There was a palpable shift in our relationship that weekend. We were no longer mother and daughter. We were two women in a kitchen together who loved to cook. Mom was finally able to share the knowledge and skills she had longed to impart, and I was open to receiving them. Simultaneously, I felt the warmth of her love, while she, in turn, relished the attention I gave her. There was no distinction between who was giving and who was receiving. We were feeding each other, trusting each other enough to expose the deeper parts of ourselves.

This trip was the start of us coming together to form a relationship.

Courting Season

"When are you going to find a Hmong man to marry and settle down?" Ah, the million-dollar question that turns our pleasant conversations immediately into a sword fight. It's the universal showdown between mothers and daughters, across cultures and generations since time immemorial. My answers never make the cut and usually just fan the flames between us. I typically end the conversation by abruptly stating I have to return to work or, if we're talking in person, by walking away.

When I was in high school, this wasn't an issue. I was still young and focused on school. Mom appreciated education; something she didn't have growing up, so she didn't push it. At family ceremonies and rituals when we were among the aunts and elderly ladies, they would ask me if I was married yet. When I told them "no," Mom supported me by saying it was best I finish school first. Of course my aunts also chimed with: "Yes, you're still young. Finish school first." They were all very supportive and understanding, despite the fact that when they were the same age I was, they already had one or two children.

The annual Hmong New Year celebrations when my nieces and cousins and I dressed up in traditional Hmong clothes to go *pov pob*, ball tossing, with boys our age were all for fun. Mom and sisters-in-law enjoyed chaperoning a group of beautiful young bachelorettes. They received a lot of attention from the elderly women and men eyeing us for their sons, telling them their daughters were beautiful. However, once I turned twenty-one, which was old-maid status according to Mom's generation, the pressure began. New Year festivities quickly changed from "dress up to go toss balls" to "dress up and go find yourself a husband."

At twenty-one my answer was, "I'm still young, Mom. I have school to focus on."

At twenty-three, after I graduated from college, I couldn't use that excuse anymore, so it became, "I'm not ready yet, Mom."

And then came a series of critiques of my non-Hmong boyfriends, none of whom were ever good enough.

At twenty-five I heard, "Your boyfriend is much too old and balding already." He was forty-two.

At twenty-eight it was, "He doesn't have any eyebrows." He was blond, and his eyebrows were light.

At twenty-nine, "He has such a big nose. Do you want your kids to have a big nose?" After that I stopped bringing home the men I was dating. If I wasn't actually going to marry him, it wasn't worth the interrogation and demeaning criticism.

Along with the critiques of their physical appearance were the lectures on, "You have to marry your own kind or he won't love you and your family."

This was the ultimate trigger that would set me off, and I always exploded into a rage. "Just because they're Hmong doesn't mean they know how to love you!" I'd go on with my rant about how Hmong women are treated as second-class citizens by their husbands and in-laws. I'd throw back that American men at least show you respect and treat you as an equal.

Mom had a comeback for everything. "You speak about love. Is it love that Americans leave their parents to live in old homes? Is that how you want to treat me? That is not the Hmong way."

There was no way to win. I might as well have been speaking to her in, well, English.

In my thirties, the pressure increased. Our phone calls didn't last longer than five minutes. The first two minutes were spent asking if and when I was coming home, the following two minutes were the lecture on getting married, and the last minute was me biting my tongue and making an excuse for hanging up the phone. The trips home were few and far between. Twice a year, at the most. Sometimes just once.

Mom always knew exactly where to plant the question. She would wait until the last day when I was packing to leave.

"Yia," she would begin, "stop playing around and find a Hmong man to settle down with and begin your life." And it stung every time, the way she saw my life as "playing around" and I needed to have a husband before I could "begin my life." It was dismissive and made me feel invisible unless I was a baby-producing machine.

"I don't want to get married, Mom," was my only comeback. I had stopped trying to argue my points. "I have a life. I'm happy. I have a job that I love and a life that I love."

"You barely have any money; you're living paycheck to paycheck. How much do you make a month, huh? How much have you saved?" That was how she dug the knife in, turned it. Not only by attacking my choice of men but driving home the point that I was "playing around" with a college degree and no high-paying job. "Look at your sisters, they all have a good job and a house, two incomes and kids."

"Yeah, and look how happy their lives are, and how much their husbands love them!" That was my slash below the belt, pointing out the flaw in her logic, pointing out her failure to ensure her daughters' happiness, because we both knew that some of my sisters' husbands had wandered. It was culturally acceptable for married men to flirt with other women and take on a second or third or fourth wife. A wife was beholden to her husband by tradition, and should they ever divorce, the whispers would be about how she failed as a wife, not him. She would be known as a *puj tsawj,* divorced woman, the term as demeaning as the word *whore,* while he had done no wrong and maintained his status and would carry on to find other wives.

These conversations were a dead end, knowing that neither of us was ever getting through to the other. So, once again, we would go our separate ways with a loss lingering in the air.

It took me a long time to understand that the generational divide between us wasn't about right or wrong; it was about experiencing life through different lenses. Mom grew up in a time when relationships were much simpler, guided by skills and strength of character. To her, you connected with the essence of a person, and that was enough. For me, raised in a world that is seemingly more complicated, relationships demanded more nuanced considerations, most of which were based on preferences and romantic fantasies. We struggled to bridge that gap, to really hear each other through the cacophony of our disparate values.

We grew up with different ideas and experiences on love. Mom's husband was not of her own choosing. Three men showed up at her door one day, and she was gone from her family the next. Love was not a factor. Love was something she grew into. It was not a romantic love, but a love based on the everyday realities of building a life with a stranger. On the other hand, I grew up reading romance novels and watching Hollywood movies. I wanted to be whisked away and fought for, to be somebody's "the one."

Despite the emotional distance that often arose from our differing perspectives on relationships and marriage, there was an area where we found common ground: the kitchen. As we stepped into the kitchen, the complexity of our divergent views seemed to dissolve into the comforting routine of creating a dish that was an ode to simplicity: pork boiled with mustard greens.

This dish has remained unchanged throughout time and place. We ate it at every Hmong event, be it a wedding, a funeral, or a blessing or healing ceremony. It is very simple, containing no ingredients other than the pork and mustard greens boiled in water with salt for flavoring. When this dish is cooked at family events, it embodies the simple nature of relationships between Hmong men and women.

This dish held even greater significance because in Laos, meat was reserved exclusively for special occasions due to its scarcity. Here in the United States, we have the luxury of preparing this dish year-round, as we can easily purchase pork and greens from the store. During a visit home one spring, with the refrigerator brimming with greens from Mom's garden, she taught me how to make this dish.

How to Make Pork Boiled with Mustard Greens

Yield: Union

Cook time: Until the essence reveals itself

Ingredients:
Play
Curiosity
Vulnerability

Step 1:
Play to Keep the Game Going

Mom took out the pork belly and pork chop that she had gotten from my half-brother Khoua Neng's house after a healing ceremony for his daughter-in-law who had breast cancer and was undergoing chemotherapy. The pork had already been cut into one-inch pieces and was ready to be cooked. Mom pulled out a pot, filled it with water, and put it on the stove to heat.

Cooking with her tended to be quiet unless she was instructing or adjusting me. I watched her move around the kitchen with ease and precision, keeping her eye on everything at once. While we waited for the water to boil, Mom opened the fridge and took out a bag of Hmong mustard greens. The difference between Hmong mustard greens and the Chinese variety is that the Hmong mustard greens are smaller and thinner. The Chinese variety has a thicker stalk and tastes slightly spicy while ours are sweeter.

She told me to wash the greens. I took the greens out of the bag, put them in a stainless steel bowl, and began to wash them under cold water in the sink. I took each piece of green, cut down to the softer part of the stalk, then washed the dirt from between the leaves.

Sometimes, watching Mom cook, I see her as a young girl moving about in the kitchen. I once saw a picture of her taken in Thailand for her immigration card before we came to the United States. She must have been in her early thirties. On the light teal-colored card was her headshot in the top right corner. She was wearing a traditional, wrapped headdress made of hemp cloth and dyed black, probably with her own hands. She had on small but thick silver hoop earrings with an arrow intersecting the loop. She had a cross-eyed look on her face. I couldn't tell if it was just in that moment she looked cross-eyed or if that was a condition she'd had that was later treated, because she doesn't have it anymore. She had a slight, open-mouthed smile on her thin face and full, thick lips, much like mine. Mom looked like my youngest sister, Leah. She was pretty without any embellishments. You could see the strength and wisdom in her face.

I had turned to her and asked if she had suitors at the New Year festivals when she was younger. Did she have someone she was interested in before it was arranged she would marry Dad? She dismissed my curiosity, saying she was *dlaab tuag*, ugly, and no one was interested.

"You couldn't have been ugly, Mom. Look at us! All your children are attractive. I'm sure you had suitors and just don't want to tell me."

"There's nothing to tell. There were either those you liked who didn't like you back or those you didn't like who pursued you."

"Okay, so who was someone you liked?"

"There's no point in talking about it. There wasn't anyone. Why do you ask such questions? I wasn't a beautiful person." She ended the conversation.

I detected pain behind her reluctance and changed the topic. In her hesitation to discuss her past, Mom carried an unspoken weight—a blend of melancholy and missed opportunities that seemed too painful to revisit.

Though she brushed it off, her words hinted at a complex tapestry of emotions and experiences she had folded away.

×   ×   ×

In Laos, the New Year festival lasts for five days. It occurred right after the last of the corn and rice were harvested and the opium poppies were planted in the ground. Each village often held its own celebration. It was a time for relatives to reunite and for young men and women of marriageable age to find their partners.

When the festivities began, Mom and her sisters were always very excited. They would wake up early in the morning to tend to their chores and feed the animals, and then dress in traditional clothes with Grandma's help.

Mom would first put on *dlaim tab*, the skirt. The skirt was made from yards and yards of hemp fabric pleated into accordion folds. The fabric was dyed in indigo ink with batik designs. Mom made the skirt herself with the help of Grandma. They kept this skirt clean so that she could wear it year after year for this occasion. The shirt, *lub tsho,* is worn over the skirt and is also adorned with colorful applique fabric. On the back of the shirt is a rectangular cloth panel called *lub laug*, with applique motifs that she had sewn together. Grandma would take out a pink *hlaab*, sash or belt, and wrap it around her waist a few times to hold the skirt and shirt in place, and then tie it to the back with a footlong fabric strip that draped behind her. In front of the skirt she put on *dlaim sev,* a long black waist-tied apron, to cover the open fold of the skirt. Next, Grandma would wrap a black hemp cloth around each leg for modesty. To finish the outfit, her mom put a thick silver necklace, *lub paug,* over her head and set it in place around her neck.

Everything she wore was a work of art, sewn by her own hands to showcase her craftsmanship at precision needlework and beautiful motifs. Adorning her body were signs of patience, dedication, and creativity. She was a work of art from the inside out.

The men's outfits were much simpler—black harem pants, a black cropped shirt with the same pattern on the lapel as the women's, and a shorter belt that tied to the front. Where a woman's outfit reflects her role in maintaining cultural heritage and the wealth of her family, his was understated and practical to focus on the ceremonial aspects rather than the attire.

Once Mom and her sisters were dressed, they took long pieces of black hemp fabric for their headdress and ran to the house of an aunt to have her fix the fabric into a turban. They raced one another there to see who got to the house first while being careful not to ruin their clothes. Once all the girls had their turbans on, Grandma walked with them to the New Year festivities in town.

At the fairground, the ritual of courting began. A few young men would walk up to a group of girls and ask them, *"Leej muam, mej yog xeem dlaab tsi nab?"* Beautiful ladies, what clan are you from? They asked to be sure the women were not from their clan, because anyone with your clan name would be considered a cousin, even if there was no blood relation. They asked where the girls were from and complimented them on their beauty. After a few minutes of introductions, they asked if the girls would like to *pov pob*, toss ball. The girls modestly agreed. They would form two lines across from one another and about eight to ten feet apart, or join other lines that had already been started. Someone would bring out a ball wrapped with yards of fabric and sewn together, and the tossing would begin.

During the tossing, the young men and women got to know one another. Their conversations were specifically intended to test each other's quick wit and intelligence with poetic metaphors, riddles, and bantering. The men often complimented the women on their beauty and skill at ball-tossing, and the women had to respond by walking a fine line between self-assurance and humility, neither boasting nor degrading themselves. Each woman would test her partner's wit with her own riddles and metaphors. The goal was to determine whether his responses were boastful and arrogant or respectful and modest.

A typical interaction might go something like this: "Beautiful lady, what food did your mother and father eat that they bore such a beautiful daughter, with hair black and soft as silk and skin white as new rice?"

Her response would be something like, "Our mother and father didn't have much good food to eat at all and did not bear beautiful daughters, but simply the plain ones you see before you who know only to love the parents who gave them life."

With this kind of bantering they tested one another's wordsmithing skills and made it necessary to stay attentive and keep the conversation flowing in a playful dance of words, drawing each other out more and more. The purpose of the chit-chat wasn't to win or show off your verbal skills, but rather to keep the game going. The courting was, in itself, the art of play.

Step 2:
Vulnerability Is a Gift

Steam was coming off the pot and the water was bubbling hard. Mom gradually lowered the pork into the pot, careful not to let any water splash out. The bubbling settled into a calm hum. She added a bit of salt and let the pork cook.

Mom directed me to wash the bowl and check on the rice she had in the cooker. There were two rice cookers on the counter—one for the regular white rice the family eats, and the other where Mom makes her *mov nplej tshab*, Hmong new rice. It has the same texture as regular rice but is slightly tan in color. Mom, who is diabetic, says it doesn't raise her blood sugar levels. This rice was specially grown in Fresno by a Hmong woman farmer who brought the seeds from Laos. It was an experiment born out of longing for the homeland. Sown with love and fed by her memories, the rice took root, bringing its nourishment to America.

While Mom and I waited for the pork to cook, she opened the sliding glass door to the backyard and walked outside. Not really sure what she was doing, I followed her. She walked over to her patch of herbs and started whistling a *lug txaj*, poetry song, lost in her own thoughts.

In 2015 on a trip home, I made a video recording of her singing a Hmong poetry song. I'd heard her whistle from time to time, but never sing an entire song. She prefaced the song by saying to the camera, "I'm old now and out of breath so I can't sing like I once did. I have many illnesses now and am not as healthy as I was a long time ago. We don't know how much longer I will be here. But here is a video of me singing so that when I'm no longer here, you can watch this and remember that this is your mother. I have a cassette of my singing, but it's only a cassette and for this, you can see me too." She laughs nervously, centers herself, and starts. For the thirteen minutes of recording her, I felt the longing and nostalgia elicited by her voice and the tone of the story, even though I couldn't understand what it was about.

× × ×

These were songs that, as a teenager, Mom was eager to learn. Being able to sing a poetry song was a valuable skill. It was something that Mom practiced through listening and repeating. After a long day of working in the field, and after dinner when the dishes were washed and put away, the teenage girls would gather together and ask one of the adult women to teach them a song. They would sit together, the only light coming from a lamp lit with pork oil and a blanket of stars in the night sky and the moon shining over the valley. The adult woman would sing a stanza of the song and the girls would repeat it. Over and over they would do this until late into the night, memorizing stanza after stanza. Since there was no written language, everything was learned by listening and repeating. During the day, as they worked in the field, the girls would practice singing to one another and helping each other memorize their lines.

Being able to sing a traditional poetry song and having the voice to go with it were indicators of grace and intelligence. It was a valuable courting skill at the New Year fairgrounds, when young men and women were tossing balls with each other. The man would request that the woman grace the group with a song, so that the "clouds would clear and the sun would shine upon them." The woman would decline, saying she didn't know how to sing and her singing would only cause the sun to hide and the rain to descend in remorse, so it would be better that she not. They would go back and forth, with the man becoming more complimentary with each request, until they would eventually change the subject or the woman would finally give in, warning that, if the rain should fall upon them, the New Year festivities would be ruined. Then, still tossing the ball, she would let out an ancient melodic sound lasting five to ten seconds and launch into a beautiful poetry song telling of heartache and lost love, or the strength and humility of an orphan child, or the love and care of parents. The verses would capture the hearts of those listening and draw them to her. At the end of the song, which might last anywhere from eight to fifteen minutes, tears would flow and smiles brighten the faces of her admirers, young and old alike. A skillful poetry song singer elicited deep emotions from those around her.

The other way to sing these poetry songs would be as a call and response. Either a man or a woman would sing a few verses and then the other would sing in response. The ultimate test of wit and intelligence would be the poetic quality of his or her response. The exchange would continue until one of the participants came up with a clever ending to the duel. The elders were touched by such displays, which reminded them of their own youth. Based on her voice and the skill of her responses, a woman developed a reputation for beauty, grace, and wit that made her desirable as a wife and daughter-in-law.

Mom was shy when it came to discussing whether she had ever sung for suitors. She downplayed my inquiries with a simple statement: "If they ask you, that's what you do—you sing." She refrained from exposing her personal experiences, but I sensed that these moments were precious and vulnerable. When she sang in response to others' requests, it was a gift—a vulnerability she shared with those who appreciated her performance.

Step 3:
Bring Out the Essence of the Other

Mom was crouching over her herbs, pulling out some weeds, although there weren't many at all. I was looking at the kaffir lime leaf tree, making plans to take some leaves back with me. She called out to me, interrupting my thoughts, and told me the pork was ready and I should go add the mustard greens in the pot. I didn't know how she knew, but after decades of cooking and building a relationship with the food, she had a keen sense of when things are ready.

I followed her instructions and headed back inside. I took a handful of greens from the bowl and dunked them into the pot of boiling water, which again calmed to a serene pool of meat and greens. I took a wooden spoon out of the drawer and pushed the greens down to make room for a second batch. The sweet, earthy aroma of the greens immediately hit my nose along with the savory smell of the pork.

The sliding door opened and closed behind me. "Put more salt in the pork."

"How much salt?" I asked.

"Until it's good."

I poured a bit of salt in and stirred it with the wooden spoon. Then I took a soup spoon out of the drawer and scooped a bit of liquid. I blew on it to cool, then tasted it. I added a bit more salt, and tried again. The flavor of the greens had infused the broth, the liquid a nuanced bouquet of peppery, earthy richness balanced by a subtle undertone of natural sweetness. Not fully trusting my senses, I took another scoop and handed it over to Mom.

"Just see if it's salty enough," she chided.

"Well, I'm not sure. You try it."

Mom took the spoon and tasted the liquid. "More salt."

I took a tiny teaspoon and poured it in.

"A little more," she told me without tasting it. I put in a slightly bigger amount. "Okay, that's good," she said, again without tasting it. "Turn it off once the greens are cooked."

"When are they cooked?" I asked once again.

"When they're soft," came her response, as she walked over to the sink to wash her hands.

I left the greens to cook for about three minutes longer and then took out a piece and tried it. It tasted soft to me, so, not wanting to overcook them, I turned off the heat. "It's ready, Mom."

Mom came over to taste for herself. "Are you sure?" She took the spoon and dished out a piece of green with a stem, blew on it, and tasted it. "No, it's still hard. A little bit longer."

These instructions were frustrating and confusing. Nothing was timed, her responses and measurements made no sense to me, and on top of that, it had been a long time and I hadn't eaten enough of this food to actually know what it was supposed to taste like. My Hmong palate had been displaced by all the other food I'd been eating. I only ate Hmong food once or twice a year. A dish as simple as the pork with mustard greens required more attention, not less, to capture the true essence of each ingredient. If the soup were overcooked, the pork would be tough and the greens would be soggy rather than tender. And if it was undercooked, the greens would be tough and spicy rather than soft and sweet. The flavors couldn't be too salty or bland, but required the perfect balance of salt with the natural sweetness of the greens.

×　×　×

The Hmong courtship ritual developed in much the same way as this simple but festive dish, according to unspoken traditions that had been handed down through generations.

After the New Year festivities, the man would go to the woman's home to call on her. There was no dating or fine dining or walks at sunset. Rather, he would generally first speak with her parents, who would question him about his parents if they didn't already know his family. The woman, meanwhile, would listen quietly and do her needlework until the parents were satisfied with the suitor. The father would then leave and busy himself with other tasks, and the mother would chaperone the "date," while doing her own needlework. The young woman, who could not show too much interest, would continue to be modest and appear to be humbled by the man's attention. After an hour or two, he would say farewell to her and her family and take his leave.

This courtship ritual continued over weeks and months, with the man coming over to the house to visit. Some of the visits would be close to dinnertime so that he could taste her food. Of course, he wouldn't be that straightforward about it. Usually, when it was close to dinnertime, he would announce he was about to leave.

The woman's parents would ask him to stay for dinner. *Oh no, I mustn't burden you with making extra food, and besides it's getting late and I should go.* It is not a burden at all! Please, he must stay for dinner. He's been here all day and has not had a single thing to eat.

After a few minutes of this, he would surrender and stay. The women would then move into the kitchen and prepare dinner while he stayed in the living room to chat with the father. When the food was ready, the father would invite him to the dinner table, where everyone ate and the men conversed some more.

Once the courting became more serious, there were other traditional ways for the man to continue seeing the woman without damaging her reputation. At night, after the woman's parents had gone to bed, the suitor would stand outside her bedroom. The houses in Laos were made of bamboo and wood, so the walls were very thin and porous. The suitor pulled out a grass blade, called a *nrab ncaj,* and blew on it to awaken her and let her know he was there. The Hmong language is a whistled language, meaning its words can be communicated through a musical instrument. Those with a trained ear will know exactly what the instrument is saying.

The tone of the grass blade is high pitched, like a bird call, cutting right into your heart. The man plays it as if he were speaking to the woman. He tells her that her beauty shines like the moon to lead his heart back home, and her smile is like the sun that warms his soul on the coldest days. All this he tells her by "playing" the grass blade. She can respond by playing her own *nrab ncaj,* telling him of her own feelings.

The courtship between a man and a woman is simple, speaking to each other's essence with genuine interest and love. Like the simplicity of the pork and mustard greens, one brings out the essence of the other, and together they create a simple melody reflecting nature in its purest form.

Step 4:
See Through Eyes of Love

Sensing the soup was ready, Mom told me to turn off the stove and set the table. I took out a small bowl for her rice, and put that along with the bowl of leftover rice on the dining table. I took out a bigger bowl and spoon for the pork and mustard greens. I thought about my first bite of this dish and my mouth watered. I put the bowl on the table along with the kabocha squash broth, *kua taub hau*, that Mom had made the day before. It's served at room temperature and can be eaten at any meal, acting as a palate cleanser between bites of food.

Mom opened the fridge, pulled out her Thai chili pepper, spooned some into a tiny sauce bowl, and handed it to me to put on the table. I pulled out some plates and spoons to set the rest of the table. I went around the house to call Cher, his wife, and the kids to eat. It was a weekday, so everyone was in front of their computer, in class or working remotely. They told me to go ahead and eat.

Niya, a brown Yorkie with hair covering her eyes, and Senpai, a beautiful golden orange Shiba Inu, my niece Nikki's dogs, followed me back down the stairs to join Mom and me at the dining table. Mom didn't like animals in the house and always complained that they left fur all over the place. Whenever Mom sat down to eat, they were waiting at her feet. She would tell them "no!" and then a few minutes later, throw them something to make them stop begging, which, of course, had just the opposite effect.

Mom and I sat down, she at her place at the head of the table and I on the side. I filled my bowl almost halfway with rice, then added pork, broth, and mustard greens. I chose the pork chop pieces, because I didn't like the fat and skin, and if I couldn't find any without skin, I would tear off the tender meat and give Mom the skin. I took a spoonful of rice with the broth and blew on it, then bit. It was warm, slightly sweet from the greens, and savory from the broth. I dipped a piece of pork into the pepper sauce and took a bite. It was tender and succulent, spicy from the pepper. The simplicity of the dish was a marvel, and it made me feel loved and warm. I followed the pork with a piece of mustard green to balance its saltiness with the sweet, soft, slightly peppery, and earthy green.

After we finished eating, I cleared the table and washed the dishes while Mom took out a lid and covered the food. Then she walked out of the kitchen and into her bedroom. Fifteen minutes later, when I'd finished washing up, I followed her. She was sitting on the floor sorting through a small plastic storage bin filled with little white bags and holding an antique Hmong *paug*, necklace, fit for a child, on her lap.

"What are you doing, Mom?" I asked her.

"There is a pair of earrings that I'm trying to find. I don't remember where I put them. My memory is failing me these days. I don't remember things as much as I used to."

I sat down a few feet in front of her and asked her to hand me the *paug*. I hadn't seen this before. It was a very old, child-size, solid silver necklace handmade by a Hmong silversmith. I wondered to whom it belonged but didn't ask Mom. It was thick and sturdy, with an opening about three inches wide that would fit around a child's neck. The two ends were bent backward and shaped into crane's heads with long beaks with fish eyes and feathers etched into them. Connecting the two ends of the *paug* was a chain of small silver rings linked together with a pendant. The pendant had fine etchings, designs of fish eyes and flowers. This was a soul-lock necklace meant to bind your soul to your body.

I watched as Mom opened one bag after another, pulling out pairs of very old earrings. She told me about the ones her mother had given her that she brought to the United States. A few years ago, when Aunt Green visited, she told Mom they could sell the earrings for money because they were handcrafted and made of real silver. Mom went along and sold those earrings. She regretted selling them because they were from her mother. Hearing that broke my heart.

I asked her why she'd sold them, and she responded with, "I don't know. It seemed like a good idea at the time, and my sister was selling hers, too." I asked her when and where she'd sold them, hoping that maybe I could retrieve them for her. But it was years ago and they would no longer be there.

Next Mom pulled out two sets of thick copper bracelets that Uncle Fang had made for her. They were an elongated C shape and had very finely detailed etchings on them. One was copper and the other a faded golden color. She unwrapped tiny silver coins for a baby's bracelet and a ring with points at both ends. She handed these to me one by one, and I tried them on.

She took out a large gold ring with a red stone. "This was your father's," she said, handing it to me. I was fascinated by all these items, none of which I'd ever seen before. "It was his favorite item. He bought it one day from a cousin who came to visit. He said that these rings were sent from Laos and the stone came from the base of the tree that grew where a monk was buried. It's for good luck."

Looking at the ring, I could see that it wasn't real gold and that the stone was an imitation ruby, but it was beautiful. It looked like the eye of a dragon. "The cousin had a blue ring and this red one, and your father chose this one."

I put it on my finger. The only piece that had belonged to Dad. It fit perfectly on my left middle finger and I could feel Dad's powerful energy in it.

"You keep the ring."

I didn't know what to say. There were no thoughts in my mind except questions about this man I hardly knew. It had been twenty-four years since he'd passed and Mom barely spoke of him. When he was alive, he was a ghost among us, lost in his world of opium. Even after his death, he remained as such. This ring was one of those things that made Dad a fully formed person.

I asked Mom if I could keep her bracelets and pointy ring, and she gladly handed them over.

Mom continued to open bag after bag, showing me ancient Chinese silver money bars that they had carried over from Laos. These bars were passed down through the generations, safely wrapped and kept. Each daughter, when she married, was given two bars as part of her dowry and for luck. She showed me silver coins with French writing on them from when Laos was colonized by the French in the late 1800s and early 1900s. The silver looked good as new, shiny and bright. Mom had kept them from tarnishing all these years. I remember, as a child, seeing her boil and clean the coins as they went from dark back to bright.

After she put all the silver away, Mom took out a suitcase. No longer was she trying to find those earrings; instead, she went through all these different items to show me what she had. For years she had carried suitcases around. Her closet was full of them. I knew they held Hmong clothes, including the pieces of cloth I had sewn as a teenager that she made into the shirts and sashes we wore for Hmong New Year. But I didn't know the history of her own personal items in the suitcases.

She took out a small handwoven, two-piece bamboo box that held some silver coins, acupuncture needles, and two old batik pens, specialized instruments used for applying hot, liquid wax onto fabric in intricate designs. The basket had belonged to her mother, and as a young girl, Mom kept her own *paaj ntaub*, flower cloth embroidery, in it. The basket must have been at least sixty years old, but it looked new and sturdy because of the way Mom kept it carefully wrapped and clean. I examined these items with fascination, feeling the essence of Laos and her childhood palpably fill the room. All these items came from a time and place where everything was all handmade. Seeing the batik pens told tales of Mom spending hours to dye the fabric cloth and design patterns on them with wax and then cleaning it up again for a dress. The French coins were a piece of Laotian history. These were the precious items of Mom, of Laos.

She took out a piece of *paaj ntaub*. It was a two-by-four-inch pouch, intricately sewn with thousands of cross-stitches forming simple yet beautiful patterns of snail designs in colorful threads. She looked at it admiringly and then handed it to me. "I made this. When I leave this Earth," she said, "you can look at this piece of embroidery and be proud that your mother was very skilled at *paaj ntaub*." She had poured all of her love and pride into that embroidery, and in sharing it, she hoped I would know her. This was the first time she revealed something she was proud of.

She went through all the Hmong clothes in the suitcase, unfolding each piece, remembering them fondly, pointing out what they were. She showed me a *paug* that had five tiers of thick silver rings stacked on top of one another and increasing in size from the neck down toward the chest. These necklaces were very valuable and displayed your wealth in Laos. Back then, very few families could afford such luxury. She also showed me two bunches of money bag sashes she had sewn that I'd worn before at Hmong New Year festivals.

As each item revealed its secrets, I saw deeper into the essence of Mom. Every artifact wove a tapestry of her history, providing me with an intimate glimpse into the woman behind the roles she had performed throughout the years. Mom generously allowed me to peer beneath the ocean of mystery that concealed who she is.

After we'd gone through everything for almost an hour, Mom repacked every item and returned them to the suitcase. It had been a beautiful and rich bonding experience for both of us. Then, out of the blue, she said, "The *paug* and two of the money bag sashes along with two outfits are supposed to go to you when you get married." She waited two beats. "But you're not getting married." Two beats. "So I will give them to Leah's daughter when she's old enough." Just like that she picked up the sword and slashed my heart.

I instinctively swung back. "I don't care. Those things aren't important to me anyway."

In the aftermath, shell-shocked, we scanned the perimeter for the damage done. Regret hung between us like a heavy cloud, weighed down by unspoken words and lost moments. Mom proceeded to stow the remaining items and closed the suitcase while I scrolled aimlessly on Instagram on my iPhone. Finally, she broke the silence by asking me to help put the suitcase in the closet. I proceeded in silence. Once the suitcase was back in the closet, I stepped back to survey the room for anything else to put away.

Mom took out two French coins from a round red case originally used to store a gold necklace. She handed me the coins and three acupuncture needles. They were her peace offering.

"What's this?" I reached out to accept them. Truce.

"If you're ever feeling feverish, take these two coins and a whole raw egg. Wrap them in a warm, moist face towel and rub the egg and coins all over your body, from head to toe. Then, puncture the tips of your fingers with this needle. It will relieve the fever and make you feel better." Her words evoked a childhood memory of her performing that ritual when I was five and had a fever.

Both of us knew this wasn't easy. We were trying to balance on two shifting sheets of ice, one under each foot—one representing the weight of tradition, the other independence. Old and new. Mother and daughter. We were trying to stand straight on this precarious surface, attempting to find our way back to each other.

Just as when we had earlier cooked a simple meal of boiled pork and greens together, the subtlety required to sustain our relationship became evident. My initial response was always to hit back and end the game, but I had to learn to absorb that bullet and play back, to alchemize what she sent me and send it back out as love. It sounded simple, but wasn't easy. It required me to have rightness about myself. This became a stabilizing ballast for those times when Mom and I found ourselves in disagreement.

Mom didn't stop asking me—actually, *telling* me—to get married and start my life after that. She would still carry on about finding a husband when we spoke on the phone or when I went home, but at least now, rather than drawing my sword, I put it down and loved her just a bit more.

MUSTARD GREENS AND
FIDDLEHEAD FERNS

"Run, the Communists
Are Coming!"

In my late thirties, I moved with some friends from San Francisco to Mendocino County to work on a 162-acre retreat center called The Land. It is a gorgeous property that came with a communal lodge attached to a commercial kitchen, thirteen cabins, and eight houses. Over the course of five years, my friends and I turned the abandoned barn that had been a storage and dumping ground for old pipes, sheetrock, and chopped wood into a state-of-the-art meditation hall with floor-to-ceiling windows, reclaimed-oak floors on the first level, and a cozy multiuse space with cork flooring on the second level.

The first year working on The Land was a hard adjustment to say the least. We showed up at the beginning of January 2017, the middle of the rainy season. Our city jeans, booties, and silk blouses wound up being packed away and stashed in the basements of several houses. But we loved to shop and we loved fashion, so we scoured the internet for chic flannel button-down shirts, Urban

Outfitters jogger pants, Timberland boots, and rustic faux-fur jackets.

We were city dwellers through and through and knew nothing about country life. We went from walking down the street to Whole Foods to driving forty-five minutes along a winding road to the nearest food co-op. We were used to and thrived on the fast-paced, thought-to-action flow of the city and discovered that the country was anything but.

At first all I saw was a lot of dirty, hard work. The previous owner of the property had bought it as a shelter for himself, his family, and close friends in anticipation of the millennium apocalypse. He visited the place twice, and when the world continued to spin on its axis with no volcanic eruptions, tsunamis, planes falling from the sky, or Wall Street crash, he up and left it in the hands of a caretaker. By the time we arrived, the only residents were mice, squirrels, and woodpeckers, and, boy, did they party like drunk frat boys, leaving a multitude of evidence in their wake.

During those first few months, in the midst of rainstorms, we spent our days scrubbing broken, rodent-infested, feces-packed, stained toilets and tubs, floors, and cupboards, and making loads and loads of trips to the dump with mustard-colored sheets and mattresses, broken dressers, and bedframes. On top of that, there were ruptured pipes, clogged septic tanks, and power outages.

Amid the chaos of reclaiming the property, we felt a beauty that called for attention and respect. The landscape, serene and mystical yet resolute, inspired a natural generosity, awakening a desire to give fully of ourselves. Its stillness drew us in. We were home.

The first year was all about building our relationship to The Land. We were building trust. We had to learn to stop and listen and feel for what she wanted, how she wanted each cabin to look and feel, how she wanted each house to be remodeled.

And then there was the garden—a magical, five-acre space with one section designed in the shape of a mandala. The garden was designed by Carolyn North and built by a group of individuals trained by the Findhorn Community in Scotland. The Findhorn community, founded in 1962 by Peter and Eileen Caddy and Dorothy Maclean, became renowned for its remarkable gardens, created in sandy soil through a blend of spiritual connection and ecological principles. Inspired by these teachings, Carolyn and the team designed a garden where the beds were aligned with the moon cycle to enhance plant growth. Vegetables were interwoven with flowers and perennials, fostering a harmonious, healthy ecosystem.

In keeping with Findhorn's practices, the garden was nurtured not just by hands, but through a deep spiritual connection with nature. Just as the Findhorn community has long been known for its belief in communicating with the plants, insects, and devas, the garden was tended with similar reverence. A Zen practitioner from the Green Gulch Farm Zen Center, who had also studied at Findhorn, helped care for the space. Statues of Quan Yin and other Buddhist figures dotted the garden, bringing a sense of peace and spirituality. At the center of it all was an open area for picnics and lounging, offering a space for both reflection and connection to the land.

At the end opposite the mandala was a little stone creek that fed into a pond we named Mirror Pond, with the idea that when you looked into it, you saw your true self. Across the pond was an orchard with a variety of fruit trees, including apples, pears, Asian pears, and plums. In total, there were eighty fruit trees spread throughout The Land.

When I first saw the garden, it made me think of Mom, as she would have loved working in it. She'd always wanted a space of her own where she could plant and grow whatever she pleased. Once she started living with my brothers and their wives, she had little gardens in their backyards, but the wives never appreciated them. To my sisters-in-law, she was taking space away from the flowers and fruit trees they wanted to plant, and they were not shy about telling her as much.

For the first two years we worked on The Land, hardly anyone went down to the garden. Having grown up resistant to working in the garden with Mom, I personally didn't want to have much to do with it. Our gardener kept up with it and continued to maintain it. From spring to early winter, he would bring us fresh produce—arugula, kale, spinach, romaine, butter lettuce, cucumber, tomato, broccoli, sorrel, basil, mint, scallion, thyme, oregano, rosemary, zucchini, yellow squash—and in the fall, different kinds of pumpkins. Fruit was abundant and fell off the trees like raindrops in a summer storm, painting the ground with a vibrant mosaic of colors and filling the air with their sweet aroma.

In our third year with the property, it became evident that we were adapting to life on The Land, growing more attuned to her language and rhythm. We gardened, harvested, and made delicious meals. We distributed the excess vegetables and fruits to the local community and made meals on a weekly basis to feed the homeless and low-income population in Ukiah and Santa Rosa. We were circulating our abundance outward.

The raging fire season of 2019, combined with the COVID-19 quarantine, served as a wake-up call. We realized we couldn't just use the property for sanctuary; we were called to focus on restoration and sustainability as well. We learned about rewilding, which involves returning the earth to its natural state without human control or influence. This led to the establishment of our Earth Program, where we practiced composting, rainwater harvesting, and sustainable gardening techniques. Life drew me toward Mom's experiences through necessity; tending land became something I loved.

I invited Mom to visit me on The Land on several occasions, telling her about the garden and how much she'd enjoy it. I'd shown her pictures from our website so she could see the beauty. Each time I asked, she declined. In April 2021, I picked up the phone one day and called to see how she was doing. Out of the blue, she said, "Come pick me up next week." I thought she was joking.

"Are you serious?" I asked her.

"Yes," she replied. "Come early so that we can go to the Hmong market to buy some food to bring up there."

I couldn't believe what I was hearing, and yet, at the same time, it felt so right. In the days leading up to that weekend, I waited for the other shoe to drop, for her to say she was too tired or had to do something else and couldn't come after all. But she never did. On Saturday I started out at seven o'clock in the morning, although by Mom's standard that was very late, and drove the three and a half hours to get her. When I arrived at my brother's house and rang the bell, Mom greeted me at the door, chiding me for being so late. "The day is almost gone, and we still have to go to the Hmong market! By the time we get there it'll be dark!"

I shook my head and laughed. "It's still early, Mom." I walked inside hoping to rest a bit before driving again, but Mom was packed and ready to go. She was as excited as a seven-year-old going on her first field trip.

"We have to go; it's getting late!" Had this been a year earlier, I would have been annoyed at her criticism, but now what I felt was her enthusiasm.

I quickly went to the bathroom, then said goodbye to the family, reminding them that I would drop Mom off at our sister Cha's place in Sunnyvale in a few days. Mom had packed some of her own food, including the Hmong rice, some greens, medicinal herbs, and pork rind. We had talked about gardening, so she brought seeds, lemongrass stalks, and herbs that we would be planting in the garden. We stopped by the Hmong market and picked up some groceries. I wanted us to cook a meal for everyone on the property, so we picked up the items we'd need to make baked herbed fish wrapped in banana leaves.

We made it to the property a little after three o'clock. As we drove through the gate and up the meadow, my heart swelled with pride. I wanted Mom to be as proud of The Land as I was. We drove past the garden, and I told her what we'd planted and that I would take her down there later. As we drove farther into the property, I pointed out the lodge, the cabins, and the houses.

We arrived at the house she was staying in and stood in front of the wall of windows looking out onto a small hill that opened to a meadow and a line of trees beyond the meadow. On the horizon were more rolling hills. "What do you think, Mom? Is this like Laos? Does it remind you of Laos?" I asked with innocent, hopeful curiosity.

I had never wanted to please her the way I did at that moment. I wanted The Land to be something with which we both could connect. I wanted to show her something she could be proud of. Selfishly, I also wanted her approval.

"It's nice," was her underwhelming response. "Laos is so different from this. In Laos there are mountains and mountains of jungle so thick you can't see more than a few feet in front of you."

I was a little disappointed by her response, but I didn't lose hope. The garden was what I really wanted her to see, and I just knew she would love it.

That week with Mom was magical and healing. She taught me many recipes and how to garden. By popular demand from my friends, she was brave enough to teach a group of us, all masked and standing fifteen feet apart, about the garden and the medicinal elements in some of the plants, like consuming aloe vera to help with digestion or using the gel to soften your skin. She spoke in Hmong and I translated what

I could. She taught us to forage for foods we had dismissed as weeds, like mustard greens, and showed us the difference between the fennel in our garden and the fennel Hmong people grew, which was sweeter and more fragrant. She scolded us for letting weeds overrun the beds and explained how to harvest cabbage in a way that allowed a second, younger, and softer cabbage to grow. She came out more than I'd ever seen her before, and everyone was captivated by her teaching and knowledge.

The Land had strict protocols during COVID-19 to ensure that all guests to the property remained healthy. Mom and I had to test upon arrival. Because we were both negative, we were able to prepare a lunch for everyone. I had been making a few Hmong dishes on The Land, but they never came out like Mom's, and I wanted everyone to have the same nourishment I got when I ate her food.

We planned to make baked herb halibut wrapped in banana leaf parcels, Mom's steamed white rice, and, since we didn't have any Hmong greens, sautéed kale. But on the second day, when we went down to the garden, Mom made a beeline for the mustard greens lining the fence.

Every spring, when the mustard greens bloomed in the garden and the ferns covered the hillside beyond the lodge pathway, I wondered if they were the same mustard greens Mom used at home all the time, and if those were the same ferns I foraged and ate once with my family on a camping trip.

We had two gardeners, and when I asked them about the mustard greens, they both told me the same thing: "They're more of a weed. We use them to attract pollinators."

"A weed? I think these are the mustard greens we ate all the time as kids. My mom would sauté them," I told the gardeners. Although they confirmed that you could indeed eat them, they didn't seem interested in them as a food source.

With Mom there, these were the two plants I most wanted her expert opinion on.

How to Forage and Cook
Mustard Greens and Fiddlehead Ferns

Yield: Humanity

Cook time: Until you see the "other" as you

Ingredients:
Courage
Acceptance
Confidence

Step 1:
The Discarded Are Gifts

The first thing Mom taught me about foraging was that not all weeds are bad. Get to know your weeds and their benefits, do not just pull them out and throw them away. Everything, unless poisonous, could be good for something.

As I followed Mom toward the mustard greens along the fence, she exclaimed, "You guys don't eat these?! These are edible." When I asked if they were the same greens we'd always eaten, she snapped off a soft stem and ate it, then snapped off another and handed it to me.

"Yes, these are the ones you eat, but these are a bit spicier than the Hmong ones. The Hmong mustard greens are sweeter."

"Hmong ones? How are there Hmong ones? Aren't they all the same?"

"No, they're different," she told me. "The Hmong ones are better. But these are still very good. Why aren't you guys eating them? Most of these are old by now, and you want to eat them when they're still young, before the flower blooms."

I told her they were more of a good weed for us, and that we didn't eat them. I didn't know how to explain in Hmong how we use them as a cover crop or to attract bees for pollination, or that it helps with the soil, so I left those out.

Mom couldn't believe what I was saying. "You're wasting food," she told me as she continued to snap young stems and directed me on how to pick them.

"We call these *zaub paaj* (flower greens). You pick the young part of the plant. It's the part of the stem where the flower buds haven't bloomed. Once they've bloomed, they're too old and tough to eat. Look." She showed me the difference between a young stem and an old stem. She snapped a piece off from each and handed them to me to try. She was right, the bloomed stem was tough and fibrous. She continued to snap young stems and I followed suit. "You guys don't know how to eat these. I'll make some for all of you to try."

We went through patches and patches of mustard greens until we filled a plastic bag and Mom was satisfied. "You can sauté them alone or with meat. You can boil them alone or with meat. All you need is a bit of salt to bring out the flavor. These are very delicious to eat. In Laos we didn't have these, but here in America we grow lots of them. They can also be foraged in the woods. They aren't just weeds. They are very good for you. Hmong people sell these at markets all the time. They are one of the main greens that we eat."

As Mom was telling me this, I realized just how disconnected we had become—from the earth and from each other as a society. One culture's weed is another culture's livelihood. We were surrounded by an abundance of food, and we didn't even know what we were missing. While we were throwing food away without understanding its value, another culture was losing out on the opportunity to eat it. It's so easy for us to discard something instead of taking the time to learn about it and build a relationship with it. We see weeds as a nuisance and never stop to wonder what the essence of that plant could be or the purpose it serves. We compare it to something else and see it as an impediment to our own agenda, and then we cut it out. Discard it. We do this not only with food, but also with material things, with ourselves, with people, and with other cultures. We've become a society of narrow-minded definitions of good or bad, useful or meaningless, right or wrong.

This was something we Hmong people understood after having been chased from our own land in China, persecuted in Laos, and then seen as outsiders in the various countries where we ultimately settled. My family, on both Mom's and Dad's sides, had experienced firsthand how terrifying it was to be hunted and killed just for being the minority culture.

The thread that wove their lives together happened long before they became a married couple. Mom, a member of the Xiong clan, and Dad, a proud Vang clan descendant, lived in the same village but on different sides of the mountain. Their families knew each other well. Mom was a teenager at the time and Dad was already married and had a few young children.

During one of our weekends together, Mom recounted the story of when their village was raided as though it were fresh in her mind. She didn't know what year it was or how old she was, but I later learned from other family members that it was January or February of 1962.

×   ×   ×

"It was the season where the New Year festivities had just ended and we were getting ready to prepare the land for clearing. One evening, two traveling *plog,* Laotians, were on their way to buy some pigs. They came through the Xiong side of the village and proceeded to the Vang side of the mountain. It was nightfall, so they stopped and spent the night in a Vang cousin's house. The following day they went on their way to another Hmong village to buy pigs. In that place there were soldiers from General

Vang Pao's army. The two men must have been carrying money to buy pigs and never made it back home. We don't know if the soldiers killed them or if they were killed by someone else.

"When they didn't return after a few days, their comrades came to look for them. They came to our village. They had guns. They were angry. They asked about their friends. We told them we didn't know what happened to them. We said they spent the night at a Vang cousin's house and the following morning they went to the White Hmong village. The *plog* went there to search for them. After not finding them, they came back and accused us of killing them.

"That day they arrested my brother Fang, three Xiong members, the Vang cousin who hosted them, and two other Vang members. All seven men were taken to the *plog* village. We didn't know if they were going to come back home. Each day we waited in hopes of their return. We didn't know if something had happened to them. They were held there for a long time. For seven to maybe ten days. Eventually, the Vang cousins were released but they kept my brother and the Xiong cousins. We were afraid that they kept them to kill them.

"That day some of our men went back to the *plog* village to look for them, but they were no longer there. The communist soldiers had taken them somewhere. They couldn't find them anywhere. The villagers said that our men were probably killed but they didn't know for sure. They saw them being taken away from the village.

"That day our men went to the White Hmong village where General Vang Pao's soldiers were. They paid them to find and rescue my brother and cousins. The soldiers went to the *plog* village, taking guns with them. They were prepared to fight.

"That day, we knew we were in danger if we stayed. Families packed what they could carry and ran to other villages for safety. We knew the communists would come after us should war break out.

"We had cousins that married into the Thao clan so we were going there. Their village was down the mountain across a small creek. It was far but not too far. Everything was happening so fast, I felt as though my heart was going to explode out of my chest. Me, Mom, brother Xao and his two wives and baby, and Sister-in-law Fang, we all set out to the Thao village. It was already nightfall, too dark to see anything but the space in front of you where the light touches. We walked all the way to the Thao farms and dropped off our things. The village was still farther down. We decided to have Mom and brother Xao and his baby and second wife continue to the village while myself, first Sister-in-law Xao and Sister-in-law Fang went back to gather and bring the animals.

"The night was still. We walked into the dark. Three of us girls reached our village. There were still a few families packing and leaving. We each carried a bamboo basket on our back and put some chickens in there and a jar of pork oil. We herded four pigs with us. We were starting on our way out when suddenly, we heard popping sounds like thunder slicing through the dense night air. Our soldiers had reached the *plog* village and war broke out. There was so much shooting that the area caught on fire. The fighting was close enough that we could hear the gunfire and see the red flames on the horizon. Soldiers were in the village shooting, while others fired from the periphery. The fire raged throughout the entire area. Many people lost their lives.

"The communist soldiers had kept my brother and our cousins at a farmhouse nearby. When they saw the flames and the attack underway, they ran back, leaving our men tied to chairs and tables, unattended. Our men managed to free themselves and made their escape. They split up to avoid being caught together. My brother and a cousin fled in one direction, while the other two ran in another.

"My sisters-in-law and I rushed on our way toward the Thao village. We had already been walking for so long. My bare feet hurt, stumbling over sticks and stones through the jungle. My eyes burned from being up all night, but I had to keep going. There was no time to stop and rest.

"The sun was just starting to wake up; the sky becoming indigo. We were walking along the river when we heard someone yelling, "Run, run, the communists are coming!" We dropped all our baskets and left the chickens and pigs. We ran into the jungle and found a cave nearby. We hid there. We could hear the commotion and bullets. We stayed where we were and didn't move. It was just us three girls.

"That morning I thought I might die. Then it was quiet. We didn't know if it was safe. We were no longer protected by the night. First Sister-in-law Xao was worried about her baby. We didn't know if Mom and the rest made it to the Thao village. She couldn't wait any longer, so she ran out to find them. Sister-in-law Fang and I told her not to go, but she wouldn't stay. I was so scared for her.

"The two of us were left. We waited. There was no time to be tired, to rest. I had to keep going. I could hear my heart thumping fast. I was so scared they could hear my heartbeat. After a long time we heard someone from a distance saying, 'You can come out.'

"We came back out. The sun was on the horizon. The sky was starting to brighten. We went back to where we dropped the baskets. The jar of pork oil had cracked and three of the pigs were eating up the oil. Another pig had wandered around the river so we had to go look for it and herd it back. We gathered the chickens back into the basket. We stayed quiet and hid as much as we could and made our way to the Thao village.

"The sun was out now and it was mid-morning. We finally reached the village. We went straight to cousin's house and found Mom and brother Xao and his wives and baby It was such a relief to see them. I didn't know if we would see each other again. Everyone was there except brother Fang. There were family members still missing. It was heart-wrenching. People cried for their loved ones. Families were separated among the shuffling and hiding. There were so many of us that ran together. Your dad's family and the rest of the Vang clan ran with us.

"It was another two days before brother Fang and our cousin found us. We were so happy to see them. First we were crying from loss, and now we were crying from joy. But it was a bittersweet joy. The kind that tells you nothing will be the same. Everything's changed.

"Family members were scattered between different villages. We didn't know who was dead or who was alive. It took a few more days to finally gather everyone. We were so lucky no one was killed. Some of General Vang Pao's soldiers were killed during the fight."

× × ×

I had never heard this story before. It was something that Mom and Dad never spoke of. I knew they were born and raised in Laos. I knew that we fled to Thailand, but never knew of the conditions or the effect of the war on our family. And because they never spoke of it, my information came from books and websites, piecing together the history of my people, of my family. But to hear her story in detail was to start filling in the gaps of who she is. To learn where her resilience comes from, her strength, her courage all born from pain, heartache, and war. She was becoming a woman to me. A courageous woman.

All these years I had discarded her. Never took the time to learn about her, listen to her stories. I had dismissed Mom the way America had dismissed its refugees. In America we were another group of immigrants. America did not know us. Did not know of the thousands of lives we saved for America in Laos. America did not know of the lives that we lost defending its democracy. Our military service, noncombatant service, and civilian contributions were not acknowledged in the melting pot. We were aliens to a country we died fighting for.

Step 2:
Start from the Seed

When I was younger, we once took a family camping trip to Silver Lake. We went foraging for curly ferns that we later stuffed, along with some herbs, into the fish we'd caught in the river. Then we wrapped the stuffed fish in aluminum foil and grilled them over an open fire. When they were cooked, we sprinkled them with salt. Every year when the ferns behind the lodge on The Land bloomed, still curled within themselves, I thought about that camping trip, remembering the bitter, earthy taste of the ferns.

After the mustard-green harvesting, I took Mom to the hillside where the ferns grew and asked her if they were edible. Most of them already had their leaves proudly fanned out, fully grown, but many were still furled.

"Yes! These are edible! We've picked these before, remember?" she said, referring to the exact trip I always remembered. "They are a little bitter, so they're best eaten with fish or chicken in a soup or sautéed."

Mom didn't wait. She immediately started snapping the stems with the furled heads and put them into another plastic bag. I took a picture of her and sent it to my friends on the property. "Fiddlehead ferns! Mom says they're edible, and she's going to make us some to try!" Everyone was excited.

"We're going to need another bag," her voice rang out just a few feet above me on the hill. In haste, I reached for my phone, texting someone to fetch a bucket while Mom and I continued our diligent gathering of fiddleheads. It was only when we assessed our harvest that her satisfaction became palpable. Her face lit up with a deep sense of pride, and in that moment, I felt it, too.

Standing on the hillside among the lush green fans of the fern, she seamlessly merged with her surroundings, as if her very soul resonated with the natural world. Her confidence radiated. She felt at peace, at home with the plants and trees, as though they were welcoming one of their own. There was a joy that flowed from her, making me feel as though I, too, belonged to the forest.

×　×　×

Mom continued her story:

"The days following the raid were hard. We had no house to live in, no food to eat. We went to live at a cousin's house, but there was no place to sleep. We lived in constant fear of the communist soldiers. We dug a large, deep hole behind their house for shelter. We covered the dirt floor with banana leaves to lie on. During daylight hours, we scoured the surroundings for food, using our cousin's pots and pans for cooking. At night, we returned to the hole for sleep, our cousins covering it with bamboo and dirt to conceal its existence.

"The hole couldn't accommodate everyone, so brother Fang and his family stayed there, while we sought another solution. We found a spot on the side of a hill and dug a deep cave, again using banana leaves for bedding.

"Sleep was difficult. Food was so scarce because we had no farm. We were afraid that the communists would attack this village, so, after just a few weeks, we left and hid in the mountains. *Oy ah*, when I talk about these times from long ago. . . ."

Mom paused and looked down at her hands for a moment, bringing herself back to the present. She cleared her throat.

"We ran into the mountains and slept wherever we stopped in areas with thick foliage and coverage. All the Vang and Xiong families and the children. . . . The babies would cry so much. You'd just pray that when they cried no one was around to hear them. We'd go to our cousin's farm to sleep there for a few nights. But it was too close to the village, and we would be scared that they could find us there. So, we went very, very far away to search for another area to stay. We'd stay there for a few nights. Then we'd be on the move again and find an old farm area and stay there for a few nights. No matter where we went, the babies would cry. We'd get to a place and sleep for a few nights, then go to another place and sleep there for a few nights. We had no direction, we didn't know where to go.

"We couldn't go anymore. We ran out of food. The children were hungry and crying from starvation. The elders were tired. Everyone couldn't keep running. We finally decided to go back to an area close to the Thao village. All the Vangs and the Xiongs were together. We had been on the run since the New Year festivities ended months ago. If we wanted to have food, we would need to start planting.

"Each family began to build their house, chopping bamboo and gathering banana leaves. We cleared a vast area of land for farming, cutting down plants and brush. We burned it and tilled the soil.

"We hadn't even finished preparing the beds for planting when a coughing illness began spreading through some families. My brother's little girl caught it, became very sick, and died. Others followed.

"After we prepared the land, we decided to leave this area for good. We had settled for four or five months. But it wasn't far enough away from the communist soldiers. We were constantly worried about being found and killed. We were on alert all the time, wary of sounds from the jungle, of walking to and from the farm or visiting relatives in nearby villages. We had to get much farther away from the war, so we decided to go west and crossed the Mekong River. The Thao clan left with us. It wasn't safe for them either.

"We walked for days and days, stopping to rest and sleep when we couldn't go any farther. I don't know how long we had been walking when we finally reached the Mekong River. At that point, soldiers were not patrolling the river. It wasn't dangerous. There were so many families. Laotian boatmen crossed us a few people at a time.

"We were now in the province of Xaignabouli. On this side of Laos, the war did not affect it. There was no fighting in the mountains, no raids, no soldiers coming to bother the villagers. After we crossed the Mekong, the families split up. I don't remember why we split. Our

Xiong and Thao cousins went to Phouhong. Your dad's side of the family went to Phihua. Some of the Vang families followed the Xiong to Phouhong.

"In Phouhong, there was a village where brother Xao's first wife's sister and her family lived. We came to join them. It was my mom and both brothers and their families. All my sisters were married and lived with their clans.

"By the time we got there, it was late in the planting season, so we couldn't plant anything. We helped the family with their farm and joined in with them. It was hard that season with food, so we made do with what we had. My mom would take me into the jungle and show me what was edible. We found cassava roots and wild greens and bamboo shoots. Once we got home, she would show me how to prepare them.

"Your father and I—we lived in our separate places for many years. Your dad's first wife passed away, and a while after that, he came to Phouhong for a wife. That's how I married him.

"For a few more years, we lived in Phihua and flowed into a natural rhythm of life. I had Mai, Phoua, Cher, and Cha already when the earth exploded and we moved to Thailand. We were in Thailand for years where I had Tang and you, then we came to the United States. This is the origin of how and why we first left."

×   ×   ×

All my life, I always felt like I began in the middle of a sentence, unable to flip back to the beginning to answer the question, "Who are you?" To fill the blank pages, I borrowed stories from others, imitated them from movies, took on others' emotions. I was living outside the pages of my own life. Now, when people ask, my mouth can speak with colors. My bloodline came from heroes and heroines, mystics and warriors, addicts and healers, love and war, bravery and courage, pain and fortitude. We are people of the earth. We survived no matter the odds, defied great betrayals, outran organized armies, and pulled one another out of death. It was the seed from which I sprouted.

Step 3:
Appreciate What You Have

Mom and I went back home after a successful day of foraging. We put the ferns and mustard greens in the refrigerator, then had lunch and rested for the rest of the day.

In the evening, we began preparing the next day's lunch. Austin, one of my friends, dropped off the halibut and ingredients for the meal. We first salted the halibut filets and put them on the side. We rinsed and chopped all the herbs—cilantro, green onion, Thai basil, and mint—and put all that mixture into a big bowl. Next we took out the packaged banana leaves and opened them carefully, piece by piece, so as not to break them. I cut them into twelve-inch lengths and stripped off the vein to make it possible to fold the leaves later. I turned on the stove and, one by one, held a banana leaf over the flame for a few seconds to soften it. The banana leaf quickly turned into a darker, shiny, earth green color upon contact with the flame. I moved the leaf back and forth over the flame to soften the whole leaf and then turned it over and did the same. It took a good amount of time to prepare thirty leaves, and I was grateful we did it the night before.

Once all the preparations were complete, we put the herbs and fish in the fridge and left the banana leaves on the counter. For the final preparation, Mom took out a big stainless steel bowl and scooped up some white rice, filling the bowl almost to the top. Then she had me rinse the rice a few times, filled the bowl with water, and left it on the counter overnight.

The next morning, we set out to steam the rice and make the halibut parcels. Mom placed a banana leaf in front of her. She placed a kaffir lime leaf and a small piece of lemongrass in the middle of the banana leaf. She put a piece of halibut on top, and scooped a spoonful of herbs on top of the fish, covering the whole filet. Then she carefully folded the banana leaf over each other, covering the fish lengthwise, and took the top and bottom pieces and folded them over each other. We used the banana leaf vein to tie the parcel together. We spent about an hour wrapping the packets. In the middle of it, Mom paused to steam the rice over the stove.

Once the rice and parcels were ready, we put them in the oven and cooked the mustard greens and ferns. Mom instructed me to put the mustard greens in a bowl and *muab tsaug,* which isn't quite "washing" them but is a method of cleaning that consists of filling a bowl with water and dunking a few pieces at a time to rid them of any dirt or bugs, then shaking off the excess water. This was how I was taught to wash greens. I washed it once and called it done, but Mom scolded me to do it twice. And that was the other thing—whenever you *tsaug* greens, you always had to do it twice. The first time got the dirt and bugs out; the second time made sure they were clean. I swore the greens were clean already, but I refilled the bowl anyway and did it again to Mom's satisfaction.

While I prepared the mustard greens, Mom worked on the ferns, snipping the unfurled heads off the stems. I watched her work, looking to see how much of the stem she kept and what got thrown away.

As Mom continued her work, she told me to boil a pot of water for blanching the mustard greens and another for making the fish soup with the fiddlehead ferns.

Once the water for the greens was boiling, she had me put them in and blanch them for a few minutes until they were "about halfway soft," so that they would sauté faster and maintain their vibrant green color.

When the pot of water for the fiddleheads began boiling, Mom added a few pieces of fish to create the stock for the soup. After a few minutes, she added half the ferns, sprinkled in some salt, gave the pot a stir, and left the fiddleheads to simmer.

By then the mustard greens were ready. She turned off the heat and told me to strain them in a colander.

Mom kept an eye on many things at once, tracking the progress of each dish, stirring the fiddleheads from time to time, giving me instructions for the mustard greens, and calculating how long it would take to sauté them both.

After a lifetime in the kitchen, with her senses fully attuned to the ingredients in front of her, Mom could play them like an instrument, always knowing when to turn something off, when it needed more salt, and what it should taste like. When I'm in the kitchen with her, I become an instrument she's also playing—guiding me on what to do, when, and how, all while keeping her attention on me to ensure my focus remains on the food. I become an extension of her, my hands commanded by her voice and confidence. If she senses me wavering or notices I'm on my phone too long, she nudges me back to stir something on the stove, and sometimes she outright tells me to stop staring at my phone. I watched her movements, and even though we were juggling multiple tasks under a tight time frame, she never lost her cool or panicked. She stayed grounded, absorbed the stress, and continued cooking with confident joy. I was witnessing a lifetime of practice at work.

×　×　×

Mom resumed her story of once again fleeing through the mountains.

"When we migrated to Thailand, we didn't have to cross the Mekong. We were already on the west side of the river. We just crossed the border and came straight to Thailand.

"We weren't chased out of our village, but at that time Hmong people all over were fleeing. People were saying that it was no longer safe for us because General Vang Pao had fled to Thailand. They said the *xam lav* won the war and took over the country. They said the *xam lav* were coming for us.

"In our village, all the families wanted to leave. Your dad didn't want to leave. He wanted to stay in Laos, his homeland. These were the mountains of his father and grandfather and great-grandfather. Of your dad's sons, Khoua Neng, the eldest, wanted to leave. They said it would be safer. After much debate, we split up. Your dad was stubborn. Khoua Neng and his family left for Thailand and followed another cousin. He took one of your father's younger sons, Dang, with him to watch over. It was two other sons, Yia Lue and Chao, who stayed with Dad. The daughters were already all married and followed other clans. The whole village left except for our family and another Yang family. We had lived at the edge of the village, and the Yang family was in the center of the village, so we moved into an empty house to be closer to them. It was just the two families left. It was so quiet and eerie. You could feel a gloom casted over our heads.

"Not long after that, Yia Lue's wife got sick and she passed away. They had one baby together, Soua, who was a toddler at that time. He needed a mother to take care of her, so he married another wife.

"It was very hard living on our own. Your dad didn't like having all the family separated. We stayed for a few more months and finally decided to leave for Thailand. Khoua Neng came back to take us.

"When we were set to go to Thailand, we took only what we could carry. We had two horses and packed what we could on them. We each carried a basket on our back. Yia Lue carried a basket with a blanket inside, and he put Soua in the basket to carry her. Your sister Mai was eight or nine. She carried Cha, a toddler, on her back. Phoua was maybe six. She carried a little packet of clothes. Cher was maybe four. He could walk on his own, but he was so stubborn and wouldn't.

"Your dad was very sick at that time and was just getting better, but he didn't have his full strength back yet. He had begun smoking opium by then, because of the pain. He carried a basket with a blanket and his opium pipe and lamp. He also put Cher in the basket, because whenever you put him down to walk, he wouldn't. Even if you left him there to follow, he would not move. He would just cry. So, your dad had to put him back in the basket. He was carried all the way to Thailand. Such a stubborn child. You would be so tired you could barely walk, and still, he wouldn't get out of that basket.

"I don't remember how many days we walked. Toward the end of the trip, we were one day away from reaching Thailand. We came upon a mountain when one of the Thao elders told us to stop and rest. It was almost nighttime. We rested until nightfall and then started up again.

"Even though there was no war on our side of the land, we still had to be careful. The communists were coming after all Hmong people, and there was no safe place to be. We heard of people being arrested for no reason, of villages being burned down. They were killing everyone, even old people and babies. Everyone's senses were so heightened to sounds and rustling coming from the jungle.

"We couldn't turn on any lamp at the possible risk of soldiers nearby catching a glimpse of any light. It was so dark and we just had to feel our way around, trying to follow the road that was in front of us. Each one following the other.

"We took a quick break on the road, because some of the people needed to pee. There was some rustling coming from the bushes. It must have been the people peeing causing the rustling. It was ridiculous. Someone got scared and suddenly yelled, 'Run, run, the communists are here!'

"Chaos broke loose. You didn't want to wait around to see if it was true. From all that we've been through, from the stories that we've heard, everyone was already on edge traveling through the mountain. Everyone reacted to those words. We all ran, afraid for our lives.

"We were in the dark feeling around for our children, for each other, colliding into each other, trying to find a direction to run. I ran straight ahead with your dad and the children. Then suddenly, I tripped on something and fell hard. But I got right back up and ran. No one wanted to fall behind, so you kept running. People going into different directions. Everyone trying to get ahead. Everyone trying to gather their children. You didn't know if the child you were running with was yours or not. You didn't know if you're still running with your own family. All that mattered was staying alive. I just kept going.

"It was so dark. No one could see where they were going. The possibility of running off a cliff to your death was real. The possibility of falling into a hole was real. Of tripping and breaking your neck. You're just running into the dark.

"Khoua Neng was with us and knew the way, so he kept on the road. Your dad and I and the kids followed him. We lost Yia Lue and his wife and other families. They went in a different direction. It was dark, you couldn't see what was happening. You couldn't see who was still with you.

"When we didn't hear any gunshots or anyone chasing us, we got off the road and found a place to hide behind thick foliage. We stayed up and listened to the stillness, to the creatures and critters of the dark. Sleep felt dangerous. You didn't want to close your eyes in case you never opened them again. But what can you do when you can no longer keep them open? You just pray to your ancestors and you close them.

"The following morning, as soon as light touched the sky, we went looking for each other, calling each other's name, hoping for a response. We retraced our steps and yelled and yelled to each other. Family by family, we found each other again. We gathered everyone together.

"It was a false alarm. There were no soldiers. There was much relief but the reality of danger at any moment was still very real. You couldn't let your guard down.

"One of our cousins had a horse that was pregnant. During the chaos the horse went into labor. We had to leave that horse and the foal behind. Once we reached the village in Thailand, I don't remember if the cousin went back for the horse and foal or not.

"Once everyone was gathered, we continued on our way for another half-day walk. We came upon a river called Nan Wa. We crossed that river and went up a mountain and finally made it to the village where Khoua Neng lived. I don't know if I felt relief at having left a country where we were hunted, or scared at being in a place that was no longer familiar. There was no time to think about these things. You just keep going.

"We arrived and were met by devastation. A few days after we got to the camp, Dang became very sick and passed away. We don't know what it was. He was only a teenager. He was such a good boy. When Dang was one or two years old he was very sick and was never able to speak from that. But he was not dumb. He was a very sharp child, very smart and aware. He was helpful and knew how to sew *paaj ntaub* and could make a Hmong outfit. He helped to take care of all the babies. If Dang was alive, he would be the most handsome son. He had a long and slender face. He was such a good boy."

She paused, reflecting on memories of Dang. She cleared her throat and continued.

"When you listen to the stories that other families tell, there is so much horror. There are those who paid Thai people to help them cross the Mekong River, and those cold-hearted people would flip the boat over and let them drown. There are those who were shot down by communist soldiers patrolling the river. There are those who would come upon rotting bodies scattered throughout; men, women, children, elders.

"When you hear these stories, it makes me grateful that we were very lucky, we didn't encounter any deaths. There are other Hmong who had half their clan killed on the way to Thailand. Some stories where the parents were killed and only the children were left, some where the women and children were killed and only the men were left, some where the men were killed and only the women and children were left. So many different stories of horror.

"Now, every day I hear these kinds of stories on the Hmong stations. So many Hmong were killed all over the place. At the time there was no way to know. It's not like it is now. There was no radio, no internet, no phone. It is so sad. Your own people being killed by cold-hearted people and you don't know about it. But you know the danger and fear they feel, because we felt the same thing. We are one people. When one is in danger, we are all in danger. You think about these things and your heart hurts for them."

She paused, her attention back in the room. She had been gently rocking forward and backward as she spoke. Her legs stretched out in front of her, folded at the ankle. I was next to her in my usual spot on her bed.

"*Auj yauj*, that's it to tell." She laughed nervously to inject some levity. "When you talk about the hardships of this life, there is no end. That is the life of a Hmong; you run, run, and run all the way to this country. I'm still running from them in my dreams."

× × ×

As children, we were always shielded from the unspeakable horrors of our parents' war. They bore the weight of those memories and the grief that came with them, guarding these secrets deep within their hearts. Much like the Secret War itself, the scars and sorrows that etched our parents' souls remained unknown to us, hidden behind a protective barrier they had constructed to spare us from their pain. Their greatest desire was not to pass down their suffering but to bestow their dreams and aspirations for a brighter future.

Inheritance, for Mom, was not the sorrow of war but the appreciation for what life offered. It wasn't to focus on what was lost but rather to cultivate our traditions and values. In her demonstration of love, Mom resolved not to burden us with her own grief. She carried those heavy emotions silently, shouldering their weight while continuing to provide for us to the best of her abilities. She sought to impart the wisdom of tending to the land, ensuring we understood the intrinsic value of cultivating our own vegetables. She always appreciated what she had, from the few pieces of jewelry her mother gave her to the food she could forage, to her children who would carry on her legacy.

Step 4:
Love the Unlovable

While the fiddlehead fish soup was cooking on the back burner, Mom pulled out two pans, added some oil to each, and set them on the stove to heat. Once the oil was hot, she put the fiddleheads in one of the pans and the mustard greens in the other. As both pans sizzled, she turned off the fish soup and proceeded to stir one pan after the other, letting them sit and sizzle before turning over the greens. Then she salted both pans.

"You don't need anything more than salt for these dishes," she said as she continued to stir them occasionally.

She told me to start washing the dishes to keep the kitchen clean. This wasn't a big kitchen, and the utensils we'd been working with were big, so she told me to dry the pots and bowls outside on the Adirondack deck chairs. I was both amused and amazed at her creativity and use of space.

After I took them outside, I went back in to watch for when the mustard greens and fiddleheads were ready. Their earthy, nutty smell filled the room. It felt comforting and cozy, like the sun on your skin, waking up your nerves after being in an air-conditioned room for too long.

The fiddleheads looked soft and limp but not mushy. Mom turned off the heat under both pans. The greens were glistening with oil. Blanching helped maintain their sheen, preventing them from becoming burnt and tough during sautéing.

We plated the fiddleheads and mustard greens, finishing right on time for lunch. Austin came back to pick up the cooked halibut parcels, soup, sautéed greens, and fiddleheads to deliver to the lodge for everyone to eat. Although we were allowed to cook the meal for everyone, The Land's COVID safety protocols prevented us from eating all together. In our haste to get the food out on time, we forgot to save greens and fiddlehead for ourselves, but we still had plenty to eat in the fridge. Besides, I'd had them both before, and I wanted to make sure everyone else had a chance to eat her food.

Within ten minutes the texts started coming in.

"OMG! So much love in the food!"

"I feel like this is the first time I'm eating rice. I can taste every grain!"

"The fish soup with the fiddleheads is so warm and nourishing. The best ever!"

"The smell of the halibut and the herbs and seasoning, superb."

"We're so lucky to have your mom's food!"

"I can't believe we haven't eaten these mustard greens before! Definitely harvesting them next year."

As they came in, I translated them for Mom. I could see love and pride beaming from her eyes. She became softer, more receptive, confident, her soul getting filled up with the love coming her way.

Throughout my life, I had experienced a critical, hard-to-please, and harsh mother. It was challenging for me to love her because she never gave me love in the way I desired. I often cut her off and avoided her when she became critical, itching to hang up the phone or leave the house to escape. We had struggled with different love languages, unable to meet each other halfway.

I believed she must be loving before I reciprocated. This whole time, I'd withheld love from her, waiting for her to give me the love, approval, and attention I wanted, which I believed was her duty as a mother to give me.

In that moment though, love flooded in and I was getting to experience Mom inside the radiance of love. She became a different woman.

In the kitchen that day, I learned to love the unlovable.

Arranged Marriage

I remember Mom spending a lot of time making a particular dish during the hot summer months of my youth. She would cut open a big, empty, polypropylene rice bag, spread it on the dining table, and pour hot, gluttonous sticky rice on top of it. As she spread the rice, huge waves of steam puffed up into the air and evaporated, producing a sweet, nutty aroma in the house. A few days later, she would hand me a small bowl of the rice with a bit of liquid in it. Upon taking a bite, I would shiver at the strange sweetness. The rice was not sweet like sugar, but rather like honey, and it smelled yeasty and sharp. I was never able to finish even a small bowl. I didn't like it. It was too strange. I opted instead for the sweetness of Snickers and Skittles and KitKat bars. Dad, however, seemed to love it and would eat it every day.

I remember that, as I rummaged around for food in the refrigerator, I always avoided the *mov cawv*, fermented sweet rice. It was something we kids referred to as "old people food." We left it for Mom and Dad.

Mom made *mov cawv* every summer, and since I didn't like it, I stopped paying attention to it. When I was old enough, she would tell me to wash the dishes as she completed making it. After the first few summers of my refusing to eat it, she had stopped giving me a bowl. In the summer of my junior year in high school, I gave it one more shot, but after a few bites, I handed the bowl back to Mom.

After Dad died my senior year, Mom stopped making *mov cawv*. Almost eighteen years must have passed before she made it again. In my mid-thirties, I visited her one summer, and out of the blue she handed me a small bowl of *mov cawv*. I took it from her outstretched hand out of courtesy and brought the bowl close to my mouth. The familiar pungent, sweet aroma filled the air in front of me. I took my first bite. The flavors exploded in my mouth. I tasted sweetness and plum and a subtle hint of alcohol from the fermentation. The light fluffy rice dissolved without my having to chew it. I had no reference for how to describe this taste and texture. There were no words for it in the catalog of foods I'd recorded on my tongue over my lifetime. It was refreshing. I felt instantly alive. It wasn't as weird as I remembered it.

While I was still relishing this newfound taste, my bowl was suddenly empty. I asked Mom for more, and, delighted, she made me another portion, spooning a generous mound of fluffy rice swimming in a pool of its own syrup into the bowl and mixing in some cold water. The second bowl was even more amazing than the first.

"This is the first time I've made *mov cawv* since your dad died," she stated unexpectedly. Her announcement brought an even sweeter nostalgia to the whole experience as I flashed back to memories of him eating bowl after bowl of this heavenly goodness.

Mom didn't talk about Dad often, and certainly not about things he liked. I sat there silently eating, waiting to see if she would offer more information, more memories. It felt like watching a feral cat circling around a bowl of food, avoiding any sudden moves that might cause it to flee. But that was all she said. I'd learned that to have Mom share her memories, I couldn't press her. I would have to wait for her to feel safe enough to open up. While I eagerly awaited further information, this single acknowledgment had been worth the wait.

In the past, when I'd asked her about Dad, she would just tell me he was stubborn and short-tempered. Nothing about love, about their time together, about how it felt to be married to someone she didn't choose, or even if she ever grew to love him. However, the fact that she had stopped making *mov cawv* after Dad passed away told me there was more in her heart for him than what I had known.

When I left at the end of that weekend, Mom made sure to send me off with a Tupperware container of *mov cawv* along with instructions on how to eat it. "The longer it sits in the fridge, the sweeter it gets. It doesn't go bad. To minimize the sweetness, dilute it with water to your liking." I took the Tupperware home and consumed the contents within a few days, each bowl reminiscent of Dad, every bite a sentimental and sweet reminder that he had loved this dish. I didn't get to eat *mov cawv* again for a few years until she came to visit me on The Land.

Before she came, I told her I wanted to learn how to make it, and since she'd be staying for a week, there would be enough time for us to make it together. When I went to pick her up, I assured her that I had the sticky rice at home, so we didn't need to buy that in the Hmong supermarket. She packed the yeast balls she had made the previous summer. After teaching me about fiddlehead ferns and mustard greens, this was the next dish she taught me.

How to Make Fermented Sweet Rice

Yield: True Love

Cook time: Until you become love

Ingredients:
Commitment
Aversion
Fortitude

Step 1:
Love Is Dynamic

My lesson started with the rice itself. I was proud that I had a bag of sticky rice in my possession. It became something I made regularly in the kitchen where I cooked and was always a popular accompaniment to the other Hmong dishes I made.

Mom asked me to *tsau tsab,* soak the rice, for the following day. I scooped a healthy amount into a big bowl, checking the quantity with her until she was satisfied. Then I took the bowl over to the sink and rinsed the rice the way she showed me when I was a teenager. I felt confident and enjoyed the whole process until she came over and noticed something about the rice.

"Oh, this is long grain sticky rice," she said. "You don't have short grain?" I hadn't even thought of that detail. I thought sticky rice was just sticky rice. "Short grain is much better than long grain. It's sweeter and fluffier and produces a better result."

"Oh," was my only response. "I didn't know there was such a thing or that there was a difference."

"No matter," she continued. "It'll be okay. Next time you come home, I'll show you what to buy."

In the past, when Mom pointed out little things like that, I would have shrunk to the floor and died of shame. But now I reveled in her knowledge, her wisdom. There's a difference in the rice! I made a mental note to buy short grain next time I was in Sacramento, and not just any short grain, but the kind that Hmong people use, which would be found only at a Hmong or Asian supermarket.

I continued rinsing the rice until the water ran clear, filled the bowl with fresh cool water to a depth of about two inches above the rice, and set it aside on the counter to soak overnight. I thought about the ritual of Mom making this dish for Dad every summer and how it, in its own small way, was symbolic of their relationship.

×　×　×

Dad, Tsaav Kuam, Chang Kua, was born in a Hmong village called Paav Kaam, Ban Kang, on the mountain called Haav Toj Pob, named for the mudslide that occurs on the mountainside during the monsoon season. He was born deep in the jungle near the city of Muang Nan in Luang Prabang Province. He was born in 1922, or at least that's the year on record. Unusual for our culture, his immediate family was small, just one older sister, Zang, and one younger brother Xeng, both of whom died before I was born. He was born to Ntsuab Ntxawg, Joua Ger, and Ntxhais Lis, Mai Lee. Dad's mom passed away before he married Mom and his dad married a second wife.

Dad's family was well known and respected by the Vang, Xiong, Thao, and Lee clans. Dad came from a line of powerful shamans. His grandfather, *yawm* Pov Yob, Pao Yao, was a well-known shaman, revered even by the Chinese. *Yawm* Pov Yob left China with his six siblings and other clan members and migrated to Laos when he was only a boy. They were no longer safe in the mountains of China and fled south, away from war and persecution, into the jungles of Laos. The elders told stories of how he received his shaman abilities when he was a young boy and had powerful spirit guides. He was smart and a quick thinker. He always carried his shaman sword on his back and used it for protection from evil spirits.

The elders told stories of times when, after the clan had moved to Laos, Chinese men would come and capture our Hmong women. As a teenager, *yawm* Pov Yob would negotiate with Chinese men for the release of our women. He would outwit them and threaten them, and because they knew of his powers and his reputation, he was always successful in getting our women released without harm. He was a well-known shaman and village chief. Many families asked him to be their leader and joined our Vang clan.

Those who respected *yawm* Pov Yob, loved him and supported him, but there were also those who were jealous of his powers. The elders told stories of jealous shamans who collectively captured his guides and put a curse on him so that no one in his bloodline would have access to his guides for seven generations. They performed black magic and caused him to become sick and die. Ever since then, Dad's father and brother have had guides but they were not the ones from *yawm* Pov Yob. After Dad's brother, we haven't had another shaman in our direct family line for the last two generations. *Yawm* Pov Yob's shaman tools are still kept with our family, wrapped and put away safely. His sword, the elders said, was lost after one of the migrations, either during the raid or during the journey to Thailand. Other shamans have come to our family to ask for the use of his gong and finger bells but to no avail. His tools still contain his energy.

After *yawm* Pov Yob, Dad's father inherited the family guides and became a shaman. The elders say he was also powerful, though less so. He once cured the pain from Dad's toothache with simply a chant. After Dad's father passed away, the family spirit guides were passed down to Dad but he didn't want to be a shaman. So, it went to Dad's brother, but he didn't want to be a shaman either.

Being a shaman was hard work; your life was devoted to serving the community. Your health depended on performing ceremonies and rituals. Becoming a shaman is not a choice; you are chosen. If you resisted being a vessel for your guides, they would become angry, causing you great pain and illness until you raised a shrine—a spirit house where your guides reside. If you still refused to comply and didn't raise the shrine, they may cause your death or induce mental illness to release themselves into a more willing vessel.

In our family, if you were chosen and didn't follow the path of the shaman, you would begin to experience such terrible leg pain that you couldn't walk. Dad wanted to be a farmer, a trader, and a father, and didn't want to take on the mantle of shaman. Both Dad and his brother suffered from pain until his brother finally took the role. Dad's brother raised his shaman shrine, setting up an altar and home for his spirit guides, and he performed the minimum amount of rituals required to appease his spirit guides. Once he did, the pain subsided for him and Dad.

When he died, Dad was left to carry the spirits, but he still didn't raise his shrine. By then, Mom and Dad were married and had my four siblings. Subsequently, his leg pain became so bad that he started smoking opium to deal with it. For a long time, he managed his opium smoking. He used it medicinally, as has been customary in the culture for generations. He would wake up early, smoke a few puffs, enough to ward off the pain, then head out to the farm. But eventually, with the displacement and grief of migrating from Laos to Thailand, losing Dang, and with no land of his own, he fell into depression and lost himself to opium.

When the French colonists arrived in the mountains of Laos in the late 1800s to early 1900s, they saw that the Hmong were growing opium. Our people have been growing it since China, using it for ritual and medicinal purposes. It was not used recreationally. We knew of its healing properties and its dangers. A plant that powerful was respected. We grew it in small quantities, only using it when necessary. But when the French came into the mountains and saw that the land was ripe for growing poppies, they saw dollar signs. They saw people who were skilled at agriculture and cultivating opium poppies. They saw cheap, disposable labor. They saw money and power.

They recruited our people to grow opium poppies and paid them for it. Furthermore they put policies in place to monopolize and exert control over the ethnic groups growing them. They controlled its sales and distribution and heavily taxed its production, forcing many growers to increase production, eventually leading to an increase in its use. They came and took what wasn't theirs. They were greedy. They were takers.

Opium became a cash crop for many families, including Dad's. The family grew and traded poppies and livestock. They were considered wealthy. They were hard workers. Dad held the title *nom tswv,* leader or chief of his village, a title that was passed down through the generations of men in our family and then to him.

Dad married at a young age. His first marriage was arranged by his family. Because of their small size, his parents wanted a daughter-in-law to help with the farming and chores. They knew of a close family that had a daughter who was a very hard worker. The only thing was that she had a baby out of wedlock. But because they needed a daughter-in-law and they liked her, they took her in.

Dad was not ready for marriage. He was smart and bright but had just come of age and wasn't even confident about girls, much less having a wife or being a father. But in the end, because he was a dutiful son, he gave in to the arrangement.

The girl, Xue, was young and pretty. Her daughter, Chao, was only a month or two when they married. Dad quickly became a father and learned to care for a wife and baby. Together they had ten more children: six girls—Lau, Aa, Zang, Bla, Yeng, and Lha—and four boys—Neng, Lue, Dang, and Chao. They were beautiful and hard-working children. Dad was a strict father and demanded excellence and discipline from all of them. He was also very frugal and conservative in how he spent money.

Dad didn't marry for love. Love was not a luxury he could indulge in, but he made a good life out of it with his relationship with Xue. He loved Chao as much as his own children. Dad was not an affectionate person, as his parents weren't affectionate with him, but he distilled in his children hard work and loyalty through his own example. It was a dynamic relationship, expressed through various forms of love.

Step 2:
Love Is Attention

The following day, after breakfast, Mom and I continued preparing the *mov ncawv.* I filled a steamer pot with water and set it on top of the stove. Then I emptied the washed sticky rice into a V-shaped bamboo steamer, put the lid on, and set the steamer on top of the pot. While we waited for the rice to cook, I asked Mom how she'd learned to make this dish.

"I learned from watching my mom and my older sisters. That's how you learn to make anything, by watching and practicing. I am very good at making this dish." This was the first time I'd heard Mom compliment herself about her food. She's usually modest and always says that what she makes isn't good. But this was different. I could hear the pride she took in having mastered this dish.

"This was your dad's favorite dish. He loved it. In Laos during the summer, it would be so hot you barely wanted to do anything, much less go to the farm. Your dad would enjoy eating it. He loved it so much he'd have two bowls at a time, several times a day. Your uncle's wife made it, too, but it was never as good as mine, so she left it for me to make. Everyone loved it." This was another first—the first time she'd talked about Dad in an affectionate way. I flashed back to seeing him eat *mov ncawv*, and it all came together—those childhood summers when she made it for him, the fact that she stopped making it after he died.

Mom teaching me how to make *mov ncawv* felt as if she were letting me into the innermost sanctum of her heart. I knew that what I was receiving was something tender and valuable, that it captured the essence of my parents.

After about fifteen minutes, with steam coming out the sides of the pot, Mom went to check on the rice. She instructed me to fill a glass with water, open the lid, pour a bit of water over the rice, then use a wooden spoon to turn it over and water the underside. She told me to mix it in carefully so as not to mash the rice. I followed her instructions, then put the lid back on to allow it to steam a bit longer.

Another ten minutes went by and it was ready. I turned off the heat. Mom covered the table with large sheets of aluminum foil and instructed me to pour the rice onto the foil. I flipped the basket upside down. Steam came rushing out of the basket, leaving traces of sweet nuttiness in the air. Mom spread the rice over the foil.

"You want the rice cool but not cold; don't make it while it's hot," she said.

I mentally took notes, watching her skilled hands spreading rice across the foil.

"In Laos, there was no such thing as aluminum foil. We would cut down large banana leaves and use that to cover the table."

×　×　×

Mom's family was poor, so poor that she had no clothes and ran around naked until she was five years old. She wore her sister's hand-me-down Hmong dresses and shirts for years, even after she'd grown out of them. She had no shoes and walked barefoot everywhere.

Although she grew up with nothing, Mom worked hard and applied herself to the handcrafts of *paaj ntaub* and batik dyeing. She was very focused and had a steady hand. As soon as she was old enough to thread a needle, she learned to make her own traditional Hmong dress, which took almost a year of hard work. Grandma diligently guided her in cooking and sewing, grooming her to be someone's daughter-in-law one day.

Grandma was smart and had a good ear for language. She spoke Lao and made friends with a local Laotian woman who taught them how to spin cotton into thread. This is one of those happy memories of Mom's childhood, and when she talked about it, I could feel the love between her and her mother, and her joy of learning these traditional crafts.

Luxury was something Mom didn't have. Luxury was flip-flops, candy, silver jewelry. She grew up watching other girls who had these things, and she would crave them so much that she could feel the silver earrings dangling from her ears. When she was a teenager, Grandma was finally able to afford a simple bracelet that she bought for her girls to share. Mom and her older sister fought each other for the right to wear it. Growing up with very little made her resourceful. Her needlework, cooking, and farming became her most valuable assets and the means by which she expressed her love.

This explained why the many summers of my youth were filled with her teaching me how to sew *paaj ntaub*. She constantly nagged me to work on my embroidery, to be more precise. She would take these pieces of cross-stitched fabric and make them into a traditional shirt and the *dlaim sev,* a thin, apron-like sash, for my New Year's outfit. I would always complain about having to spend so much time working on something I would wear only once a year. My complaints only frustrated her, and she chided me for being lazy, comparing me to my nieces, who were very skilled at needlework. That always made me feel bad about not being the kind of daughter she wanted.

I understand now what she was trying to do. She wanted to make sure I had the clothes she didn't have growing up. Teaching me the skills she had learned was a way to pass on our culture, and perhaps to create those memories she had of her own mother teaching her everything she knew.

Sewing was more than a craft. It was what distinguished a good Hmong woman. It was a skill passed down for generations. In China, our ancestors were persecuted and forced to assimilate into Chinese culture. Our written language was outlawed. Our women created a system to sew our language into the beautiful embroidered patterns on our clothing. It was a way for them to pass messages to each other; a silent women's code of survival and strength. Eventually our language became lost in the intricate patterns of mountains, rivers, flowers, snails, and elephant footprints. Today, *paaj ntaub* are looked at and admired for their precision and intricate beauty, but each still carries with it a woman's lineage of unity and power.

This explained why, whenever I came home while I was in college, she would send me back with bags of groceries, from rice to chicken to vegetables. I would tell her I didn't need them, that I could buy them from the store, and besides, my friends would freak out at seeing chickens with their heads and feet attached. To this day, Mom still cooks for me when I visit her and sends me home with my favorite dishes.

Mom's love was not expressed in phrases or gifts, but with her attention through food and service.

Step 3:
Love Is a Discovery

Mom put two of the yeast balls, *xaab*, she'd made the previous year, in a Ziploc bag. With the spine of the high-carbon steel Hmong knife, she pounded them until they turned to powder. While she was doing that, I washed the pot and the bamboo steamer.

I asked Mom how she made the yeast balls, and she explained the complicated three- to four-day process. They were made of steamed sticky rice that had been pounded into a glutinous dough. Then you roll them into little balls and dry them for a few days. As the dough dries, it develops a yeasty mold, which is what keeps it active. Summer is the best time to make these because the heat helps to dry the dough quicker.

I asked her to show me how to make them, but she said it was a lengthy process, and she wouldn't have time to show me on this trip. "I can't make them as good as I used to. I'm getting too old and my sense of taste is not as good as it used to be. The foods that I love to make don't taste as good anymore."

That was all the more reason why I wanted to learn, I thought, but didn't say it out loud. We were now living on the fragile edge of time, where each moment had taken on a newfound preciousness. I was hungry to learn as much as I could from her, not only about her recipes but also about her life with Dad.

×　×　×

When Mom's family and Dad's family went their separate ways after crossing the Mekong River, he faced heavy grief and heartbreak. He lost four lives all within a short time.

Dad lost his second daughter, Aa, to a fever. By the time they had settled in a new village, it was already too late to plant crops for food. To make matters worse, the fields were ravaged by rodents, which destroyed much of the harvest. Hunger gripped the village. One day, Aa and some family members went into the mountains to forage for root vegetables and other edible plants. While they were out, the monsoon rains struck. That night, Aa returned home, but she and a few others had caught a fever. Her condition worsened, and despite efforts to save her, Aa did not recover. The illness claimed her life.

A few months after losing Aa, another tragedy struck. It was right after the New Year celebration. His oldest daughter, Lau, and two other girls went to the poppy farm for the day. On their way back home, with the setting sun, they walked innocently along the same path they always took. Two of the girls were talking and walking way ahead of Lau. The girls came upon a group of Laotian communist soldiers. They turned and ran, but not before the soldiers spotted them. The girls ran, saw Lau, and told her to run. It took a moment for Lau to catch on to what was happening. The girls ran past her, and Lau turned around to run when the soldiers opened fire. Lau got hit. The two others continued to run, not aware of what happened to Lau. In the chaos, the girls lost their way and didn't make it home before dark. They took refuge at a cousin's house in a nearby village, praying and hoping that Lau had made it safely. The following day, they returned, but Lau was still missing. The girls told the family what happened.

Dad and some uncles went to search for Lau. They looked and looked, calling out her name, but to no avail. They came to a road near a town with a random, freshly dug, unmarked grave. After consulting with the nearby village to see if that grave belonged to anyone, the villagers said they did not know of any burials from their village. Following their intuition, Dad and the uncles dug up the grave, each handful of dirt weighing heavier and heavier on Dad's heart. There he found his daughter. Dad crumbled.

The uncles dug Lau out and carried her body back home to give her a proper burial. No one knew what happened to her. They don't know if she was already dead before she was buried or if they buried her alive. Grief swept through the town.

Before Dad had a chance to recover, death struck a third time. His wife went into labor. It seemed like a typical delivery, and no one anticipated complications since she had already given birth to many sons and daughters. But this time, the spirits were not kind. As if losing two daughters wasn't hard enough, Dad's wife died in childbirth, taking both her life and that of their unborn child.

Dad found himself a widower, alone with his remaining eight children to care for. After the mourning period was over, the elders told him to find a new wife for companionship and to care for his children and the farm. He was told about a widow who lived in Phouhong. He packed up a blanket and some rice and chicken for the road, and with two of his uncles and a *mej koob*, a wedding negotiator, he made the three-day trek to Phouhong.

Once Dad reached the village, the elders there told him that the widow was not healthy enough for him to marry and that he should find another wife. Dad's family knew that Mom's family now lived in that village and that they had many daughters. Dad, his uncles, and the *mej koob* went to Mom's house to see who would be available for marriage. By then, Mom, being the youngest and a teenager of marriageable age, was the only daughter left unwed. Her family knew that Dad was a good man. He had wealth and a good reputation, so they knew she would be marrying into a good family.

Her mother came to her and told her she was to marry this man. Her brother Fang reassured her that he was a good man from a respectable family. She was frightened and protested, saying she didn't want to marry. But they persisted—she had to do what they told her. She looked for a way to escape, but there was none. Despite her tears and protests, in the end, she had no choice. After the uncles negotiated with her brothers, they accepted the marriage proposal.

"My mother and brothers were so desperate for money that they were willing to accept a bride price of only one bar of silver," Mom told me as she recounted the story, bitterness evident in her voice.

As is tradition, her mother dressed her up in a simple wedding outfit that she had made for this occasion. Everything was handmade, from the fabric to the thread that held the pieces together. What her mother could not give her in wealth, she expressed through this precious outfit. As she dressed Mom, she imparted the same words that had been passed on by her own mother. "*Miv naib Ntxawm*, go and be an obedient daughter-in-law. Learn their ways and become like them. Don't be lazy. Be the first to wake up before your in-laws and make them food. Serve your husband. Follow your husband and do what he does. If he's working at the farm, go work with him. You do not rest until he rests. Take on their ways and customs. They are now your family." She gave Mom a pair of bracelets and packed Mom's clothes and two money sash bags into the bamboo basket for her to carry to her new life.

They invited relatives from the village and had a simple wedding feast to tie the union. As Mom parted from the comforts of a familiar and safe world into an unknown life with this stranger, she mustered up all the courage in her body and forced herself to walk forward onto the road ahead of her. "You must not look back," the elders told her at the table when they recited the wedding vows for the couple. It was considered bad luck to look back at your family when you set foot toward your new life. It took everything she had to not turn back and run home.

They set out to return to Dad's village, walking for three days, stopping at villages at nightfall to sleep at relatives' houses. For those three days, few words were exchanged between them. Mom did not want to marry Dad. She did not know him. He was old enough to be her father.

When they finally arrived at Dad's house, Mom saw that he had eight children, three of whom were older than she was. The children didn't like her. Why would they? Their own mother had just died and now they were supposed to call someone their own age *nam*. Mom didn't know anything about being a mother, and she didn't want to be the wife of a man she didn't choose. Every day she wanted to leave, fantasized about running away. But where would she go? She would not be accepted at home and the very act itself would bring shame to her family. She had to force herself to stay, telling herself, "Just one more day." Every day, she repeated the same mantra: "Just one more day." It became a daily battle, taking it one day at a time.

When she got pregnant, she could no longer think about leaving. No one would want a runaway woman with another man's child. It was the ultimate disgrace, worse than death. Mom banished all thoughts of leaving, putting away all her escape plans, and decided to stay. She told herself to find something to love about this man, to find little things that she could appreciate.

She noticed that he was wise and kind and took in other families who needed a home and clan to belong to. Dad was very family oriented and other clansmen respected him. She came to learn what made him angry and what made him happy. She learned his favorite dishes and how he liked to eat them. They fell into a routine together: waking up early as Mom prepared breakfast and food for the day's trip to the farm, while Dad got the corn and rice ready to feed the animals.

Their relationship started on a blank canvas, each stroke deliberately crafted. There was no template for them. There were no promises to live up to, no bitterness from unfulfilled expectations, no disillusionment from unmet hopes. Their love unfolded naturally; each day was a discovery of the other.

Step 4:
Love Calls for Our Full Expression

Once the rice had cooled, Mom lined a large stainless steel bowl with aluminum foil. She filled a small bowl with water and placed it next to the larger bowl. She started by wetting her left hand to prevent the rice from sticking, then placed a handful of sticky rice in the foil-lined bowl. With her right hand, she took a small handful of yeast powder and sprinkled it over the rice, working the powder into the rice with her left hand. She wet her hand again and repeated the process—her left hand placing the rice in the bowl and working in the powder, while her right hand sprinkled more. Her hands knew exactly what to do.

I asked her how much powder to use, and she said simply, "Just watch and you'll know. You just keep sprinkling yeast over the rice to cover it." But as I watched her, I still had no idea. My mind raced with questions: *What if it's not enough? What if it's too much? Would that affect the taste of the final product?* But I didn't ask. She kept working and talking.

"When we were in Laos, we didn't have bowls or aluminum foil. We would go out into the jungle and cut off banana leaves and use them to cover the sticky rice. We knew so little in Laos. We never thought of using water to wet our hands. Our hands got so sticky that it became harder to work with the rice. What we did was have two people make this. One person would handle the rice and the other person would sprinkle it with the powder." As she was telling me this, she laughed at the memory of how little she knew compared to what she knew now.

"When sprinkling the powder, it's okay if you use more or less." She reassured me that the amount didn't matter and you just do it based on feel, but I wasn't convinced that it would work for me. I was a stickler for measurements, especially if I wanted it to taste like hers. She continued to artfully powder the rice, breaking it apart and powdering it some more, grabbing another handful and repeating the process.

Once she'd used up all the rice and all the powder, she washed her hands, then came back and folded the aluminum foil over the rice. Finally, she covered the bowl with a kitchen towel.

"If you don't want it too sweet, it will be perfectly ready to eat after twenty-four hours. But if you want it sweeter, let it sit for two nights. I prefer to let it sit for at least two nights so that it's light and fluffy and syrupy and sweet."

I put the bowl on the kitchen counter and washed the rest of the dishes.

We planned to go down to the garden to plant the lemongrass and herbs she had brought, but it was too hot, and Mom had used up her energy for the day. We decided to wait until the next morning.

It was close to lunchtime, so I opened the fridge to see what we could heat up, mother and daughter standing side by side in the afternoon glow.

×   ×   ×

Mom found joy in raising her girls. While she was pregnant with her first child, Mom made peace with her situation. Her child became the reason for her to keep going day to day. She settled into life with Dad, into the daily work of farming, cooking, and needlework. Dad's youngest son, Chao, was old enough to help with chores and didn't need tending to. When she had her baby girl, she named her Mai, which was a common name for a first girl child. The following year, she had another girl, Phoua.

Dad had some good qualities, and he also had some that were challenging. He was jealous and possessive. Mom was still young and beautiful, and he feared she would run off. He wouldn't let her go anywhere on her own except to the farm and back, or to the river to fetch water.

One day Mom went to the farm and took Mai with her, who was about four years old. She was gone a little longer than usual, and Dad became very angry, thinking that she was flirting around. He went out looking for her and found her walking by the road. He accused her of having gone to talk to boys. He yelled at her, and without giving her a chance to say anything, picked up a rock and threw it at her head so hard she bled.

He turned and walked away, leaving her there, crying and bleeding. Mom had no choice but to follow him. When she got home, in pain, with her head still bleeding, she cried and cried. She told her little girl that she was going to die and not to be scared, telling her to take care of her little sister. Seeing her mother bleeding and crying, Mai too cried and cried at the thought of her mother dying and being alone in the world. Mother and daughter cried together for hours until they were both exhausted.

Dad felt remorse for what he had done and never hit her again, but his jealousy still came out in the way he prevented her from venturing on her own. Mom came to make peace with all of it—with Dad's possessiveness and temper, with his frugality, with his strict rules. She knew that she couldn't change nor control these aspects of him.

There were unpleasant memories of fights, jealousy, and harshness, and there were also memories of cocreation, love, and sweetness. Neither set of memories was better than the other; both were equally necessary for the full expression of love, encompassing both the light and the dark.

Step 5:
Love Is a Choice

We let the rice sit on the counter for two days and two nights. On the second night, Mom pointed out the sweet perfume exuding from the rice. "This is how you want it to smell. It's starting to ferment."

On the third day, Mom opened the aluminum foil to see how it was progressing. Just by looking at it and smelling it, she could tell it wasn't ready. It needed another day to break down the rice some more and draw out its sweetness.

"It's only April, so it's not hot enough to ferment the rice in three days," she said. "We need another day. In Laos it would be so hot that you only needed two days." She covered it back up and we left it for another day.

With experience came patience. Mom did not feel rushed that the rice was taking a day longer to sweeten. She simply gave it time, trusting in the process that age and love had granted her, in the same way she had done in her relationship with Dad.

× × ×

Mom found herself alone once more when her mother passed away. She had just given birth to Phou and had barely recovered when she received news from relatives that her mother had died suddenly. Her mother had gone to visit one of her daughters in another village to care for her while she was sick. However, within a day or two of arriving, she contracted the illness and passed away shortly after. When Mom heard the news, she crumbled. She desperately wanted to see her mother, but she was still weak from giving birth, and it was a three-day walk. The little strength she had left was drained by grief. Every day, she cried for her mother and clung to her daughters. They were the only things tethering her to this world.

Despite her overwhelming grief, life continued. Slowly, new bonds began to form. Mom was not in love with Dad, but, over time, a companionship developed between them and a mutual love and respect. They were both hard workers and had skills that complemented one another. Mom had to find something to love in Dad, because it was the only way to be with him for the rest of her life. She came to love the fact that he was *nquag nquag* and patient, and that became the foundation on which she built a life with him. To be *nquag nquag* meant having a resilient spirit for hard work, someone who stayed in flow with the daily activities of life, who knew what to do without being told, as though moved by a deeper purpose.

Mom loved that he woke up with the roosters and worked hard, never complaining. He was always the first to be ready, to pick up a shovel and till the land, and the last to stop, always taking advantage of the last rays of sunlight. He was a helpful partner who worked alongside her and helped around the house and with the animals. He was not one to sit around while she was hard at work.

There was a subtle sweetness about their relationship. On the third day of waiting for the rice to ferment, Mom and I were eating lunch and, out of the blue, she told me a story about Dad.

"One time your dad and I were eating together. I had hiccups and couldn't stop them. Out of nowhere, your dad said he told his brother and sister-in-law that I stole some silver bars from them. I was furious and yelled at him: 'Why would you tell such a lie! I have done no such thing! Can you not stand the sight of me? Why do you hate me so much?'

"Then he said, 'I only said that to stop your hiccups.' Realizing what he said, I stopped yelling. He was right! My hiccups were gone! Your dad laughed at me for taking it so seriously. He said of course he would never say such a thing, but he scared away my hiccups! I was mad at him at first but then I started laughing with him too."

When Mom married Dad, she had no choice in the arrangement. However, she did have a choice in how she wanted her life with him to go. She had a choice in who she wanted to be and how she wanted to be with him. She could have been a victim of her circumstances. Instead, she chose love over allowing her heart to grow rigid and cold. She chose life and to make the best of what she had.

I once asked her what made a good marriage. "Find someone who you can talk to. So long as you can talk kindly to each other, that is what matters."

"But what about love?" I asked. "Shouldn't you marry someone you love?"

"Love may not always be there in the beginning," she replied. "Find someone you are compatible with, someone you can talk to. That's the foundation of a good marriage. From there you can work on love; you will find love."

I wanted there to be romance in their relationship, hoping that Mom had been "in love" with Dad, and that Dad had treated her well, giving her a world of affection, gifts, and romance. I wished that Mom hadn't endured the hardship of living with someone controlling and possessive. However, her response revealed the wisdom of someone who understood and experienced True Love. Through her stories, I felt the essence of love radiate from both of them. Dad didn't provide her with a world. They provided each other a world.

Step 6:
Love Is an Act of Becoming

On the fourth day, Mom opened the aluminum foil, releasing the sweet, fermented smell I remembered from my childhood. She gently stirred the rice with a wooden spoon. It looked soft and fluffy, drenched in its own syrup with a slightly thick viscosity. My mouth watered as I imagined the taste. Mom spooned big heaps of rice and liquid into two bowls and handed one to me.

"Don't you add water to it?" I asked, since that's how I remembered eating it.

"You don't need to. At this stage you can eat it as is. If you let it ferment for at least a week, you can add some water to dilute the sweetness. The longer it sits, the sweeter it gets. This rice can sit for a long time, either in the refrigerator or on the counter. If it's on the counter, it'll ferment faster, so it's best to put it in the refrigerator and take your time eating it."

I took the bowl from her and held it close to my nose to inhale the fragrance. There isn't any smell like this anywhere else—bright, fermented, sweet, nutty, with even more intricacies than that. I put a spoonful in my mouth and closed my eyes so I could really get inside the taste. It was sweet like honey but not as thick. There was a fuzzy fermented taste like plum wine, but the sugar would need much more time to break down into alcohol. The rice was like fluffy clouds that dissolved in my mouth. It was refreshing and woke up my senses. I savored each bite as if it were filled with Mom and Dad's love.

This was the dish I've now come to associate with them. It was a simple combination of sticky rice and yeast and, given some time, patience, and care, it broke down to become a complex, intricate, sweet, and fragrant dish. It rewards you with something new and beautiful.

I couldn't help thinking about my own relationship with Mom and how it has fermented over time and developed a sweetness of its own. It had less to do with Mom changing than it did with my own heart breaking down over time, turning my critical emotions and memories into a sweetness that has its own distinct flavor. I went from being a child who saw Mom as a disciplinarian to an awkward child who was ashamed of her, to a child-victim who blamed her for the pains of my life, to an adult who accepted her for who she is, to a woman who saw her as a woman that I continue to discover. I now delight in the depths and complexity of her thoughts and emotions, recognizing that she has always been driven by only one thing, and that is love. Our relationship has allowed me to evolve into *being* love. Instead of looking for love *from* her, I am able to reflect love back *to* her.

The Ways of Hmong Women

In every culture, there exists a special dish that always nourishes us on a bad day and heals our soul during sick times. Mothers throughout time have bestowed this dish upon their loved ones—the soothing embrace of chicken soup.

When we lived on Farmington Road in Stockton, we would buy *khao piak sen*, Lao chicken noodle soup with handmade tapioca noodles, from Laotian families who lived in the apartment complex across the street. During my college study abroad in Chile, my host mom would make *cazuela de pollo*, chicken soup with chunks of carrots, corn on the cob, and whole small potatoes. My Jewish friend, Rachael, would always make her famous "Jewish penicillin" when a friend was sick or wanted something loving in the middle of winter. My Yemeni friend, Hesham, would share his mom's recipes when we cooked together and tell me about her chicken soup, *maraq*, which was served to women for healing and strength after childbirth.

The Hmong version of this soup for the soul is *nqaj qab tsau tshuaj*, medicinal chicken soup. This soup has been in the community for centuries, the recipe and herbs passed down through the generations from woman to woman, with very little modification, based on the availability of herbs.

When Mom made it, the whole house was engulfed in the aroma of the soup—earthy, like fresh-cut grass, woody, and soft, with a sweet, musky scent. When I breathe it in, I feel the medicinal properties of the herbs making their way into my bloodstream and bones and muscles.

Growing up, I didn't understand the significance of medicinal chicken soup or the healing properties of the herbs. To my young taste buds, it was pungent and bitter and not appealing. The herbs were available from spring through fall, during the hottest months in Stockton, California, and I didn't particularly want to eat it then. Later, in middle school, I understood that Mom made the soup when someone in the family was sick. Occasionally, she made it when I was sick, but I still didn't enjoy it very much. Then, when I was in high school, that smell became pervasive when Sister-in-law Cher had her first baby. It was the only thing she was allowed to eat for thirty days. I didn't envy her, and by the second week even she started to tire of it and would sneak in bites of spaghetti or egg roll.

It wasn't until I was away at college, my taste buds having matured, that I developed a craving for the smell and taste of this soup. It became something I longed for, that my soul called out to. Whenever I went home, I would ask Mom to make it, which she happily did.

On a trip home in June 2022, while I was collecting recipes from Mom, I asked her to show me how to make

medicinal chicken soup and to tell me about the significance of the herbs. A portrait of Hmong food wouldn't
be complete without it. I received not only instructions
for the recipe but also a deeper understanding of the
strength and power of the women in my lineage.

Mom's garden wasn't very robust that year, so she
didn't have all the herbs needed. However, she called up
Aunty Blia, and after a few minutes on the phone, told
me we'd be going to her place to pick some up.

In the car, I pulled out my phone to open Google
Maps. "Stop looking at your phone and let's go!" Mom
said impatiently in Hmong.

"Mom, it's just the GPS! What's the address?" I
defended myself.

"You don't need that. I'll tell you how to get there,"
she responded. I put my phone away and we drove off
with Mom directing.

Mom sometimes commented on her memory slipping away, but when it came to driving and directions,
she remained as keen as a compass needle. She couldn't
always read street names, but she recognized the spelling of the words. "Turn right at the sign that spells
B-R-Y-A-N-T," she would tell me as though she were
in a spelling bee.

"In Laos there are no signs," she once told me. "You
mark everything. At the huge tree by the river is where
it is shallow and you can cross. In the jungle, it is easy to
get lost for days."

Her mind is a map for getting back home.

Here in America, where she didn't know the language, she continued to mark everything: Turn right

at the second light, make a left at the white house with the big tree; their house is the fifth one. It's brown, with a green car in front. In America, it is easy to get lost for days.

Here in America, her mind is still a map for getting back home.

When we arrived, Aunty opened the door and greeted us with the traditional Hmong greeting. "*Meb tuaj los?*," you have come?

To which we responded, "*Aw tuaj os*," yes, we have come.

Mom asked, "*Mej pua caiv?*"

The only way for me to translate that is, "Is the house restricted?" This is something you traditionally ask before entering a Hmong person's house. A family would *caiv* after a spiritual house cleansing or after someone had a baby. *Caiv* could last anywhere from three to five days. *Caiv* is an indication that no one is allowed to enter the house and no one is allowed to leave the house for a period, so that evil spirits do not find their way in. Normally the residents wouldn't even have to open the door because there would be a sign outside the door informing visitors that they had *caiv*. The sign could be a small branch of leaves nailed to either side of the door, or a hexagonal mesh object hanging on the door, or a wooden cross tied with red fabric leaning outside the door.

Aunty replied, "*Tsi caiv os. Lug tsev, lug tsev.*" No, it's not. Come in, come in.

With that invitation, Mom crossed the threshold and I followed her in. One is not allowed to enter the house until verbally invited, so as not to provoke the house guardian spirit who resides above the door and protects the house.

Once inside, we took off our shoes and left them with the tens of other pairs—flip-flops, sneakers, and house slippers of various sizes—clustered near the front door. Aunty invited us to sit down, then walked in the kitchen and disappeared into the garage. Her daughter-in-law, who was in the kitchen, greeted us "*Meb tuaj os*" and went back to her work.

The house was very quiet, clean, and uncluttered, with no kids running around. This was an atypical scene in a Hmong household. Aunty, who is a widow, was living in the house of her son and daughter-in-law, who are more Americanized.

On the wall opposite the couch was the biggest *thaaj neeb*, shaman altar, I'd ever seen. This was my first time inside Aunty's house. I didn't even know she was a shaman. I'd seen pictures of shaman altars online and in documentaries about Hmong people, but I had never visited a shaman's house. Our clan's shamans always came to our house for rituals.

Hmong families who aren't Christian have maintained the practice of having a family altar, *xwm kaab*, facing the front door. The altar acts as a spiritual house for the ancestors. It is also a place of worship and provides protection for the whole house. It serves as a place for offerings, prayers, and rituals, fostering a strong connection between the earthly and spiritual realms. A typical family altar is about one foot wide and one foot deep and hangs on the wall.

Aunty's *thaaj neeb* was about three feet wide and stood about six feet high, adorned with meticulously cut joss papers in white with red and gold accents, hanging in symmetrical patterns across the top and sides, creating a visually striking and sacred space. The natural fiber paper glimmered with gold and silver squares in the center. Joss paper is known as spiritual money and is burned by many Asian cultures as an offering to ancestors. Diamond- and triangle-shaped patterns are cut into the paper, creating delicate designs, much like paper snowflakes. There was a tapered candle at each end of the shelf of the altar, along with many different types of bowls for offerings of water and rice, and two smaller bowls filled with rice grains to hold the burning joss sticks in place. There were also Aunty's divination tools: A set of split bull horns used to communicate with the spirits, and a pair of finger bells shaped like donuts with red fabric tied to them to announce the shaman's presence. On the floor, leaning against the wall, was her wooden spiritual sword to ward off and kill evil spirits. There was also a gong for calling all her spirit guides together and an iron rattler, about twelve inches in diameter, shaped like a circle with a pointed iron tip, smaller rings encircling the bottom, and flat, jagged iron disks between the rings. When a shaman shakes this tool, all the rings clang together, making a loud rattling sound that informs the spirits she is entering their world. The rattle is also used to raise a fallen soul. To the left of the altar was her bench, which was the flying horse she rode once she was in the spirit world.

I was fascinated and continued to study each element of the altar. Above it was a long bamboo stick tied with a few strands of thick string that stretched across the room to another stick above the lintel of the front door. There are nine to twelve levels to heaven in the spirit world, depending on the elder shaman you speak to, and the sticks represent the first three levels of the physical realm. The next levels after that are in the spiritual realm.

Being a shaman is not something people boast or brag about. Hmong people are humble and don't promote their services. But then again, being a shaman is simply a normal role for us and not one that warrants any special advertising to others. Every clan has its own shamans who carry on specific clan rituals and ways according to their *dlaab qhuas*, ancestral spirits. It is very rare for a family to seek a shaman outside their clan unless one isn't available from their own or they've already consulted their clan shamans and more help is needed. That being said, if a shaman has a reputation for being powerful, it is not uncommon for people to seek out his or her services.

Men and women may both be shamans because shamans are chosen by spirit guides. Gender doesn't factor into who is better. There is no such thing as a male shaman being better than a female shaman, because it is all based on the power that your guides possess. The person is the channel for their guides. When someone comes to a shaman's house to seek their service, they have to ask and kowtow to the spirits in front of the altar, not to the shaman. The spirits then inform the shaman whether or not they can help. If they can, the shaman performs a healing ceremony, invoking their spirit guides, *qhuas neeb*, to assist in the healing process similar to the way Balinese shamans, or Balians, invoke their spirit guides, Hyang, during rituals. In Balinese culture, these spirit guides, which can include ancestral spirits and deities, are consulted and honored through elaborate ceremonies.

×　×　×

My concentration on the altar was interrupted by Aunty's high-pitched voice giving her daughter-in-law instructions about some sort of preparation they were in the middle of making. She seemed to be in a hurry to do something, but that might just have been her energy. Her petite five-foot frame maneuvered around the house with quick and precise motions. Minutes later she came back into the living room and directed Mom in Hmong.

"*Tais*, you want some medicinal herbs, is that right?" *Tais* means older sister or aunt.

"Yes, my daughter wants some medicinal herbs for chicken soup and that's why we have come." And with that, Mom handed Aunty three joss sticks with a twenty-dollar bill rolled around them. I had seen her carry them into the car, but didn't think to ask her what they were for. Aunty took the bundle, turned toward her altar, and lit the joss sticks with a lighter. After a few seconds, she blew out the flame. The tips of the sticks glowed. Smoke danced in the air, perfuming the room with a sweet musty scent. I wasn't sure what was happening, but was fascinated that our simple visit to gather herbs had turned into some sort of ritual.

Aunty got on her knees, kowtowed toward her altar, and muttered some words I didn't understand. Then, as quickly as she started, it was over. She stood up, put the twenty-dollar bill on the altar with other cash that was already there, and placed the joss sticks in one of the bowls of rice grains. She walked back into the kitchen where she took out two plastic bags from a cupboard. She opened the sliding glass door and disappeared into the backyard.

I looked over at Mom, curious to see her reaction. She was completely at home with everything that was happening. I continued to watch the joss sticks burn in the bowl and surveyed the altar in silence.

In less than ten minutes, the sliding glass door swooshed open again. Aunty returned with two very full bags of herbs and handed them to Mom. They carried on with a bit of small talk as Mom accepted the bags. Aunty was telling her something about the herbs and her garden and how unsuccessful the growth had been that season. She apologized for not being able to give her the best herbs or very many of them. All of that didn't make sense to me, considering that she handed Mom two full bags, which was more than I expected. Hmong people never boast about their abundance, but, quite the opposite, apologize for handing you something that may not be worthy of you or your efforts.

Mom responded, "Whatever you have we will accept. We don't mean to be a burden."

"Not a burden at all. Take it with you and make a few meals out of it to fill you up," replied Aunty.

Mom and I took our leave, with Aunty calling after us, "*Moog mej hua tuaj os.*" Go and come back.

We responded with the traditional, "*Aw, tuaj tim tsev hab os.*" Yes, come visit us, too.

Everything in the Hmong language is a ritual, a series of calls and responses—from greetings to giving and receiving offers to how you eat, how you conduct weddings, rituals, and funerals, and coming and going in the house. Even the way a traditional household is set up: A home is a spiritual sanctuary, with house spirits that protect its residents. Spirits and humans are believed to live in the same realm. We can't see or initiate exchanges with spirits, but they can with us. And if they want us to see them, they can make that happen. Some shamans have the rare gift of being able to hear and/or see them in the everyday world.

In the car, I took out my phone and tapped in my brother's address before Mom could protest. As I was pulling out of the driveway, I asked her why she had given Aunty the joss sticks and money.

"Aunty's spirit guides won't let her touch medicinal herbs without asking for their permission first. If she did, they'd make it painful for her hands. So, the money and joss sticks are offerings to assuage them." She said it matter-of-factly, with no further explanation.

Having grown up with explanations such as these, I didn't need her to say anything more and left it at that. The rest of the drive home was quiet, both of us lost in our own thoughts, with the exception of Mom pointing out that my GPS was taking us on the longer route home.

How to Make Medicinal Chicken Soup

Yield: Womanhood

Cook time: Until you pass knowledge to another woman

Ingredients:
Pain
Power
Strength

Step 1:
Start from the Roots

Mom took all the herbs out of the bags and laid them on the dining table. With quick eyes and hands, she started sorting through them, picking them up and snipping away the older leaves that Aunty had included in her rush to get us the herbs. As she sorted them, she made bundles that included each variety and the correct amount that would be good for a meal.

Each bundle contained purple Okinawa spinach, *Artemisia lactiflora*, *Acorus gramineus*, *Artemisia annua*, and *Cupatorium fortunei*. As she went through them, she told me what each one is called in Hmong, and what they are good for. She was quick to tell me that she's not an herbalist but that we'd used them for centuries. She grew up with them, and she'd learned from the elders what they are good for, and when and why you would need them.

In researching these herbs I found that most had originated in China and some were found in Southeast Asia. These plants have different names in various cultures, making their scientific name the easiest way to identify them in the plant kingdom.

Mom held up an herb with big pointed leaves that were green on the top side and purple on the underside called *tshuaj tsog lab*, purple Okinawa spinach. She snipped the young pieces and let go of the older leaves. Then she picked up another kind, *tshuaj tsog ntsuab,* green Okinawa spinach, whose leaves are green on both sides, and added it to her bundle. Okinawa spinach has been known to lower cholesterol. Not all Hmong herbs are meant for eating. Some are used to flavor the soup and then removed, just as Western cuisines use bay leaves. Okinawa spinach was one you eat, and it was my favorite—soft and hearty, with a slightly sweet nutty flavor.

She picked up *taab kib lab*, *Artemisia lactiflora*, which is a member of the mugwort family, with purple stems and leaves shaped like duck feet. Mom told me it was good for blood circulation, especially during a woman's menstrual cycle.

Next we moved on to the *pawj qab*, *Acorus gramineus*, also known as Japanese sweet flag. Mom went over to the counter, tore off a piece of paper towel, and started rubbing the dirt off the root and leaves. They are thick, yellowish-green blades that are thicker than most wild grass and about ten to twelve inches tall. As she meticulously cleaned the blades, she told me *pawj qab* were good for increasing strength. When you're feeling tired and have low energy, you'd boil the whole plant to make a tea to drink. She gave me a blade and told me to rub it and smell it. It literally smells sweet. *Pawj qab* is also good for digestion and eliminating gas from the body. Because it's a tough blade, you only use it for the flavor, not for consumption, so take it out after the soup is cooked or leave it in to continue adding flavor if you reheat it.

Next we looked at the *tshaab xyoob*, *Artemisia annua*, also known as sweet wormwood, native to China. It is one of the Chinese herbal remedies used for treating malaria, reducing fever and swelling. Like *pawj gab*, it is also used to add flavor to broth and not for consumption, because the stems and leaves are tough. It is very pretty, with slender, finely divided leaves that have deeply cut edges, giving them a feathery, delicate appearance, almost like a fern, but much smaller and lighter.

Last, Mom held up the *txaj lab*, *Eupatorium fortunei*, and I asked her to repeat the name. Most of these names were foreign to me, and it was hard to wrap my tongue around them. *Txaj lab* is good for revitalizing a person's appetite and treating nausea and vomiting.

These were the main herbs that went in the soup, but others could be added. In making *nqaj qab tsau tshuaj*, any combination of these medicinal herbs would work, with no requirement to use them all. If you had more variety, you could include more herbs; if you had fewer, you used what you had.

When Mom finished assembling all the herbs, she proudly put together five large bundles for me to take home, so I could make soup for my American friends. She also included a bundle of lemongrass, *tauj qab*, which she had harvested from her own garden. The term *qab* means "chicken."

"We call this *tauj qab* because it's always used in chicken soup," she informed me. "During seasons when these herbs were unavailable, we'd make chicken soup with *tauj qab* and black pepper. It is good for warming and cleansing your body. It is such a luxury to have. In Laos, my mother and I would walk a whole day to a Laotian town to buy it at the market. Sister-in-law Xao's sister's husband has a house there where we would spend the night. To use it, we'd take a few whole peppercorns, wrap them in a cloth, and crush them with a stone to grind them."

I had no idea that something as simple as black pepper could be good for your health. Black pepper has merely become a seasoning that adds a kick to a meal. Its healing properties have been lost to us.

As we concluded, she told me she would also give me two freshly killed chickens to take back. These chickens, purchased from the Hmong supermarket, taste very different from the organic chickens you'd buy at Whole Foods.

I asked her how she learned to make the chicken soup.

"Aah, I learned this by watching the elders. You just watch what they do and learn," she told me, sounding as though she couldn't fathom why I had to ask in the first place. I'd been hoping for something a little more romantic, conveying the special bond between mother and daughter or mother and daughter-in-law created by the passing on of this cultural gem. But alas, she gave it to me straight, because making the soup, like being a shaman, is just a part of our culture. Knowing how to make *nqaj qab tsau tshuaj* is what makes you a Hmong woman.

Step 2:
Dilate through the Pain

Once Mom had discarded the unused herbs in the backyard for compost, it was time to make the delicious chicken soup. She took a medium-size pot out of the cupboard, filled it halfway with water, and put it on the stove to boil. She took a fresh chicken out of the refrigerator (and by fresh, I mean with head and feet still attached). A surgical line cut through the center of the breast from the neck down indicated that it had been gutted and cleaned. We used to kill our own chickens, which we bought live from Hmong or Mexican farmers. However, once my sisters were married there was no one to help Mom with the killing and cleaning, so she began buying them from the Hmong supermarket. I asked her about chickens from American supermarkets, and she looked at me as if I had asked her to cut off her arm. "Kill your own chicken or buy one from Hmong supermarket," Mom said. "Get black chicken or brown chicken. They make the best broth and are more nutritious to eat." I recalled sometimes seeing black-colored skin on chicken in the soup.

She chopped off the head and neck, then the feet, followed by the drumsticks and thighs, then the wings. Next, she cut the breast in half and cut each half into three pieces. Finally, she flipped the chicken over and chopped the spine into smaller pieces. By the time she finished chopping, the water was boiling. She put all the chicken pieces into the pot of boiling water.

We went to the backyard, and Mom cut a stalk of *tauj qab*, lemongrass. The sweet citrus aroma was immediately released into the air. We took the stalk into the house and Mom rinsed it. Then she used the back of a knife to pound it so that it broke slightly, releasing some juice and fragrance. Starting with the bottom end, she folded the stalk at about four inches twice to form the base. Then she wrapped the leaves tightly around the folded stalk, starting at the bottom and moving upward. When she reached the top, she secured the bundle by making a loop of the leaves and pulling the ends of the leaves through the loop a few times to the end. Voilà, there was a tightly wrapped bundle of lemongrass.

As the soup continued to cook, I moved around the kitchen gathering dirty dishes. Mom headed over to the counter where my sister-in-law had a tea set and pulled out a gold-colored, unmarked packet. Holding an edge of the packet, she tapped it against a finger, shaking the contents to one end. Then she punched a hole in it with a paring knife to open it.

"What's that, Mom?" I asked, curious.

"*Tshuaj mob laug*," medicinal tea for old age. She poured the golden brown powder into her blue-and-white Chinese mug and added hot water. She stirred the mixture until it turned a brownish coffee color and set it on the counter to cool. "It's for body pain. These days my body aches so much—all those years of physical labor and hard work in Laos and never resting."

"Well, you still work hard, Mom. You haven't stopped." I was teasing her but also being honest.

"It's true. I can't sit still." She stirred the tea again and blew on it, then took a sip, lost in her thoughts.

×　×　×

When Mom was pregnant with her first baby, Mai, she didn't know that she was pregnant. She didn't have anyone to tell her what signs to look for. It was opium harvest season, which was around February or March. Mom would go to the field and the smell of the resin was so overwhelming that she constantly threw up. Between craving food and throwing up, she thought that there was something wrong with her. No one told her she must be pregnant; even Dad either didn't know or didn't think to tell her. She would feel nauseated, with a heaviness in her chest. She thought it might be due to something she'd eaten, so she took medicine to help with the nausea and vomiting.

After coming back from harvesting opium one day, Mom told Mother-in-law how she had been feeling, that she had a lot of cravings for foods like sugar cane, pineapple, and liver, but after she ate them she would vomit. Mother-in-law, who was not a very talkative person, told Mom she must be pregnant.

For three months, she went through intense morning sickness that lasted into the night. She slept with a bucket next to her. She either had no appetite at all, or she'd have intense cravings for specific foods. She couldn't stand the smell of fried food or pork fat. Usually, on her way home from somewhere, she could smell the pork oil even before she made it home. Her senses were very sharp and sensitive. Even the smell of steamed rice became hard to bear. Eventually the nausea subsided.

Mom continued to work hard throughout her pregnancy. Dad's family wasn't like other families in which there were many people to help, but they were all *nquag nquag*, hard workers, and Mom kept up with them. All of Dad's previous children were teenagers and young adults, and everyone helped with the farm. Yeng, the youngest girl, was married and lived with her husband's clan.

Mom continued to carry heavy items in her basket. During pineapple harvest season, while Dad and everyone went to the farm, Mom would take the horse and go pineapple picking by herself. She had two baskets with her and filled them with pineapples. The baskets were so heavy that she could only fill them halfway and then lift up the baskets to hook them onto the horse. As the weeks progressed it became harder for her to lift them. She devised a plan to get there early, fill up the baskets with pineapple, and ask passersby to help her hook them to the horse. However, once she got home, she had to pull the baskets down on her own. She took the pineapples out of the basket two or three at a time and walked them into the food storage hut. Even that was arduous work for her.

Months later, while she was getting ready to go to the farm, Mom suddenly felt an intense wave of back pain. She knew she was going into labor. She and Dad were the only ones at home, everyone else was at the farmhouse. It was customary that Dad couldn't be there with her during childbirth, but he helped her prepare. Mother-in-law had told Mom what to do once she was in labor. They had saved and dried the husks from harvesting corn, and Dad now laid out a pile of them in their bedroom where she would give birth. He then set a small bamboo stool in the same area so that Mom could sit on it while she was going through contractions. He put a pair of sterilized scissors to cut the umbilical cord on a small bench, along with a thick white hemp string, two clean cloths, one for the newborn baby and one for the placenta, and a very small, silver necklace, handmade by an uncle for this occasion. Dad laid out a blanket in front of the fireplace, and on top of it, he spread out the corn silk and rice stalks saved from harvest. Then he added a pillow to complete the bed where Mom and the new baby would sleep for three days after the birth.

Hours later, as the contractions became stronger, Mom squatted over the dry corn husks in the traditional childbearing position. She went through unbearable pain during the contractions, her young body feeling as if it were on fire. It was a pain like none other she had experienced. She focused all her attention on the pain, breathing deeply and, instead of screaming, opened herself to the pain and used it to strengthen her body and mind to keep from collapsing. She didn't know how long she was in labor, and with each breath, she prayed to the ancestors for the baby to be okay and for her to make it through. When she finally felt the baby slipping out, she reached down with both hands and caught her baby before it touched the ground.

Mom held the baby girl in her arms, exhausted, still in pain, and elated all at once. When Dad heard the baby crying, he came in to assist. Mom was still in her squatting position, waiting to expel the placenta. Dad immediately put the silver necklace around the baby's neck to lock in one of the baby's souls. Then he used the string to tie off the umbilical cord near the baby's navel and cut the cord with the scissors. Minutes later the placenta came out, and Mom put it on one of the clean cloths.

The placenta, known as *lub tsho* or original shirt, serves as the first garment for the soul as it enters the earthly realm. After death, the soul journeys back to the place where the placenta was buried, slipping back into it before embarking on the path to reunite with the ancestors. The retrieval of the original shirt is essential for the soul's reincarnation in the next life.

Since Mai was a girl, her placenta was buried under Mom and Dad's bed, symbolizing the eventual departure from the household upon marriage. For boys, their placenta finds its resting place at the main pillar of the house, where all the family spirits reside. As boys carry the lineage forward, their placenta is interred alongside the ancestors.

Mom wrapped the baby in the second clean cloth and prepared to clean herself and change her clothes. With every ounce of strength left in her exhausted body, she picked up the baby and prepared to wash her with the heated water Dad had prepared. Once the baby was clean, Mom wrapped her back up and made her way to the bed in front of the fireplace.

Dad cleaned up the corn husks and took Mom's sarong out back. He dug a hole in the ground to dispose of the corn husks, then washed the sarong in a basin. After he'd completed those tasks, he carefully poured the water from the basin into the hole with the husks and buried it, being careful not to leave any trace of blood that would attract evil spirits.

Dad came back in the house and dug a hole under the bed to bury the placenta, again being careful to not let any liquid drip on the floor where it would attract insects. It is believed that if any insects eat the placenta, it would harm the child's health. He made Mom a poached egg with ground black pepper. After eating, Mom gave in to her exhaustion.

Mom birthed six of her nine children in this fashion. Each one was a deliberate ritual of welcoming a new soul to Earth. Her second baby, Phou, was born at the farm prematurely at seven months, but turned out healthy and thriving.

In America, she had my three younger siblings in the hospital. The first time Mom was in the hospital, everything was new to her. She was confined in a room, on her back, with doctors and nurses and machines all around her, speaking to her in a foreign language. She didn't know such things as epidurals were available to reduce pain and had her babies naturally. The doctors and nurses were surprised she was so calm and quiet, and by the same token, Mom was surprised by how loud Western women were. She laughed and joked that Western women can't bear pain. She told me she was proud that when she had her six babies in Laos and Thailand, not one of them ever touched the ground.

Step 3.
Tend to the Soul

Mom sipped her tea, put it down, and checked on the chicken. It was almost ready. She had set aside some of the herbs earlier for this soup. She gave them a rinse in the sink a handful at a time, shaking out any dirt. She brought them over to the pot and added them to the chicken, pushing them down to bathe in the boiling water. She then added salt and black pepper, tasted the broth, and kept adding and tasting until it was exactly the way she wanted it.

I stood over the pot for a few minutes, watching as the herbs softened and danced with the chicken, releasing their healing properties into the soup. The broth darkened slightly into an earthy golden green with droplets of chicken fat floating on top.

"How do you know when it's ready?" I asked her.

"When it's softened," she replied.

She left the soup to cook for a bit longer and told me to start setting the table.

After a few minutes, Mom went back to check on the soup, turned off the stove, and the bubbling ceased. The herbs clung to the chicken pieces to stay afloat. The musty, sweet steam evaporated into the air. The smell alone was soothing and warm and healing. I couldn't imagine ever being tired of this soup if I had to eat it for thirty days.

× × ×

For thirty days, during the postpartum period, a new mother has to *caiv,* restrict going out of the house. For three days, the household must follow certain guidelines to tend to the souls of Mom and the baby. Mom is still recovering and her soul is, therefore, more likely to wander off or to be attacked by evil spirits. The same is true for the baby, whose soul, being in a new body and not integrated with the main soul, is also susceptible to being taken by evil spirits.

During the three days Mom and baby sleep and bond on the bed of corn silk and rice stalks in front of the *dlaab qhov cub qhov txus*, guardian spirit of the fireplace, to keep warm and be cleansed by the fire. In postpartum, the mother's body is considered "cold" as it has expelled a lot of heat while giving birth. For the healthiest recovery and to get her body back in balance, she must keep herself warm by staying in front of the fireplace, resting, and eating *nqaj qab tsau tshuaj* with freshly made rice while the baby sleeps peacefully next to her.

Other household customs during this period include restricting who can enter the house. If someone is sick, they can't come in because they might bring unwanted spirits. Those who are sick are usually susceptible to spiritual attacks. Pregnant women not part of the household must also not come in because the soul of their fetus could steal the milk from the new mother, thereby reducing the amount of milk available for her baby. Furthermore, anyone who is allowed in must leave their shoes and bags outside the door so that unwanted spirits don't hide in them and sneak in undetected by the guardian spirit at the door.

When Mother-in-law arrived home from the farmhouse, she helped take care of Mom and made her *nqaj qab tsau tshuaj*. It was the only smell that soothed Mom. The soup cleansed her body, eased her blood flow, dispelled any toxins and stale energy from the birth, and restored her strength and vitality. Bringing balance and blood flow into her body also made it possible for her to lactate properly for breastfeeding. Mom couldn't eat anything but the soup in order to keep her body warm. She bathed with warm water in the house since she wasn't allowed to go outside, and she couldn't wash her hair so as not to get a cold.

The third day is a significant day for the baby; it is the day of *hu nplig*, the soul-calling ritual to guide her main soul from the ancestral world into her body. She is then given a name and officially becomes Hmong.

Early in the morning of the third day, before the rooster crowed, Dad was already awake and preparing the items he needed for the ritual. He gathered joss incense to wake the spirits and the spirit money that would later be burned as offerings to the baby's soul parents to guide the journey. He cut pieces of the hemp strings that would tie the hands of the baby, Mom, and Dad to bind them together, and the eggs to capture the souls before boiling the eggs for consumption by Mom and Dad.

The final preparation was for the baby's name. Typically, the name is chosen by the paternal grandfather of the baby, but since he was no longer with them,

Dad's brother, Xeng, chose the name. He chose Mai, an honorable name meaning daughter whose traits are grace, beauty, and dignity, which is typically given to the first-born girl. Dad asked one of his uncles to perform the soul-calling ceremony and invited all our relatives to this joyous celebration.

Once all the preparations were complete, Uncle began the ritual. He opened the spirit door, which was in the back of the house, not the front door. He stood looking out with a rooster and a hen in his left hand, both facing him and slightly tucked under his arm with their feet tied together to keep them from clawing their way to escape during the ten-minute chant. Chickens are used in rituals, because they know everything in both worlds and are the best guides in the spirit world. In his right hand, Uncle held his split bullhorn. In front of him was a bowl of uncooked rice with two eggs on top and three lit joss incense sticks planted in the rice to keep them standing.

He hit the side of the door frame with the split bullhorn and began the chant calling to Mai's soul. He told her to get up and come home, guiding her soul all the way from the gate of the ancestral village in the sky to the mountains and roads on Earth, then to the backyard of the house and through the door to be with Mother and Father, to be a sister to the hearth and a sister to the house pillar. Along the way he told Mai's soul that the chicken was there to guide her, the rooster was there to protect her with its claws, and there were eggs waiting for her to eat. He told her to keep coming, to not wander into the dark sky, to not stop and rest by the roadside, to not go into the mountains, but to keep coming home. Once he'd guided her soul all the way home, he concluded by giving thanks to the soul parents, the spirit of gold money, and the spirit of silver money, for protecting Mai's soul.

After the ceremony, the chickens were sacrificed, cleaned, and boiled whole. Once they were cooked, they were taken out of the pot to cool in a bowl. Uncle came to look at the feet of each chicken. All the talons were curled up close together. Then he pulled out each tongue one at a time, observing them carefully. Both tongues were bent inward in the right direction. Mai's main soul was indeed home in her body and she liked her name. Dad burned the spirit money as promised to the soul parents and ancestors for the healthy baby and offered them a meal.

The chickens were chopped up and put back into the pot with lemongrass, salt, and pepper. A few more chickens had also been prepared for the meal for all the guests.

Uncle gave a blessing to Mai. As Mom held this precious new life in her arms and took out her tiny hands, Uncle brushed the bundle of white strings over her palms and the backs of her hands, sweeping out the bad luck. He recited a chant to welcome her to Earth and blessed her with 120 years of good health and wealth. Then he took three strings from the bundle and passed the rest to other family members.

He tied the first string around Mai's tiny wrist, binding her soul to her body, and chanted a blessing over her. He did the same with Mom, tying the second string and saying a blessing over her, and then the third string with Dad. The rest of the family members followed suit, wishing all three of them a long life, good health, and good luck. Afterward Uncle cut off the ends of each set of strings and burned them together, binding the souls of Mother, Father, and baby under this household. Mai was officially Hmong.

During her postpartum period, Mom was expected to rest, but as soon as she regained her strength, she busied herself around the house, tending to chores and caring for the animals. In the midst of her tasks, she would gather her needle, thread, and various fabrics, fashioning a little hat for Mai adorned with intricate flower and mountain patterns. This hat served as a protective measure. Once Mom and Mai *puv hli,* completed their thirty-day postpartum period, and Mom could venture outdoors with her, she would place the hat on Mai's head. This precaution was taken so that if spirits were to approach Mai, they might mistake her for a mere flower and not an adorable baby and attempt to steal her soul.

In addition to the hat, Mom also crafted a *naab nyias*, a baby carrier, adorned with floral prints and protective symbols. This carrier would be used when Mai became a toddler. It could be carried on Mom's back or chest. From the silver necklace around Mai's neck to the strings on her wrist, as well as the hat and baby carrier, her soul was well protected from any spirits that might wish to do harm.

Hmong people believe there is a direct relationship between the body and the soul. When the soul is happy, loved, and cared for both by the individual and by others, the body is healthy and thriving. Should the soul be neglected or frightened away, it would affect the body's health. Tending to our soul requires us to be in tune with our body and our feelings. It is a relationship and an art that calls us to be our own beloved, paying attention to the nuanced impulses, feelings, and intuitions it tells us. To be an advocate for our soul through the body.

Step 4.
All Knowledge Is Shared Knowledge

While I set the table, Mom disappeared out to the backyard for a few minutes and came back with some sort of medicinal plant and a piece of green onion. I eyed her curiously as I spooned rice from the cooker into a bowl and placed it on the table. She stood in front of the sink with the faucet turned on to a trickle and started to rub the two pieces of greens together, dabbing on some water as she mashed them with her index finger into her palm. I worked my way through putting the chicken soup into another bowl.

"What are you doing, Mom?"

"My ear has been ringing," she said, continuing to mash the greens, which were becoming a thick, aromatic pulp, into the palm of her hand. "At various times my ear rings with a loud, sharp sound. I don't know why. I went to get it checked, but the doctor says there's nothing wrong. It's so bothersome. This remedy helps stop the ringing."

I didn't know how to diagnose what she was telling me and made a mental note to google what it could be. Mom divided the thick pulp in two small mounds and stuck one in each ear. They stood out like tiny Bluetooth earbuds. As much as I was concerned about the symptom Mom described, I was also glad she had a natural remedy.

She went to the fridge, took out the fresh Thai chili pepper dip she had made weeks earlier, and spooned some into a sauce cup. I went around the house to call everyone to eat, but my nieces and nephews weren't hungry, and Cher and Sister-in-law Cher were both busy and told us to go ahead and eat.

I put some rice in my bowl along with a drumstick and some of the herbs and broth, and topped it off with pepper dip. I took out my phone, snapped a few pictures, and made a video of the delicious-looking soup.

I held the phone up to Mom, who had started eating. "Stop filming me, especially with my ear like this! It's embarrassing!" she exclaimed, laughing.

"I want a video of your food, Mom! It's for my TikTok channel," I replied. "You're popular on TikTok!"

"No. They're going to say '*Ewww*, look at that old ugly lady with that thing in her ears!'" We both laughed.

"Nah, Mom, you're popular! People love you in my videos." Which they did. My most popular videos were of Mom cooking through my narrative of her life.

I took a quick clip of myself attempting to get rice, herbs, and pepper onto my spoon with one hand and bringing it into my mouth off camera. I turned off the camera and put it down to savor the healing magic happening in my mouth. It tasted warm, soft, earthy, with a touch of citrus sweetness, both medicinal and soothing. I chewed, savoring every change of flavor in my mouth. After I swallowed, I exhaled deeply.

I asked Mom where we found the medicinal herbs, since they were not originally grown in the United States. She told me that when the Hmong came over, we were not allowed to bring the herbs, but some people brought over the seeds. Family by family, they were shared, and they grew from there.

This was one of the things that united Hmong people—you always share what you have, especially important and distinct herbs like these. "Every Hmong household has these herbs in their backyard," she said. "Any herbs I don't have, I know someone who does have it, so I ask them for a cutting or seeds that I can plant myself. That is how these herbs are passed down." Woven into the fabric of Hmong women is this sharing and passing of knowledge and goods. As soon as one woman learns something of value, she passes it on to other women, and that's how it becomes part of the culture.

Mom had been eating this chicken soup her entire life. The recipe was passed down from her mother, who got it from her mother, who inherited it from her mother, and so on for centuries. As Mom and I ate in silence, we both felt that the *nqaj qab tsau tshuaj* had planted its seed in my body. We knew, in the way women do, that the tradition and knowledge would live on in me. And we knew that, although we didn't know exactly how, I would pass this knowledge on to others.

Beyond the medicinal qualities of the herbs, *nqaj qab tsau tshuaj* was a soup that provided solace to my soul. I reminisced about my college years when I yearned for this soup. Whenever I caught a sudden whiff of its musky, sweet, grassy scent or tasted its soft, earthy, citrusy flavors, it was as if my soul were longing for home. I had, at times, felt lost in the world of appearances and achievements, and I had temporarily forgotten my true values, trading them for a sense of belonging and acceptance. Perhaps it's my soul's way of reminding me that true belonging originates from returning to my body, not seeking external validation. That home, in the body, is where I come back to.

As we ate, I felt my body absorbing the nutrients, each molecule unlocking something deep within me. Warmth slowly spread throughout my body and my soul felt lighter. Each bite brought me back more to myself, transporting me into the kitchen of all my grandmothers and great-grandmothers and ancestral grandmothers, *puj koob*. I was embraced not just by Mom, but the collective embrace of all the women who had given birth to me. Centuries of strength and power enveloped me in their arms.

Refugees of War

There is a term the elders use when they talk about the Secret War in Laos: *"Thaum teb chaws tawg,"* When the world exploded. It depicts the metal birds unleashing fiery missiles from the sky that shattered their fertile lands. The soil torn asunder by the detonation of grenades. The scattering of guts and limbs through the air as hidden bombs were triggered. The relentless symphony of gunfire echoing through villages, through the jungle, through their dreams. The yellow rain that poured down on skin, in rivers, in the earth, leaving millions—American soldiers and Southeast Asian civilians alike—with fatal health issues and death, followed by hundreds of thousands of babies born without limbs, deformed limbs, underdeveloped brains, and abnormalities.

The aftermath of the war extended beyond mere physical devastation. *"Thaum teb chaws tawg"* encompassed not only the literal explosions but also the emotional upheaval that shattered the Hmong world. The United States and other countries opened their doors to the wave of war refugees who poured in, desperate for a better future. However, neither America nor the refugees were prepared for what lay ahead. Neither anticipated the emotional or psychic impact this relocation would have on their souls. The diaspora of Hmong people in the United States after the Vietnam War quickly revealed deep emotional rifts within their culture, caused by uprooting individuals from their natural environment and relocating them to a foreign land. These divisions appeared between husbands and wives, parents and children, and traditional elders and the evolving younger generation.

The blueprint etched across centuries, resilient against the ravages of war, bigotry, and China's assimilation efforts, was abruptly overturned. The life and customs we once knew, tasted, and touched, were whisked away on iron birds to a different world. The stark divide between tradition and the American way gave rise to an epidemic of low self-esteem among Hmong men. Once respected as village chiefs, landowners, and collective providers, they now struggled on welfare or worked long hours in corporate factories for low pay and few benefits. Heroes and soldiers were reduced to garbage collectors and field workers. Unable to grasp the new language, they were seen as weak and lazy in the eyes of Americans, dismissed as freeloaders clinging to archaic customs.

The women emerged as the primary breadwinners. Alongside their husbands in factories, they leveraged their sewing, cooking, and cleaning skills to secure additional work and income, sustaining the family.

Suddenly, women who had often been subservient to men found themselves wielding power through their artistic abilities.

In Laos, most families couldn't afford to send their children to school. Those who could prioritized sending a son, typically the youngest, while the eldest assumed the role of preserving traditions and rituals. Education was deemed unnecessary for women, whose primary role was to care for the family.

In America, however, women enjoyed equal access to education. With schooling being free and mandatory, girls attended eagerly and adapted swiftly, often outpacing their brothers in academic achievement.

The men, traditionally the stewards of the family's lineage, lost their foothold, not only within their own households but also in society at large. Roles reversed as children assumed the responsibilities of parents, and parents began to rely on their offspring for translation and guidance in navigating the world. This added pressure compounded the challenges children already faced in school as they sought acceptance and belonging. Consequently, resentment and shame toward their parents grew. At the same time, parents, frustrated by their children's perceived failure to meet expectations at home and in school, lost both their authority and respect.

The war that ravaged the men in Laos carried over into a silent battle that eroded their sense of self-worth, casting a shadow over family life. In our culture, there are no terms for mental disorders such as depression, anxiety, or PTSD. Everything is perceived through the lens of body and soul, and in this new world, the soul was very much displaced. Struggling to find their place in the world, men succumbed to depression and withdrew from their families, while others grew increasingly controlling. Tragic stories of men committing suicide increased in the community. At family rituals, the elders lamented heartbreaking accounts of husbands killing their wives and children and then themselves. It washed over the community like a death sentence.

In the 1980s and '90s, whispers began circulating about a mysterious phenomenon: Healthy young men were dying in their sleep, with no prior symptoms or identifiable causes. This enigma was dubbed Sudden Unexpected Nocturnal Death Syndrome (SUNDS), haunting the Southeast Asian and Filipino communities alike. Neither the medical community nor the shamans could offer explanations. Survivors recounted waking in a state of lucidity, only to find themselves paralyzed. They described feeling a presence in the room followed by a weight upon their chest. Their mind struggled for release but physically they couldn't move or scream. Across the globe, our community grappled with the turmoil of unraveling this mystery.

Families fractured, with dropout rates among teenage boys rising as they sought belonging in gangs. Meanwhile, teenage girls experienced newfound freedom, which clashed with cultural norms of being married and raising a family as young as thirteen years old. While such ages were considered normal within the culture, the girls were labeled as child brides by American standards. Social services were called to intervene in homes, with parents facing accusations of abuse and exploitation. Both cultures struggled to accept, adjust, or understand each other. A barrier existed between the two groups, each judging the other by their own standards.

To seek some sort of safety, and to recreate the same kind of community that's always existed, Hmong people sought to live together in enclaves. These enclaves provided a sense of familiarity and support in an otherwise foreign and often challenging environment. Within these close-knit communities, we were able to maintain our traditional practices, language, and rituals. This preservation of identity offered a buffer against the pressures of assimilation. To America, that was detrimental to the purpose of "civilizing" us. To us, it was the only thing we had left that held the culture together. The culture is under the threat of extinction, disappearing with each generation born in America as children forget their mother tongue and forgo the value of family and tradition, instead prizing the American way.

I grew up in Stockton, the Central Valley hub of Asian diversity in California, and home to some of the best, most authentic Southeast Asian food in the United States. I'm talking about made-to-order papaya salad and egg rolls at 8th Street Park on a Saturday afternoon or noodle-stuffed chicken wings with Thai chili pepper fish sauce dip and purple sticky rice from Laotian neighbors. Kids knocking on our apartment door to sell pandan and mung bean three-layer cake fresh from their mother's kitchen. And *naab vaam* from the Asian market on scorching summer days when our only relief was slurping the iced, sweet coconut tricolor drink with red tapioca pearls, green cendols, and yellow water-chestnut balls under a tree because Dad was too frugal to turn on the air conditioner.

These were some of the foods of my childhood whose memory provides the blueprint for how I make them now. Memory is the secret ingredient to my recipes. When people tell me they taste love in my food and look up at me with surprised pleasure at their first bite, what they are tasting is history passed down through the generations in various shapes and sizes, ranging from creative to survival, from criticism to discipline. Like nutrients passed from mother tree to baby tree, the intention to preserve and pass on a lineage is the thread that connects mother to daughter, infusing each dish with a legacy of nourishment and tradition.

I grew up in an apartment complex on Farmington Road that was home to ninety-six Hmong families. We called it *zog vib nais,* Vinai Village. When I was little I didn't understand why it was called *zog vib nais.* Much later into my adult life, upon doing some research, I learned that Ban Vinai was a refugee camp in Thailand. The original Ban Vinai Village was built in 1975 to house more than forty thousand Hmong refugees who had escaped Laos and crossed the Mekong River.

A lightbulb went on.

×   ×   ×

In Thailand, my family didn't live in Ban Vinai. They settled in a refugee camp named Soptuang, nestled in Mae Charim, a district in the eastern part of Nan Province.

Despite sprawling across several hills and valleys, the camp was quickly overcrowded by tens of thousands of refugees. Our camp was not encased in barbed-wire fences, nor patrolled by Thai officials with rifles who took advantage of the vulnerable immigrants, including women on occasion. But like all refugee camps, the conditions were poor, food was scarce, and clean water was hard to come by.

Life in the refugee camps was strikingly different from life in Laos. The land belonged to the Thai so the Hmong couldn't scout for their own land to farm. There was only a tiny plot where some people had access and could grow corn and vegetables and sell the extra in the camp. Every day, rice was brought into camp and rationed among the residents based on the number of family members and age of each person. If you were older, you got a little more rice. For this reason, Mom and Dad forged the age of Mai, Phoua, Cher, and Cha so they could get more rice for the family. And even then, it was barely enough.

The first two years were especially hard and miserable. There was hardly anything to eat. Because of the scarcity of vegetables, the women would forage in the mountains, digging for root vegetables or any edible vegetation they could find. Cassava was a common find. Mom would cut it up, boil it until it was soft, then squeeze out all the excess bitter liquid, and mix it with cooked rice to bulk it up.

In contrast to the smaller Hmong villages in Laos whose residents consisted of three or four related clans, this refugee camp had eighteen clans mixed together, along with Laotian officials, soldiers, and their families who had escaped the communist regime. They lived in a subsection of the camp.

As the years passed in the camp, the women started to sew our *paaj ntaub* into decorative pieces to sell for money. Mai and Phoua were going to school to learn English, but seeing that they could make their own money, both girls decided to help Mom sew instead. Mom would teach Mai and Phoua how to make book-marks, little cross-body purses, and big decorative wall pieces. They would take them to the American women who came to the village to collect them and sell them at the bigger markets away from the camp. Mom and the girls would come back days or weeks later and wait for their name to be called to see if they made any money.

It was so satisfying for them to make their own money! With that money, they could buy new foods to try. Mom remembered the first time she ate pho. She had never had noodles before and recalled it as distinct and delicious. The savory and spicy flavor of the broth, the chewy texture of the noodles and the herbs were all enlivening. It was such a luxury to eat something new. It was so special that on days when Mom and the girls went to collect money, they packed some rice with them so that they could put that in the broth once all the noo-dles were eaten. Not a single drop of broth was wasted.

They would also bring it home to share with the younger siblings.

Living in camps with people of different cultures had its advantages and disadvantages. We Hmong people have always adapted to our environment while also maintaining a deep connection to our roots. One of the things to which we adapted was the food. Hmong food was simple, because living in the mountains didn't provide access to the variety of spices available in town. In the mountains of Laos, there was very little Laotian influence in the dishes that made it to the Hmong table. In the refugee camp, however, food became a point of connection and commonality. The Hmong palate expanded from mainly vegetable dishes like boiled greens to more meat and noodle dishes such as pho, *khao poon*, red curry noodle soup, egg rolls, and *thom khem*, Lao caramelized pork egg stew.

General Vang Pao sought asylum in the United States after the fall of Saigon. In the following years, the United States, along with other countries such as France, Australia, Canada, the Republic of Guinea, New Zealand, and a few others opened their doors to war refugees.

The debate about whether to leave Thailand was rampant among the tens of thousands of residents in Soptuang. The conditions in the camp were poor and overcrowded. The camps were not meant to provide permanent residency, only to be temporary placeholders while the United Nations decided what to do with these war refugees.

The same discussion carried on in our family. We had never heard of America and had no concept of it aside from the missionaries who distributed clothes and candy in the camp. Yia Lue, Khoua Neng, and Chao wanted to come to America. It would be a way to have a new life. General Vang Pao was already in America, so we should follow him there. Dad did not want to leave home behind. He was waiting for the day when we would be allowed into Laos again, when it was safe. He did not want to leave the mountains of his father and grandfather. He dreamed of going back, to be buried in those same mountains.

His sons were adamant about leaving. They wanted to start a new life, a better life. We would be part of the first wave of Hmong people going overseas. After weeks of discussions and arguments, Dad finally relented.

A few times a month, officials came to the camp to help families register with the United Nations for sponsorship into different countries. With the help of Hmong translators, we completed and submitted our paperwork.

Mom was pregnant with me at the time. On April 9, 1980, I was born in the early hours of the morning, before the rooster crowed. I kept her up all night with my kicking and urgency to come out into the world. Once born, Dad dug a hole and buried my original shirt, as the placenta is called in Hmong, underneath the bed so that when it was time to return to him and Mom and our ancestors, my soul would come here first to retrieve it. I have not been back to Thailand or Laos, but I hear them calling. My body absorbs the nutrients consumed from Thai and Lao food. I find familiarity when I hear names like Hongvilay, Saeng, Phonesvanh. I glimpse myself in the memoirs of Southeast Asian authors, their stories unfolding like a map of my own roots.

On August 9, 1980, our family was approved for resettlement. We each received an acceptance letter from the American Embassy US Refugee Program that included single headshots of Dad, Mom, Mai, Phoua, Cher, Cha, Tang, and me at four months old, with a number in front of each of us. The letter read:

> *To Whom It May Concern*
> *Re: Chang Kua Vang*
>
> *The United States Immigration Service has accepted these person for resettlement in the United States and has asked the Ministry of Interior to transfer them to Bangkok on August 13, 1980.*

×   ×   ×

As kids, *zog vib nais* was our little slice of heaven, with so many neighborhood kids to play with. The mothers found their way of connecting and continuing the life they had left behind in Laos. They traded tips on cooking and sewing. They grew buckets of herbal medicine at their front door. They called on one another to come and join in the weekend ceremonial festivities. Within the bounds of that complex, we were allowed to be exactly who we were without feeling like foreigners, and our parents could speak to one another in our native tongue.

Hmong mothers had a creative entrepreneurial spirit and used their skills to start their own little businesses to feed their families. Mom's strength was in gardening and sewing. There was a man who lived next to the apartment complex with a little plot of land, which he offered to the Hmong women to start a community garden.

Every day, Mom went there for a few hours to tend the garden. In spring she would bring back a mini bucket full of cilantro and green onion. We had more than we could eat, so she made bundles with the excess for one of us kids to sell in the neighborhood for twenty-five cents each. I loved going around to sell them because I got to keep half the money, which I would use to buy candy. Each time, I would come back with an empty bucket and a pocket full of coins and dollar bills.

Other little girls would also come knocking on our door to sell vegetables their mothers had grown, food they had cooked, or little handmade Hmong embroidered ornaments for decorations.

One rainy winter day, when I was eight years old, a little girl came by selling mung bean sesame balls, my favorite. They were only twenty-five cents, but my frugal mother refused, saying they were a waste of money. I was so upset, but it only fueled my appetite to figure out how to buy one for myself. I didn't have any money, and I knew that Dad, who was even more frugal than Mom, wouldn't say yes if I asked him.

I remembered that there was a stash of coins in the ashtray in Mom's car. That was my plan. Mom was in the kitchen preparing lunch. I went to her sewing basket in the living room and carefully took her car keys without making a sound. I put the keys in my pocket and put on my shoes. I opened the front door and walked outside without a jacket so that it looked as if I were going to Yia Lue's place a few doors down. Instead of turning right to their apartment, I went to Mom's car, which was parked out front. The window curtains were closed, so no one could see me from inside. It was raining and cold, but my hunger for the sesame ball blocked out all thoughts of the cold. I unlocked the door, and got in. I opened the ashtray and pulled out a bunch of coins. There were no quarters or dimes or nickels, so I went to work counting out twenty-five pennies. Once I had the money in hand I ran around to the other side of the building to look for the girl with the sesame balls. I found her, very happily gave her the coins, and took a sesame ball from her basket.

I was thrilled. I felt the warmth of it in my hand, and my mouth started to water. I knew I couldn't eat it in the house, so I decided to go back to the car and eat it there. When I bit into it, the fried mochi dough crunched in my mouth, followed by the sweet mung bean in the center. For those few minutes, I was in heaven. The sweetness of the treat erased any anxiety I had about sneaking out of the house, stealing money from Mom, and secretly eating the sesame ball in the car. After making sure there was no evidence left on my face and no lingering sesame glued to my clothes, I got out of the car and went back into the warmth of the house.

Everything would have been perfectly fine; I could have spent the rest of the day watching cartoons without anyone the wiser. That sweet little secret could have been mine alone. That memory could have been lost and forgotten with no real drama and no need to retell this story at all. But I guess the universe wanted to make sure that the mung bean sesame ball made a big enough impact for me to remember how to make it much later in my life.

I was back on the couch watching cartoons with my siblings, and we had all forgotten about the girl selling sesame balls. Then a knock came at the door. *Knock, knock, knock.*

Mom stopped what she was doing in the kitchen and opened the door. There was a girl's voice outside muttering something I couldn't quite hear. But I heard Mom's voice saying, "No one here bought a sesame ball."

The tasty delicacy I had consumed earlier turned into a tight knot in my stomach. "Yes, someone bought a sesame ball," the little girl replied. "It was the girl who bought it. She gave me twenty-four pennies instead of twenty-five."

I was done for. Mom turned around, her eyes shooting daggers at me. "Yia!" she shouted. "Did you buy a sesame ball?"

What was I supposed to say? The little girl had already outed me. I couldn't deny it. My face burned with shame.

"Where did you get the money?" Mom continued, visibly holding herself back from giving me a whooping right then and there.

"I got it from the coins in your car." I said weakly, looking at the floor. That, of course, made her even angrier.

The little girl remained standing there in the cold, patiently awaiting her penny. Mom marched over to her purse, visibly irritated as she rummaged through it. With controlled frustration, she retrieved a penny and gently placed it in the girl's hand.

The front door closed and Mom turned back to me. "You stupid girl. How dare you take money and spend it on something worthless like that. I told you not to buy it. It is such a waste of money. You don't ever listen to me. What kind of daughter are you, you disobedient, stupid girl."

My entire body burned. I held back the flood of tears that wanted to spill out as my body caved in on itself. I knew she was right, so I couldn't do anything but swallow the shame that came after that one impulsive desire had dared me to defy my mother's rules. I hung my head, unable to look at anyone. There was nothing I could do except to make myself smaller, wishing I could disappear, wishing I had a different mother, wishing I were never born. That was the first time I experienced such a deep feeling of wrongness about desiring something. It left behind lasting beliefs about desire—how it's deemed bad and must be concealed, how the only way to indulge in it without consequences is through secrecy and not getting caught.

Mom was quick to discipline but would soften later, not through words but through food. Sometime after that incident was forgotten, I found her one afternoon preparing something curious.

"What are you making?" I asked her, looking at a bowl of yellow kernels. I almost never asked her what she was making, but I'd never seen this before, so my curiosity got the better of me.

"I'm making sesame balls," she said nonchalantly. "I haven't made them before. I went to visit a cousin who made them, so I had her show me how to do it."

I couldn't believe what I was hearing. Mom was going to make sesame balls! I had forgotten whatever it was I was going to do, and stayed with her in the kitchen. I wanted to see how my favorite treat came about.

How to Make Sesame Balls

Yield: Art

Cook time: Until creativity flows

Ingredients:
Obstacles
Innocence
Resourcefulness

Step 1:
Connection Heals

I took a closer look at the bowl of what she called *noob nav,* mung beans, soaked in water. These must be the sweet balls in the middle, I marveled to myself. That was my favorite part. She took the bowl to the sink and turned on the faucet, adding more water. She then drained it until all the water was gone. She pulled out a pot from under the cupboard, poured the mung beans into it, and added water again. She brought the pot to the stove and turned it on. I watched her every move, not wanting to miss anything.

Once the pot of mung beans started to boil, Mom came and stood by the pot. She turned down the heat to a medium simmer. The mystery of how a sweet yellow ball could be made to float inside a bigger ball without being attached to it was going to be revealed! That was one of the best things about eating a sesame ball— wondering how it was done.

With a spoon, Mom scooped out the white foam that had started to form on the surface and tossed it in the sink. She continued doing that until all the white foam was gone. After a while, the water from the mung beans boiled away. She then added a lot of sugar and a little bit of salt and stirred the contents until the beans started to become mushy. She poured in a bit of oil and continued to stir until the mixture suddenly became a thick paste, and then transformed into something even thicker, almost doughlike. That was the sign that the mung bean paste was ready. Mom turned off the heat, poured the filling onto a plate, and set it aside to cool. The steam from the mung beans gave off a sweet and musty aroma.

×   ×   ×

On August 13, 1980, my family boarded a bus bound for Bangkok. That day, a fleet of buses arrived in Soptuang, each one set to disperse countless families to different parts of the world. Every family clung to their few remaining belongings, often crammed into a handful of bags. Mom,

Dad, and we children stepped onto one of those buses, with me cradled in Dad's arms. Mom gripped Tang's hand tightly, while Mai, Phoua, Cher, and Cha followed close behind. She carefully seated us, ensuring we stayed within her and Dad's sight, then settled by the window, her mind swirling with uncertainty. She had no idea where we were headed or how long the journey would be. All she knew was that she might never see her brothers and sisters again, never set foot in Thailand or Laos again. All she knew was that she must keep going.

As the bus prepared to depart, Mom leaned out the open window to where her brother and sisters, and sons Chao and Khoua Neng and his family stood, bidding us farewell. She stretched out her hand to her *tais lau* and *txiv dlaab*, older sisters and brother. They grasped her hand, and in that moment, all the emotions that had been swelling in her eyes burst forth. She and her siblings cried out, long wails of sorrow and farewell.

Dad reached out to his eldest and youngest sons, not wanting to leave him behind. This farewell was different from when it was Khoua Neng who had left for Thailand. Back then, Dad had been certain they would reunite. But now, uncertainty weighed heavily on his heart, though he promised they would see each other again.

A wave of wailing swept across the field of hundreds gathered near the buses. Hands reached out, grasping desperately. Hmong hands clung to one another, memorizing every line and callus, absorbing every last fragment of home. Children sat quietly on the bus, watching their parents cry. The ones old enough to understand wept for the friends they were leaving behind, while a flicker of excitement for the new adventure ahead danced in their eyes. The younger children, unaware of the gravity of the moment, merely wondered about sitting inside this big box on wheels.

Off in the distance, someone captured this raw, emotional moment in a photograph that I later found in an old album of Mom's. Her expression bore the heartbreak of leaving home and venturing into an unknown world, a pain that spoke louder than any picture could ever capture. Those memories are etched in the lines of her face and the deep grief in her heart.

Mom and Dad held on to Laos for as long as they could. The bus engine roared to life. With a heavy heart, Mom let go of the last remnants of home.

The next few days were a blur—traveling to a different city, being shuffled around in a foreign language, and sleeping in strange places. Everything felt unfamiliar to Mom When we finally boarded the plane, fear crept in. She felt lost and scared for the first time in her life.

In the thick branches of the jungle, Mom always knew where she was. Her feet knew where to take her. She could ask the praying mantis for directions if she got lost, look to the sun for guidance, or, like a moth, follow the moon's light to find her way home. Even when traveling from Laos to Thailand, Mom was certain she could find her way back if they were ever allowed to cross the Mekong again. But now, on this metal bird, surrounded by pale-skinned strangers, she feared she would never make her way back to her mother and father. She yearned for them deeply in that moment, the ache burning a hole in her heart. Despite her fear, she stayed calm and held me tightly to her chest throughout the flight.

During the journey, she didn't know how to ask for what she needed—food, water, or the bathroom. When I soiled the cloth she had wrapped me in, she didn't know what to do or how to change me. The bag immigration had given her contained a few diapers, but no one had explained what they were or how to use them. My feces soiled the cloth, and Mom did her best to wipe it away with napkins she had saved.

People stared at her; some rolled their eyes. She avoided their gazes and kept her eyes downcast for the entire flight. For the first time in her life, she felt truly lost. But when she looked down at me, at her children, and at Dad sitting next to Tang, she told herself she had to keep going.

Immigrants who came to America had to be sponsored by someone living in the United States, often members of faith-based organizations. We were sponsored by a Christian family in Minnesota, Bonnie and Roland. The family lived in a small town called Le Sueur, which was an hour away from Minneapolis. They were in their early forties, a white, all-American, Christian couple with kids of their own. Their property was a few miles outside the main town surrounded by acres of cornfields. They lived in a lovely single-story house that had been passed down from Bonnie's father to them. The house had a huge basement that they turned into a two-bedroom unit with a kitchen and bathroom. When we arrived, there was already another Hmong couple living there so we shared the space with them.

Bonnie and Roland showed Mom and Dad around the house, pointing out the refrigerator, stove, cupboards, sink, toilet, bathtub, and running water, but they had no concept to comprehend what they were seeing. These were alien objects to them; they had never encountered such modern appliances before. The sponsors, not equipped with the training, information, and knowledge to handle a family who had never seen electricity or indoor plumbing, didn't realize the extent of their bewilderment. While their hearts were in the right place, they couldn't fully comprehend the profound cultural differences and challenges faced by Mom and Dad.

The first time Mom made food, she used water from the toilet for cooking, thinking it was a well. She didn't know that the tall steel box with two handles, one opening to cool air, and the other opening to freezing air, stored produce and meat. She kept the raw meat purchased from the groceries in the cupboards, noticing that a few days later it would start to smell.

The first time Bonnie and Roland took them to the grocery store was an adventure. They had never seen so many strange fruits and vegetables—apples, oranges, broccoli, mushrooms, and more. There were no animals being butchered but rather rolls of meat wrapped in plastic. They didn't know how to pick food or what to eat. Bonnie and Roland told them to take whatever they wanted, but they didn't know how it would be paid for. Bonnie and Roland would leave apples, oranges, and bananas on the dining table, but Mom and Dad didn't know they were for eating.

They didn't know a single English word. Luckily the husband of the other couple had a Laotian-to-English dictionary, so he would look up words in Laotian and point to them to let our sponsoring family know what we needed. That was how they communicated.

We lived with our sponsors for a month until they moved us into our own house in town. We were surrounded by Caucasians. There were no Hmong people or any other Asian people in our small town. Mom's hands itched to touch soil, to grow her own greens, to harvest her own rice and to eat fresh chicken. Mom and Dad craved pepper so badly that they wrote to Khoua Neng in Thailand and had him send pepper to America. She had no fabric or needle and thread to sew any new outfits. We wore American clothes that our sponsors collected from their church. Even the clothes felt foreign, the pants tight and uncomfortable.

Yia Lue and his family came to Minnesota a few months before us and settled in Minneapolis with their sponsor. They were in the city where hundreds of other Hmong families had settled and started to create a community. Once we settled into our new home and contacted them, Yia Lue came to visit.

Yia Lue noticed that there was not a lot of food around our house. The refrigerator and cupboards were nearly empty. He grew concerned thinking that our sponsors were not treating us well. He went back home and must have reported to the sponsorship authorities because one day, all of a sudden, our sponsors came to our house and Roland was very upset. He was yelling things that they didn't understand, but Mom could feel it was probably about the food in the house. Probably about how we told the authorities that they weren't taking care of us. Mom and Dad didn't know how to respond to him but clearly there was tension.

Yia Lue came back to pick us up shortly after that to live with him in Minneapolis. It was a heartbreaking end to our relationship with them. After that we never heard from them again and lost touch with them for forty years. Mom remembered our sponsors as being very nice, the lady being gentle and kindhearted and the man tall and talkative. Years later, Mom saw me watching *Mister Rogers' Neighborhood* and said, "Our sponsor looks like that man."

Forty-two years after we left them, I found where they were, and we corresponded. In July 2022, five of us sisters and two half-sisters took a family trip to visit them. Mom wasn't able to come because of her health. Bonnie was absolutely gentle and lovely, and Roland did indeed look exactly like Mr. Rogers.

Mom had me tell them that she was sorry for what happened, for how we left abruptly, and under an intense situation. She told me to thank them for sponsoring us, and to let them know that life in America would not have been possible without them. Even though she wasn't there to see them, the message I passed on was healing for all of us.

Step 2:
Resourcefulness Brings Out Creativity

While the mung bean paste was cooling, Mom moved on to make the mochi dough for the sesame balls.

She took out two packets of flour that she had purchased from the Asian supermarket. One was glutinous rice flour and the other was regular rice flour. She opened the glutinous rice flour and poured all its contents into a big bowl. With the rice flour she only poured half the bag into the bowl. On the table was a box of mashed potato flakes. Mom couldn't read the writing, but our cousin showed Mom the box of what to buy. Mom memorized the color and the illustration and then went to the American store to find the same one. "She said to add this," Mom said, showing me the box. It said "Mashed Potatoes" and had a picture of a bowl with a mound of white stuff in it. I had never had mashed potatoes and had no idea what it was. Mom added some of the flakes to the bowl of flour, added a bit of salt and some sugar and gave everything a stir to mix all the contents together.

Mom brought over a pot of water that had been boiling on the stove. Bit by bit, she poured the hot water into the bowl, stirred it with her spoon, poured in a bit more, and stirred it again. As I watched her do this, I could see her imitating our cousin, recalling the amount of water she had poured, trying to create a dough of the same consistency. Mom kept doing this until the little clumps of flour started to cling together into a bigger and bigger ball. Within minutes the powdery mixture became a big ball of dough. She set the pot and spoon down and, using her hands, started kneading the dough. I watched her, fascinated by the whole process, anticipating biting into my favorite treat.

Hmong people don't have desserts or sweet treats, so this was something I'd never seen Mom make. When she didn't know something, or when she wanted something, she found ways to learn how to make it herself. She was a quick learner and a self-starter.

×   ×   ×

In Minneapolis, among familiar faces, Mom began to thrive again. Mom and Dad both attended an English class for immigrants. They experienced their first winter in Minneapolis with wild snowstorms. They walked in the middle of winter with two socks on, treading in snow to drop us kids off at daycare on the way to school then pick us up again on the way home. Dropping us off at daycare became harder so Mom would go to the day class so Dad could watch us kids, and then she'd come home, and Dad would go in the evening. Mom was a quick learner. She had a good ear for learning new words and picked up English quickly. She could comprehend phrases and repeat them back. She also had a notebook in which she wrote her alphabets and simple words and phrases. The other women in class with her, our sisters-in-law and cousins, envied her and copied her writing.

Dad stopped going to school after a few months. He found it difficult to pick up a new language at his age and was discouraged. Eventually Mom also stopped going to school because Dad didn't see any value for her, a woman with a family, to attend school. She didn't want to give it up, but had to. Later, when we moved to California, she again attended an English class at the skills school in the neighborhood. Mom loved learning and did really well in class, but again, because of Dad's disapproval, she stopped attending and concentrated on raising us.

I grew up not knowing that Mom took English classes. I thought she'd just learned to spell her name and picked up English words from us kids. One of us kids always had to translate for her when we took her to the store, to see our teachers for parent conference, and to the quarterly welfare office for a quick meeting with our case manager so that we could get our monthly government assistance checks. I was thrown off guard when, in college, I brought my friend Martha home one day and Mom had a short conversation with her. She knew more than I'd given her credit for. Mom asked her how she was doing, where she came from, if she was hungry. All this she prompted on her own. She was quite at ease with Martha and completely herself. It was a different mother than I was used to seeing. She displayed a self-confidence that I had often overlooked behind her downcast eyes and slower gait that was always two paces behind Dad or someone else of authority. This mother was courageous and had a history of strength and resourcefulness.

When I was in college, I came home one weekend to see Mom with a pile of Hmong turbans on her bed. These were the kind of turbans the women wore with our traditional clothes at Hmong New Year. To fit the turban, my sisters and I would gather our hair into a tight bun on top of our heads. We took turns in half-hour sessions, during which Mom would meticulously wrap yards and yards of indigo-dyed fabric around our heads. Each layer formed an inverted V, with each subsequent layer less than an eighth of an inch above the one beneath it. The turban was then adorned with a coin belt featuring bright neon green and pink appliqué designs. I asked her what all these turbans were for.

"I made these," she said nonchalantly. "I make them and I sell them." I was both fascinated and shocked. She had made two different types of turbans that went with different types of outfits. I picked up one of them. It was much lighter than the ones we usually wore because Mom had found a way to decrease the layers of fabric one would typically use. "Some of these are specially made to order," she said, and sure enough, she had names written on a piece of paper pinned to each turban.

"Wow, Mom, how much do you sell these for?" I asked.

"Twenty dollars."

"Twenty dollars? Mom, you should be selling these for fifty dollars," I exclaimed. "They take so much time to make, and you have to cover the expense of the fabric and your time." But Mom seemed to think twenty dollars was a fair price.

Mom was resourceful, and that resourcefulness drew out her creativity. She didn't allow the limitations of language, status, time, or money to stop her from learning and creating. Once she learned a better way to do something, she replicated it and made a business out of it. She'd find a way to make something work so that she could have access to it for life, and she brought that same resourcefulness to making the sesame balls. Instead of spending money to buy the treats, she invested in learning how to make them so that she could have them whenever we wanted.

Step 3:
Learn for the Art of Learning

The dough was ready and the mung bean filling had cooled to the touch. Mom took out a bag of sesame seeds and poured them onto a plate. Then she set the bowl of mung bean filling between the two of us and proceeded to tell me what to do. "Take a little spoonful like this and roll it into a ball like this." She took a small amount and rolled it between her hands with light to medium pressure so that it formed into a ball, then put it on an empty plate. I followed suit, scooping a little in my hand and rolling it into a soft ball. Once it looked like Mom's, I set it down on the plate next to hers. Cha had joined us by then and was helping with the rolling.

Once we completed the filling, we moved on to the dough. "We do the same with this. Take a little bit more into your palm and roll it the same way." Mom demonstrated, and we both followed suit. The texture of the flour dough was smooth like the mung bean filling but a little bit thicker.

It was exciting to help make something I loved to eat. It felt as if the sesame balls were revealing their secrets to me. The finished product looked and tasted completely different from what it looked like while it was being made. During its life, a sesame ball goes through many stages of transformation. The sweet treat was once finely ground glutinous flour, rice flour, potato flakes, and mung beans. Both flours were once grains of rice; the potato flakes were once potatoes, and the yellow mung beans were once whole green mung beans. All these dry ingredients were once living entities that absorbed sunlight, water, and nutrients from the soil. And prior to that they were mere seeds, but seeds that came from plants that were also once seeds.

× × ×

Mom took the opportunity to learn something new because of who she herself became through the process. When Mai lived in Pittsburgh with her husband and had to stop working to take care of their newborn baby, she started quilting to make money. She had connected with the Amish community near Pittsburgh and learned how to sew the beautiful traditional patterns, layering fabric upon fabric to design birds, wreaths, and more. Mom went to visit one summer and Mai taught her how to quilt. She picked it up like a natural. After that, Mom sewed quilts, which she then sent to Mai, who sold them to the Amish. Even though Mom wasn't paid very much, she did it because it was a new skill she could learn. Once she learned it, she became creative in playing around with the patterns and designs. She made them into decorative pieces that you could hang on the wall and sold them to other Hmong women. She began to teach other women how to sew the quilts and wall pieces.

Mom created a king-size quilt for herself that is her cherished possession and joy. She never uses it on her full-size bed, because it's so large and because she wants to keep it clean. On one of my visits home, she pulled it out and showed it to me, her eyes shining with satisfaction. We laid it on her bed and took pictures of her with it. Holding one corner and wrapping it in front of her, she told me, "When I am 120 years old and no longer here, put this blanket in my house and wrap me in it with the birds in the center." Hmong people never speak directly about death. It's all done in metaphors, so "her house" was a reference to her coffin. Everything Mom made with her hands was for someone else: for her daughters, her sons, her grandkids, cousins, and strangers. This was the one precious gift she had made for herself. The tone of her statement was not one of sadness but of fulfillment.

She treated food the same way, learning new dishes that she ate at family events or were shared with her by one of her friends. It kept her feeling alive and intimate with life. The vulnerability of Mom trying sesame balls for the first time with me exposed the tenderness of her heart, her willingness to be seen in a place of newness. She was making the sesame balls by feel. There were no step-by-step measurements or list. She used her senses to guide her, touching the dough our cousin made so she could get the right texture, tasting the balls at the end to get the right sweetness, watching for signs of doneness so that she'd know when to take hers out. She had full citizenship in the present moment.

The pleasure of experiencing something new evolved into enjoyment—she wasn't just replicating a quilt or a recipe, but discovering how it transformed her into a new version of herself, becoming intimate with the ingredients, time, and space. Her guesswork gave way to intuition, and following directions turned into creating art. She followed her inner knowing, guided by her senses, which revealed her own natural gifts.

Step 4:
Tend to Others

After we had rolled all the dough into balls, Mom picked one up and flattened it into a thick disk between her hands. Then she picked up a ball of mung bean filling, placed it in the center of the disk, covered it with the dough, and rolled it between her palms into a smooth ball, making sure it was the same thickness all around. Finally, she rolled it in the sesame seeds, which magically stuck to the dough, each seed finding its perfect place with no two piled on top of one another. When the ball was covered with seeds like a second skin, she put it on a clean plate.

Cha and I watched her and did what she did. At first it was challenging for me to get the disk the right size and thickness. My first one was too flat and too big so that when I put the mung bean in and rolled it into a ball, the end where all the dough came together was too thick while the other side was too thin. Mom watched and told me how to adjust. My next one wasn't big enough, so it didn't cover all the filling, and I had to open it back up to flatten it some more until the edges overlapped just slightly. I still didn't understand how it was that the finished sesame balls were bigger than these or how the filling stayed perfectly round inside the dough. It even bounced around when you shook the sesame ball. I wondered about that as I rolled more balls.

We worked in quiet, joyful unison, Mom tending to us as needed to make sure that we were on the right track. As we rolled the last of the dough, Mom poured a lot of canola oil into a pot and put it on the stove to heat for deep-frying the balls.

Mom had a way about her that was always looking out for others, tending to them to make sure they felt cared for, not through words, but through her actions.

At family ceremonies and rituals, she always woke up early to eat and make sure she was well nourished, and then set off to our cousin's house to join other women in creating the day's meal. She was a good worker. She was often the first one there, ready to greet the other women and cook alongside them. She wasn't one to direct and she didn't need to be told what to do, rather she felt what was needed and flowed into a natural rhythm with the women.

When I would go with Mom to these events, she was always quiet and in the background. She didn't speak loudly nor did she exclude herself from the connection. I was ashamed that she wasn't more social, more engaging like the other mothers around me. I felt like she was the odd ball out, which mirrored my own awkwardness in social situations, and therefore blamed her for why I turned out this way. But what I didn't see was that Mom didn't need to boast about her expertise or be the life of the party. She also didn't complain about the amount of work and the backache she was experiencing. She constantly had her attention on the room, making sure that the elderly women had drinks, food, and a place to sit. She kept the house tidy as she moved about the room. She jumped in when needed and sat down while the food cooked. She'd noticed if the men needed more drinks in the living room or the bowls of fruit needed to be filled and directed me or another sister-in-law to fill them.

She had a quiet way of tending to others that didn't draw attention or require acknowledgment. She didn't take credit for the work she did, but rather allowed the younger daughters-in-law to shine. She simply did what needed to be done, not because of orders from authority figures, but from her soul. In turn the environment reflected the alignment and harmony that she felt inside.

Step 5:
From the Ground Up

Once the oil was hot, Mom gently put a ball in the pot, and as soon as it made contact, the oil sizzled around it. She put in a few more, leaving some space in between them. After a few minutes, the balls floated to the top and Mom turned them over with a slotted spoon. They bounced and bobbed on the surface of the oil, transformed once more into another phase of life. Soon they started to turn yellow and then golden brown, beginning to look like the sesame ball I had eaten a few weeks before. Mom took the golden balls out of the oil and put them in a colander. I could smell the nutty aroma of sesame seeds. My mouth started to water and I wanted to eat one right away, but Mom told me to wait for them to cool. I stood there counting the seconds until I could finally eat one, as she continued with the next batch.

What seemed like a very long time had passed when Mom finally took a ball out of the colander and broke it in half. The dough was thick and seemed stickier than I remembered, and the yellow yolk remained perfectly round inside. Mom gave me the okay and I grabbed one from the batch, still slightly hot and oily in my hand. All the waiting was finally rewarded as I bit into the ball, and the explosion of warm, sweet nuttiness danced on my tongue. It was absolutely delicious. I quickly gulped it down and was ready for my second one, but Mom put the balls in a bowl and told me to pass them around to the rest of my siblings, who were watching TV in the living room or doing their homework in the bedroom.

When the bowl was empty, I made my way back to the kitchen where a second batch of balls were already in the colander and a third batch were in the pot. Mom kept going until all the dough had been transformed into golden balls, by which time I was working on eating my third ball. She turned off the stove, took a cool ball in her hands, and bit into it. I watched her taste the result of her hard work and critique her first effort. "It didn't come out right," she said. "The dough is too thick and sticky and it's not as sweet as it's supposed to be." But her words were lost to my eight-year-old ears, because the only thing I cared about was the fact that I could eat as many of these as I wanted, and now that Mom knew how to make them, I could eat them forever without having to buy them. To me, that was the best thing in the world, and the fact that Mom had taken the time to learn how to make them meant they were all the more delicious.

It was a healing experience that afternoon as mother and daughters learned how to make sesame balls for the first time together. The shame that I had experienced weeks before with the treat turned into an enjoyable connection. It made me think about how Mom, too, was once a girl who desired treats, jewelry, and clothes. Knowing what I know of her now—her intelligence, entrepreneurial spirit, leadership among her peers, natural memory, and creativity—I see many similarities between us. As a teenager, I was so defiant and determined to be different from her, to live a different life, that I couldn't see how much alike we really are. The qualities I see in her are the same ones that others have used to describe me.

I now see that the skills and talents that make me who I am are also the ones that defined her. Based on the stories she has told me about her mother, I could trace those same qualities back to her mother. After three generations, I'm convinced that if I were to trace the lineage of the women in my family even further back, I would find that their bloodline flows through my fingers onto the food I touch, the plants I tend, the systems and structures I build, the innovative ideas and resourcefulness I carry, and the intuitive nature and insight I possess.

Each of us has undergone our own transformation, yet we can always trace who we are back to a source nourished by the interconnected web of relationships, care, love, and guidance passed down through generations.

Like the mycelium network beneath the forest floor, unseen yet vital, our growth is sustained by collective wisdom and resilience from the generations before us. Just as mycelium connects trees and plants, all of us, like hyphae, exchange nutrients, thoughts, and moments in this network of intimacy and connection. We all shape and influence one another, breaking each other down and building each other back up with the exact nutrients that we need to shape who we are today, contributing to the intricate tapestry of human intimacy. This web of connection is what sustains us, even as we move through time and space. It keeps us rooted home while venturing into new territories.

Almost three decades after Mom left Thailand, she returned to visit her sister for the first time. While there, she and Aunty took a day trip to visit the remnants of the camp. Over time, one section of the camp transformed into farmland, while the area where we once resided remained enveloped by trees and jungle. There were no roads leading to that secluded spot, and Mom and Aunty couldn't venture into the dense jungle. Instead, they ascended a hill and gazed toward the place we had once called home.

There, amid the lush hillsides on a warm afternoon, the only constant that hadn't changed was the blazing sun. It had witnessed Mom's life then and now welcomed her back with its familiar warmth. Overwhelmed by nostalgia, Mom and Aunty sang a traditional folk song, paying homage to the memories they held dear. Mom couldn't do it without crying. She thought of her daily trek to the village center to collect our rationed rice. She thought of the tiny river from which she fetched water to filter and boil for the day's meal. She sang to the souls who met their fate on this land, my half-brother Dang and half-sister Zang, Khoua Neng's daughter who died as a young girl from sickness. She sang for her brother Xao, who passed away years ago before she could hold his hand again. Her song stretched into Laos, searching for her mother, her father, and the sisters who died before she was born. Closing her eyes, she could still see the road that led to our village, and as she sang, she imagined walking through the door of the house where my brother and I were born.

Vang Sisters

When we have lost our way, are battling personal demons, or when external pressures overwhelm us, there is a thread that connects women, weaving us back into the core essence of womanhood. This thread is our fundamental joy. It happens in kitchens, at restaurant tables, in bars, in knitting circles, in fields under the sun, and reading groups all across the world and in every culture. The aim is always to come back to joy and power, to gather enough strength to laugh at daily challenges. To add resilience and insight to hardships, to be reflective in areas of shame and doubt. This joy transforms complaints into desires, victim narratives into gifts of power, and poison into medicine. We replenish our spirit with care and reflection from sisters, filling ourselves with love so that we have a buffer to absorb the world's demands.

I have a lot of "sisters": nieces, first cousins, second cousins, clan cousins, daughters of aunts and uncles who aren't real aunts and uncles but I call them aunts and uncles, sisters-in-law and their sisters. Whether we're related by blood or clan or through marriage, we're sisters.

But there has always been a group of us who are very close—the daughters of my half-brothers as well as some first and second cousins—eighteen of us altogether. My nieces, Ker, Chao, and Tracy, are from the eldest brother Khoua Neng; Soua, Lisa, Annie, and Pang are from the second brother Yia Lue; and Julie and Jenny from the third brother Chao. My first cousins are May and Sanyang (whom we called Sunny), the daughters of Dad's brother. And then there are my other cousins, Tru, Christy, and Mee, whose fathers I call uncle. From my immediate family there are, of course, my five sisters, Mai, Phoua, Cha, Mary, and Leah. There are many more, but we were the main crew.

In the Hmong culture, your network of "sisters" extends beyond your biological siblings. Every girl within a clan is considered a sister, and whenever there is a big family event, be it a healing ceremony, a wedding, or a funeral, the whole clan comes together. The women gather with their daughters in the kitchen to prepare the family feast while the men assist with the ritual, sacrifice, and butchering of the animals.

We were a diverse group of girls—serious to pranksters, family-focused to academically focused, conservative to rebellious, traditional to Americanized—but despite our differences, we did everything together. We shared clothes and food, laughter and tears. We attended each other's family ceremonies and events to help with the cooking and cleaning. Some of us went to school together, and we went through puberty and our teen years together.

Each of us had our own gifts; we were unique. There were times when we would lose ourselves in the world and forget who we were, but when we came together, we reminded one another of our brilliance, not through words, not through telling someone she was a genius, but by recognizing each other's gifts and allowing each of us to do what she did best so that we all got to shine.

During the summer months of our youth, we came with our mothers and learned to sew *paaj ntaub* together. Our mothers constantly compared us to see who was the slowest sewer and who would not be good daughter-in-law material. In the Hmong culture, you did not boast about your own daughters, you compared them to someone else's by complaining about yours while complimenting the others. But, regardless of our parents' pride or critical words and the competition they created, we simply loved being together.

Our summers were filled with all kinds of adventures: slumber parties, barbecues at the river, outings to San Francisco, hours spent chatting at McDonald's, and movie nights—all the fun, innocent things that teenagers did. The wildest things we did were binging on brownies and ice cream and watching romcoms until three in the morning.

In the winter, during Hmong New Year, we all got dressed up in our traditional clothes and went to the celebration together, drawing attention from suitors and the elders who sought wives for their sons. In Hmong, a group of sisters was called *viv ncawg*. The Vang clan *viv ncawg* were well known because my two eldest sisters and their crew were beautiful and charming and had great reputations before they got married. They paved the way well for us younger girls.

Our favorite thing to do when we were together was cook and eat. We'd make massive meals for ourselves to enjoy with enough left over to take home to our families. One of the things we loved to make was Hmong egg rolls, *kabyaub*. They're filled with glass noodles, vegetables, and ground meat, with an additional "bite" from Thai bird's eye chili peppers. Each of us would work on one or two of the ingredients, and then we'd put them all together and roll them up. It was a great way to bring us together to chat, laugh, fight, cry, and love.

How to Make Egg Rolls

Yield: Sisterhood

Cook time: Until each of you shines

Ingredients:
Joy
Reflection
Turn on

Step 1:
Connect with Your Sisters

The gathering of the *viv ncaws* always began with a phone call, often from me to Christy. A simple "Let's have a slumber party this weekend" would be enough to start the phone tree. This was before cell phones and group text messages, so the excitement of planning what we would cook, eat, and do would buzz for days in advance.

Saturday would finally come. We'd pack our clothes and pillows and blankets, and meet at the house of the "hostess" in the late afternoon. Once everyone was there, we designated some of the girls to do the grocery shopping at Food 4 Less, some to go to Blockbuster or Hollywood Video to rent movies (no Netflix back then), and the rest of us would start cooking the rice and making room for all the supplies that would be coming in.

Cha, May, Soua, Ker, and Tru were the oldest, and all about the same age, so they were the drivers and the responsible ones. Because they were born in Laos and Thailand and at least five years old—Ker was thirteen— when they came to the United States, they carried more of the family traditions and knowledge than most of us who were born here or arrived when we were very young. They set the bar for the rest of us younger girls.

Cha often kept track of the finances, divvying every- thing up among us at the end of the weekend. Naturally, she became an accountant and now manages a team of accountants herself. May, flamboyant and talkative, would tell dirty jokes or say something crass that had us all screaming with laughter or pretending to be offended.

Chao, Tracy, Christy, and I were the next oldest. We were the more outgoing and feisty ones; the visionaries of the group. We often initiated these gatherings and came up with the ideas for what to do and where to go. Christy and I were known to be more rebellious, probably because, even though we were born in Thailand, we came to the United States as babies and were more Americanized. Chao and Tracy came to the United States when they were seven and nine years old. They had more of the FOB (fresh off the boat) experience as well as some of the old country's conservative style.

The youngest group consisted of my sisters Mary and Leah, sisters Jenny and Julie, and sisters Lisa, Pang, and Annie. They were all born in America and didn't have any ties to the old country. They were the most Americanized, and by the time they were old enough, we older girls had already paved the way for them to have more freedom to pursue nontraditional life choices. Some of them would later break the mold even further by marrying outside the culture.

Sometimes we went a few weeks without seeing one another, but when we did, there was an ease and joy to our connection. There was always a lot to catch up on: who was backstabbing whom on *Days of Our Lives*, what's happening with Brenda and Luke on *Beverly Hills, 90210*. If there wasn't anything to catch up on, we found new things to talk about. The excitement of being with one another eventually led to a natural, more grounded rhythm of connection and a deeper revealing of our thoughts as the day progressed.

Step 2:
All Parts Make a Whole

After about an hour of catching up, shopping for food, renting movies, and organizing our personal belongings, it was time to prepare dinner. The older girls typically started the cooking because they were more experienced. It would be hard to say who was the best cook because each had her own unique flavors and specialty dishes.

They would bring out the ingredients for the egg rolls: mung bean thread noodle, ground pork, cabbage, carrots, dried shredded wood ear mushrooms, green onions, cilantro, a few eggs, and the egg roll wrappers. Someone would gather the condiments: oyster sauce, fish sauce, soy sauce, fresh Thai bird's eye chili peppers. We'd gather around the ingredients and each of us chose a few items to prepare.

We didn't need a "leader" or head cook to tell us what to do. We'd all cooked together so many times that we naturally knew how to work together and what role to play.

Cha started with the noodles and the mushrooms. She emptied the packets of noodles into a big bowl and soaked them in hot water to soften. She did the same with the mushrooms into another bowl, allowing them to rehydrate. Tru followed after her, throwing away the bags and sweeping up any noodles that had escaped onto the floor.

Chao pulled out a cutting board and knife, peeled off the tough outer layer of the cabbage, then cut it into quarters, and each quarter into threadlike slices. Christy peeled the carrots and passed them along to Soua, who grated them into a bowl. Ker washed and dried the green onions and cilantro and chopped them into fine pieces. Tracy, noticing that Ker needed a bowl, pulled one from the cupboard and set it in front of her before she even thought to ask.

May, who loved making pepper sauce, chopped a few red and green Thai bird's eye chili peppers and put them in a small bowl along with a handful of Ker's chopped cilantro and green onion. Then she added fish sauce and lemon and stirred everything together to make the dipping sauce.

As the dirty dishes piled up, I would wash them and put them on the dish rack. Mary would notice that there was no more space on the rack and put away the dry ones to make room for the ones I was washing. Annie and Julie emptied the packages of egg roll wrappers and separated them onto a plate to prepare them for rolling. Anyone who wasn't involved in preparing the egg rolls would either start on one of the other dishes we'd planned for dinner or would clean and tidy as we cooked. Some of the younger girls chatted among themselves or looked through the magazines we'd brought—usually *Seventeen, Cosmopolitan,* and *Soap Opera Digest.*

As we made egg rolls, we chatted constantly, flowing in and out of one another's conversations, communicating on different channels simultaneously, and listening, working, and talking all at once. In chaotic unison, we moved around the kitchen, bringing order to its motion and cadence. A silent understanding enabled us to move as one, slipping effortlessly into a rhythm.

As each ingredient was completed, we'd throw it into a large bowl. The noodles were drained and cut with scissors into bite-size pieces. The mushrooms were drained. The ground pork was broken apart and added to the bowl as were the carrots, cabbage, green onions, and cilantro. Soua, who was a great cook of traditional meals, added oyster sauce, fish sauce, salt, black pepper, and a bit of Thai bird's eye chili pepper, then she cracked a few eggs and mixed the whole thing together. She'd taste a small portion of filling and continue to add condiments as necessary until it was exactly the way she wanted it. There was no measuring or following a recipe. Her tongue would tell her when it was perfect.

No one thought about whose role might be more or less important than anyone else's. Everyone put everything she had into whatever she was doing, whether it was chopping vegetables or sweeping the floor. But, at the same time, we were aware of everything that was happening around us so that we could jump in to lend a hand when needed and then return to our task.

We recreated a Hmong village in the kitchen where there were many things happening at once, and everyone was working together toward the same thing. Just as all these different ingredients made an egg roll, each of us together made a village. Each ingredient was required as part of the whole. The weaving together and making of a dish was the embodiment of the way Hmong people lived. Food creates connection, and connection creates a community, where the individual has her uniqueness and also becomes more of who she is in the community. The fundamental joy of who each woman is starts to come out and shine.

Step 3:
Women Love Sex

Once Soua was satisfied, we gathered around the big bowl of filling with a plate, a spoon, and a small bowl of egg yolk to use for sealing the wrapper. Each of us put a wrapper on her plate with one of the points facing us. We put a spoonful of filling at the end closest to us and folded the bottom part up toward the middle to cover the filling. Then we brought the left and right points to the center and continued to roll upward, gently but firmly, from the bottom to within an inch of the top point. Finally, we'd scoop up a bit of egg yolk with a finger and brush it over the empty part of the wrapper before folding it down and pressing it gently to seal the roll.

There were a few minutes of silence while we got into the rhythm of the task, making sure we were using just the right amount of filling and that the roll was tight enough without breaking the wrap. Then, as we got into the groove, the conversation naturally picked up. Eventually someone, usually May, would break the ice and make some remark with a sexual innuendo regarding the size of each woman's rolls. Tru, without missing a beat, would jump on the joke. Those two made a great comedic pair. From there the conversation about sex was off to the races. It didn't matter that none of us had any experience with sex. It was still a topic we all loved to tease one another about. One person made long thin rolls, another made short thick ones, and someone, of course, made long thick ones. There were tight ones, and there were floppy, airy ones. There were some that were perfectly shaped and some that kept breaking. We joked about sex and sizes and what would feel better or maybe would be too much or not enough. We predicted our husband's endowment based on how we rolled our egg rolls. The spirit of the conversation was light and fun as we teased one another and basked in the innocent arousal we created.

Our conversation reminded me of the many conversations I overheard at family gatherings when the "old ladies," meaning my aunts and sisters-in-law, talked about sex. One time I eavesdropped on one of my aunts making the sound of two bodies slapping up against each other, and I was shocked. Those old ladies seemed modest and shy in public, but when they were alone together they really let loose. They teased one another much more than we young ones did, and they were rowdier and more graphic. Some of the women who were the first wife and second wife of the same man, would share their feelings and talk about jealousy. There was no shaming, no judgment. They supported and empathized with each other. They didn't complain about or disparage their husbands to the other women. They just shared their feelings and encouraged one another.

It was captivating to hear them speak openly about sex, a topic typically considered taboo at any other time. This allowed me to connect with them as women, rather than judging them for being relegated to second-class citizens. Witnessing their strength and courage, I realized these qualities were not exclusive to my American friends. I began to comprehend something about being a woman: that women of any ethnicity and age, traditional or liberal, conservative or Americanized, would find any opportunity to talk about sex. Women love sex, and we love talking about it. That was a thread that wove us together.

Step 4:
Follow the Thread

Before we knew it, the bowl of filling was empty. It was time to clean up the kitchen and fry the egg rolls.

While we'd been talking, Ker had filled the wok with oil and fired it up so that by the time all the rolls were filled, the oil was ready for frying. That's who Ker was, always thinking ahead so that there was a seamless transition from one task to the next. She carefully dipped one of the egg rolls in the oil. It sizzled around the egg roll. She added a few more rolls—but not too many at a time, because that would reduce the temperature of the oil. Once they turned golden, she carefully flipped the rolls to the other side. As they turned uniformly golden in color, she transferred them to a colander that Chao had lined with paper towels to drain off the oil. Ker and Chao made a great cooking team. They complemented each other's skills and techniques. Where Ker was more traditional, Chao liked to try other ethnic cuisines, which she then brought back to Ker. Now, as Chao helped Ker with frying the egg rolls, the rest of us turned our attention to preparing the other dishes for dinner and cleaning up the kitchen.

As the egg rolls started to cool enough to eat, Lisa and Annie, two of the younger sisters, rolled them up in paper towels and passed them around. We dipped them in either the spicy Hmong pepper sauce May had prepared or the sweeter, store-bought, Mae Ploy Sweet Chili Sauce.

The mood of the evening flowed from laughter to seriousness to intimacy to dreams and secrets. We revealed everything to one another because we knew it would only strengthen us individually and as a group. We had no secrets from one another, no shame, and no judgments. We pushed and challenged each other.

Joy and laughter were the foundation of our relationship. We worked out kinks in our relationships, because we knew that, for the whole to be strong, there had to be an open connection among us. Tension between any two people created tension among the whole group. For us to work together as a unit, we had to work out any tension until there was connection and laughter. There was no competing, no proving, no scarcity, no grabbing or holding on to mine, because it was all ours. We each added something to the pot of our relationship, and we were all able to draw from it when we needed to.

My sisters taught me the essence of being a woman: we are joy and power. That is what we are meant to bring. And it's the thread of sisterhood we return to when we've lost our way.

Mother. Daughter.

Growing up, one of the dishes I loved was Mom's squash shoot soup. I loved the simplicity of it, the earthy, nutty taste, the soft texture, and the warm nourishing feel it left in my body for hours after eating it. It was a dish I saw her make every summer into the fall, as the winter squash ripened in her garden. Mom would go to the backyard and, a few minutes later, show up in the kitchen with a handful of prickly greens, baby squashes, and a few big yellow blossoms. To me it appeared that she'd just throw it all in a pot with water, lemongrass, and a few pieces of fried pork rind, added salt, and, voilà: a bowl of magic.

As much as I loved that soup, I didn't pay much attention to her garden. I was always too busy with schoolwork or sports or socializing with my friends. I didn't know what she grew or how she grew it, and I was never curious enough to ask. My entire experience of her backyard was occasionally stepping outside to look for her and being told to water the plants, which immediately caused me to regret having gone out there in the first place. Sometimes she'd tell me to go pick a few things, such as green onion, cilantro, mint, basil, or *rau ram*, which is Vietnamese coriander, for the meal she was cooking. She would ask for what she wanted in Hmong, since she didn't know their names in English. Sometimes I understood what she needed, and other times I would come back with the wrong item, which caused her to make fun of me. When I stared at her blankly or asked if she meant such and such, she'd tease me for not understanding Hmong, and I would be embarrassed. The garden was a mystery, primarily associated with difficult tasks that highlighted my lack of fluency in our mother tongue, which further distanced me from it as well as from her. At that time, my relationship with Mom was already on rocky territory, compounded by hormones and teenage insecurity.

When Dad died during my senior year of high school, our relationship plummeted. My heart was so filled with rage that I took it all out on her. I blamed Mom for everything. I blamed her for spending eighteen years not learning English, which left us relying on government assistance. I blamed her for moving us to California, where many Hmong people were farmers and lived on welfare, instead of staying in Minnesota, where they seemed more sophisticated and successful. I blamed her for living under Dad's strict and controlling thumb. I blamed her for not being Americanized. I blamed her for Dad's opium addiction. I blamed her for making me translate English for her my whole life. I blamed her for being my mother. I blamed her for my existence.

When Dad died, there was nothing I could do to satisfy her. I wasn't enough. I wasn't obedient enough. I didn't cook enough, and when I did, I wasn't doing it right. I wasn't good enough at sewing. I wasn't home enough. I wasn't Hmong enough. I wasn't helping around the house enough. I wasn't the daughter she wanted enough.

When Dad died, everything I did or didn't do boiled down to not having a father. Many of our seemingly mundane conversations erupted with her yelling, "It's because you don't have a father that you are like this!" or, "They will say you are *pug laib*, bad girl, because you don't have a father!" or, "It's because you don't have a father to discipline you that you think you can do whatever you want."

When Dad died, I couldn't look at Mom. I couldn't talk to her without being angry. Another of our seemingly mundane conversations would erupt with me yelling, "I can't wait to leave here!" or, "I'm never coming back when I leave!" And if it got really bad, "I wish I was dead!" And when it got really, really bad, "I wish you were dead!"

When Dad died, both of us were heartbroken and neither one knew how to reach the other; we were barely able to put ourselves together, let alone care for the other.

When Dad died, I had to look life in the face and confront the awareness that none of this would last. Everything would one day be gone, including me. The reality of life shattered into a million pieces like a glass breaking through space. Dad had always operated in the background, in the shadow of my life. He carried my shadow. He was my shadow. And with him gone, I felt empty. I knew who I was with a father in the dark, but I didn't know who I was with no father. Death pierced the protective membrane of my once-safe reality, violently introducing itself into my life. It loomed in the shadows on the walls, a constant reminder that life inevitably ends. I did not know how to operate in the reality that life is impermanent.

When Dad died, something cracked open in me that I couldn't put back together. The world, the reality I had lived in, which always felt small and constricted, broke open. I didn't know what to do or where to go. All I knew was that I had to get away. I had to run. I needed to breathe. I needed something different. I needed to break out of the too-tight box that had bound me to being a "good" person.

I fantasized about the freedom I would have if I weren't under the strict, controlling, and critical gaze of Mom. I fantasized about the freedom I would have if I were completely without the burden and emotional weight of Mom. All the fantasies that I used to have of Mom being an American mother, being a loving and affectionate mother, stopped. Now, I just wanted to get away.

In the following eight months of senior year, I descended into something that I wouldn't call depression. It was the opposite of that; an awakening of sorts, and in the midst of that, I felt exhausted. My soul felt exhausted. I started to fall asleep in class. I would be so tired I'd go to my badminton coach's office and sleep in the side room during class. I was part of the International Baccalaureate program at Franklin High School where thirty to forty of us students spent four years together working with the best teachers at the school. Because it was a small program and we had the teachers for multiple years, it was an intimate group. My teachers knew what I was going through and let me sleep in class as needed. They didn't attempt to wake me up unless class was over.

I was an A student, top five of my class. I loved school, learning new things and absorbing knowledge. Sophomore year I would read Tang's books for his senior English class and wrote his book reports for him. My junior and senior years, I attended Cha's astronomy and sociology classes at Delta College for fun and wrote her papers for her. All for fun. I was the setter on the volleyball team and number one on the badminton varsity team. I held positions in the Art Club, Asian Club, Friday Night Live Club. I was the MVP defendant attorney in Mock Trial and studied with friends on Academic Decathlon.

When Dad died, I didn't see the point anymore. What was all this hard work for? The A grades and extracurricular activity, the extra book reports and advanced classes and sports. I worked at McDonald's for spending money, and even there I moved quickly up the ladder. All of it, all the achievement and awards and school clubs, felt dry and monotonous.

Within four months, my grades dropped. I received my first Bs and Cs . . . and a D. Gone were the straight As. My advanced calculus teacher had to talk to me. My history teacher had to talk to me. I had to tell my advanced biology teacher I wasn't going to complete my science paper on the genetic study of crossbreeding fancy guppies. I wasn't going to take the IB test to see how

I scored with students from across the world to get an extra boost for my college applications. I started giving away food to friends and family and even strangers at McDonald's. I got fired at McDonald's. Who gets fired at McDonald's?

There were days when I didn't go to school at all. My five best friends and I would skip classes or skip school altogether. We'd go out for long drives on Highway 4 toward Angels Camp or along Eight Mile Rd, anywhere that took us out of the confinements of Stockton, of high school, of teenage life. We'd get warm apple fritters at Yum Yum Donuts, or Pralines 'n Cream ice cream at Baskin-Robbins where two of them worked. We'd eat chow fun and shark fin soup at the Cambodian/Chinese restaurant owned by one of their relatives. On late nights when we couldn't sleep, we'd sit at Denny's and talk about life until four in the morning, go home and sleep for two hours, then go back to school, where I'd either sleep in class or go sleep in my badminton coach's office. I gained twenty pounds and went up six sizes.

In those last few months of high school, my relationship with Mom continued on a downward spiral. We grieved in our own ways, separately. Things were distant between us. We were careful not to trigger each other. I would be out late to avoid being home for dinner. We didn't have anything nice to say to each other. When fights blew up, I continued to threaten to leave home and never come back.

On graduation day, Mom presented me with a 24K Asian gold necklace with a heart pendant with a monkey on it, since I was born in the year of the monkey. It was a gift that Mom presented to each one of her graduating children. Bought from the money that she had saved her whole life so that she could bestow unto us a token of her love and pride. I kept the necklace but hardly wore it. The gold was too yellow and didn't go with any outfits. American gold was more delicate and classy.

When I left for college, I left her garden and her food. I left her. *I was finally free*, I thought. Little did I know that her food was what had kept me anchored to who I am, that it was planting seeds of my value, my culture, and my people. Embedded in her recipes were the ingredients of love.

In college, out of the fire of Mom, I started to see my culture and our food in a new light. My appreciation for and knowledge of our culture grew, but my relationship with Mom remained distant. I went home every other month for weekend visits. For the first two years, the tension between Mom and I remained. It wasn't as explosive as before and much of the anger was quelled by the distance between us.

× × ×

At twenty-five, I landed a job in the Bay Area and started my own life. I only went home once or twice a year. Caught up in the demands and freedom of adulthood, I didn't feel the need to visit more often. As I matured, changed, and grew more confident in myself, I began to see Mom's food through new eyes, taste it with a different palate, and watch her cook with growing curiosity. The seeds that had been planted in me slowly began to germinate as I nurtured them with love and attention. Not only did I start to see our food differently, but I also began to experience Mom in a more intimate way through our time together in the kitchen.

One weekend home, I asked her about squash shoot soup.

How to Make Squash Shoot Soup

Yield: Wisdom

Cook time: Until poison turns into medicine

Ingredients:
Anger
Attention
Approval

Step 1:
Come Back to What's Natural

We walked out back to Mom's garden. The fence was lined with a variety of herbs and vegetables. Her plants were tall and brimming with life. I had no idea what most of them were called, but I did recognize the cilantro, which was by then about hip high and flowering, and the lush bunches of mustard greens, some of them with yellow flowers on their tips. Behind the mustard greens was a trellis of pea shoots.

"The peas are from the woods. They're wild peas. I like pea shoots much more than peas themselves," Mom explained, letting me glimpse her internal world.

I didn't ask her exactly where in the woods she got them or what that entailed, but was touched that she shared this intimate detail about herself and her garden. With a little bit of interest and curiosity from me, she was quick to share about herself, something that I hadn't noticed or done before.

Lining the back fence were buckets of mint, Thai basil, and green onion. The lemongrass grew in a corner by itself, towering over the other herbs.

Her winter squash had started to spill over onto the grass beyond the garden beds. Baby squash were starting to form with their blossoms still attached. When I asked Mom how she'd learned that the squash shoots were good to eat, she just shrugged and said, "That's how it's always been. That's what I was taught when I was little. You didn't eat winter squash only when they were fully grown. At each stage, there was something available to eat."

I asked if they hadn't been afraid that by picking the shoots there would be fewer mature squash for them to harvest, to which her response was, "There is always more than enough to eat. Squash tastes different at different stages of growth. When you eat them young, they are tender. There is an in-between stage where they are no longer young enough to be tender, but not grown enough to enjoy. When planting and gardening, you must keep your attention on what you grow. They change so fast." With that, she showed me how to pick the shoots. "You snap them at the point where the shoot meets the main stem. You only want the tender leaves."

I followed her lead and carefully snipped off a few of the young shoots. It wasn't as easy as she had made it look, and she went twice as fast, her hands moving by feel and memory. She snapped off a few baby squash that were no more than an inch or two in diameter, and a few blossoms. Now we had a handful of shoots, baby squash, and blossoms.

We moved to the lemongrass, and she cut off a stem at the root. The sweet citrus smell quickly filled the air. I loved the smell of lemongrass.

I asked Mom to put the plants down so I could take some pictures of her hands.

"Why would you want to take a picture of these hands?" she asked, seeming embarrassed. "They are so old. They are not young like they used to be. These hands have known hard work all their lives. They have sewn many *paaj ntaub* and worked in many fields. They can't sit still. They are always working."

She rubbed her hands together and turned them over as she spoke. "My index fingers are getting so stiff now. I can't sew anymore. I haven't done much sewing in the last three years."

To me, however, her hands looked strong and earthy.

For as long as I can remember, Mom was always grow-ing something in her backyard. Her garden was her life. It was the beating of her heart. She grew up with dirt beneath her feet and between her fingers. The pulse and rhythm of nature were etched in those hands. She knew by touch, by sight, by smell the exact stage of growth a plant was in and how much longer it needed to ripen or exactly when it was ready to be picked. She could identify plants even when they were barely four leaves out of the ground. Without consulting a calendar or listening to a weather report, she knew when it was time to plant, when to harvest, and when to break down her garden and prepare it for the winter. Intuiting nature required her to be prepared for the unknown, to relax into uncertainty as she listened with curiosity, open to possibility. If some plants didn't grow, she didn't fuss about it. She just figured out what to do differently next time.

Mom showed courage despite her limited grasp of English. I vividly recall the first time she returned home alone with a bag of burgers and fries from McDonald's. It surprised me because, usually, she would only go there accompanied by one of us kids to make the purchase. "I want six cheeseburgers and two large fries," she shyly said with her accent. Before approaching the counter, she meticulously studied the words, repeating them aloud to herself to make sure the pronunciation was understandable. She bravely walked up to the counter, made the purchase, paid for it, and returned home to delight us with burgers. With time, she learned that she could simply order three #2 meals and get three drinks with them. As her confidence grew, she started ordering from the drive-thru. Eventually, she added Chicken McNuggets and apple pies to her orders. Over time, she'd return with Burger King or Taco Bell.

Mom displayed far more courage than I did. When faced with something I didn't know, I would often avoid it altogether. If I had to confront it, I would hide, working quietly to figure it out on my own without drawing attention to it.

×   ×   ×

College was freedom and independence. I was finally able to allow my mind to expand as far and wide as it could. My imagination was my only limitation. And my imagination was based on TV shows and movies like *Revenge of the Nerds*; *Real Genius*; *Saved by the Bell*; *The Fresh Prince of Bel-Air*; *Beverly Hills, 90210*; and something with more sustenance—*Good Will Hunting*. College was an open canvas where anything could happen. College was fraternity parties, sorority sisters ruling the campus, and crushes on handsome, geeky philosophy majors. College was late-night partying on weekends and trying pot for the first time. I was full of ideas of what college would and could be like.

Needless to say, the fantasy of college and the reality stood on opposite ends of the pole. It was vast. It was scary. It was exciting. I grew up in a small city where people like me were the majority. As long as you didn't cross northwest of Hammer Lane, you were surrounded by Asians, Black folks, and Mexicans. Your white folks in this part of town were the ghetto, low-income Caucasians and they were the minority.

At UC Davis, not only was I the minority of the colors, I was the minority of the Asians—the Southeast Asians. There was a clear distinction between the ABCs (American Born Chinese), the Hapas (half Asian, half white), and the FOBs (fresh off the boat Asians who were born and raised overseas), and then there were the Southeast Asians: Laotian, Thai, Cambodian, Mien, and Hmong, excluding the Vietnamese because everyone knew what pho was and everyone knew where Vietnam was on the map since the war.

I grew up in schools where I was easily identifiable. I grew up with Hmong students all around me. Where I had to be careful and maintain a good reputation. I grew up needing to be and wanting to be the smartest kid so that I wasn't grouped as an FOB. I had something to prove. I stood out. Here, on campus, no one knew me. That was both lonely and thrilling. I could be anyone I wanted. I could do anything I wanted. But my fantasies were far more ambitious than my courage.

The first day on campus, I drove from Sacramento to UC Davis. I mapped out the location of the buildings for each class, trying to memorize the route so that I didn't have to pull out a map and look lost, like a freshman. I needed to look confident, like I belonged on that campus. I tried to recall the routes from the freshmen orientation I attended a few days before. I made it to my first class with ample time. I sat in a big hall, toward the middle of the room to not be completely invisible, but also not at the front to be known. There were easily more than two hundred students in that class.

En route to my second class, I had twenty minutes to walk from one end of the campus in the social sciences building to the other end, the engineering building. Now there were two issues. I didn't want to pull out a map in public, and I didn't have a watch. To remedy issue number two, I had stuffed a clock in my backpack that morning. Yes, a wall clock, a big round clock with ticking hands. That was how scared I was to talk to strangers, to look lost and not know what I was doing. I found a bathroom in the Student Union, went to a stall, unzipped my backpack and looked at my clock, then pulled out the map and memorized the next route. "I can do this," I reassured myself. I put both away, flushed the toilet, and walked back out into the dry summer heat. I crossed the quad, head held high, looking exactly as though I knew where I was going.

That was my first week. Walking from place to place with a map and clock in my backpack. Not once was I brave enough to just be lost and ask for directions. By the second week, I had memorized my routes and bought a watch.

When a Hmong person is in a new location, the first thing we do is seek other Hmong people. For survival, for safety, for connection, for belonging, for family. We connect back to what is natural for a sense of home. Once connected to that place, that home, there is more courage to wander and explore.

I knew there were Hmong people at UC Davis (UCD). Cher had graduated from Davis in 1993 and, while a student, the Hmong Student Union (HSU) held a college day for the cousins and siblings of the Hmong students there. Cher brought a few of us to be part of the day that was filled with bonding, workshops on higher education, and food. So, the first thing I did when I got to campus was look for HSU. For survival, for safety, for connection, for belonging, for family. With other Hmong students, I felt stronger.

I've always believed my family was different. Or maybe I just felt different. It's hard to describe the limitations that you live with until you've gone outside the box and seen how things can be vastly different. I just always thought there was only one way to be Hmong. Maybe Hmong mothers just aren't affectionate. Maybe all Hmong mothers are critical. All Hmong fathers are absent. Hmong parents just want you to get married and have kids. Hmong parents don't tell you they love you. Hmong parents are strict disciplinarians. My experience of Hmong families was limited to my family. We were traditionalists. We still practiced Shamanism. Our parents saved everything and bought nothing extra. We lived within our means.

To keep from being targets, we didn't befriend people outside our culture. In elementary school, my summer camp counselor invited me to a barbecue with her family, but Mom wouldn't let me go, saying, "If anything goes missing, they'll blame you. No, you are not going. They won't like you. You're not like them." I was devastated. I didn't understand why she kept me in such tight constraints. She kept me within the confines of her walls, and it was suffocating. The world I knew was through her eyes, and from her eyes everyone threatened our safety. We had to keep ourselves as small as possible, invisible, out of the sight of others so that they couldn't get us. Through her eyes, we were still trekking through the jungle, vigilance on high alert for the rustling of soldiers charging, for the sound of someone yelling, "Run, the communists are here!" For the bang, bang, bang of gunshots in the night. In her world, we were still hiding in the musty caves of Laos.

In my world, there was no war outside our door. We were supposed to be free here in America. But the war she fled from, the war her mother fled from, and her grandmother, and great-grandmother, and her before that, where scars were physical, imprinted in me the shadow of otherness war, and within that, women's war.

The cloak that kept me safe from the accusing eyes of others also kept my gifts invisible to others. I could never let others know what was happening in here, because it would leave me exposed and vulnerable, a target. If I needed to know what time it was, carry a clock, don't ask a stranger.

As I made Hmong friends at UCD and became involved with the Hmong Student Union, my experience of who we are expanded. Some had much more loving relationships with their parents. Some of them were born in Thailand or Laos and came over when they were young, but still had memories of living there. Some of them were the eldest in their family and knew more Hmong customs. As I saw our culture through their eyes and learned about our history from them, I began to glimpse the beauty of who we are.

Through HSU I found a new family, one where I expanded my knowledge and my ideas of our culture. Where I challenged myself and them about who we are. Where I engaged in conversations about our traditions and beliefs instead of being told that I shouldn't ask such questions because I am a girl.

Through HSU, I explored the variations of being Hmong. There were about fifty of us out of a student body of twenty-seven thousand. We were a family. We studied together, ate at one another's homes, laughed together, learned together, and reached out to Hmong high school students in the Sacramento and San Joaquin counties to promote higher education. We participated in Asian Culture Night, showcasing our heritage, and later hosted our own Hmong Night on campus. The event featured traditional Hmong dances, folk songs, and a fashion show highlighting the unique outfits of various Hmong subgroups—Green Hmong, White Hmong, Hmong Leeng, Striped Hmong, Red Dress Hmong, and Chinese Hmong, among others. Some of these groups were identified by their clothing or the regions they lived in within Laos.

Through HSU, I connected my attention back to my culture and what was more natural for me. When I strayed too far, all I had to do was come back to my roots.

Step 2:
Strip Away the Extra

We brought the squash and lemongrass inside and set them down on the kitchen counter. Mom took a pot out of the cupboard, filled it with water, and set it on the stove to heat.

She washed the lemongrass of soil, pounded on the stalk to release some of the juice, and folded it into three-inch lengths. Then she wrapped the top few inches of the leaves around the stalk and tucked the tips inside to make a neat little package. When the water started to simmer, she added the lemongrass to the pot.

She went into the fridge, took out a few pieces of the pork rind that she had fried a few days earlier, and added them as well. The oil from the pork rind was going to contribute a delicious flavor to the soup.

"Mom, can you make this soup with other kinds of meat?" I asked. As much as I liked the flavor of pork rind, I didn't like the texture of the fat. I always passed the fatty part of the rind to Mom and only ate the meat if there was any.

"Yes, you can make it with chicken or with none at all," she reassured me.

I asked her about Hmong spices and sauces and why Hmong food is so plain and simple.

"In Laos, we lived in the mountains and didn't have access to all these different spices. All we had was salt and fresh herbs. Salt is all you need to flavor food and draw out its taste. You don't use anything extra. You make things simple and easy. You don't have much time to spend cooking. You want to make what's necessary and have more time for sewing, farming, and taking care of the family. There was always much more to do. Food was for sustenance, to give you energy for the day."

In Laos, Mom would wake up early in the morning to make breakfast and prepare lunch to take with her for the day. The rice would have been soaking overnight, and she'd cook enough for dinner also. During harvest season, she would make the rice at home and cook the greens at the farm, using the little firepit in the farm hut. If the greens were not yet ready to harvest, she'd use whatever vegetables were available to her. The meals were simple, consisting of rice and greens that were either sautéed with pork oil or made into a soup flavored with lemon-grass and salt. The food was mostly vegetarian. Meat was for special occasions such as celebrations or ceremonies.

There was no electricity, so life revolved around the sun and the moon. Nothing was wasted. Food was not wasted, sunlight was not wasted, warmth was not wasted. Mom cooked only what she harvested, seasoning it with pork rind, chicken, or occasionally beef or bison jerky, which was made once a year during the New Year celebration when a cow or buffalo was sacrificed.

×　×　×

It was through a friend from HSU that I learned a new meaning of my name. I grew up with the name "Yia," the word for iron skillet or frying pan. My siblings had a great time making fun of my name. It wasn't fun to tell people my name meant frying pan when they asked me. In school, my name was hard for Americans to pro-nounce. I wanted to fit in and be cool. I wanted to be an American. In seventh grade, I picked a nickname, Vicky, and had used it ever since then.

I wanted the name Yia to mean something import-ant, to have depth, to justify why I was named after a frying pan. I asked Mom one day how I got my name.

"I don't know. I don't remember why we named you that. Why are you asking? It's just a name."

"But Mom, it must have come from somewhere." She looked at me blankly. I tried another tactic. "Who gave me my name?" Thinking that maybe that person was someone important and must have a reason for my name.

"I don't remember. Maybe it was Mai." My sister didn't feel significant enough. I had hoped it came from an elder who dreamed about it and gave me that name at my three-days-old soul-calling ceremony. Or maybe my parents gave me a name, and then my soul didn't like it, so I became sick, and our shaman had to ask the spirits what name my soul wanted to be called, and my soul told him that I shall be called Yia.

I tried again. "Do we have anyone in our family named Yia?"

"Well, we have an aunt named Yia."

I'll take it. Anything but frying pan. So, I'd tell people I was named after my Aunt Yia, fantasizing that she must have been a significant, important woman for me to be named after her.

One evening, our HSU crew were having one of our usual hang-out nights at someone's house, eating pizza and drinking root beer. Someone asked me, "Vicky, what's your Hmong name?"

I looked up from my pepperoni pizza. All eyes seemed to redirect over to me. Heat crept into my cheeks. I was the only person who went by a nickname. Everyone else was Ger, Tua, Ia, Phou, Ge, Tou Lee, Kao, Patong, with the exception of the brothers Julien and Stephan, who were born and raised in France, and my three best friends, Ann, Sue, and Betty, who were born in the United States, so they had American birth names but still had Hmong names.

"Yia," I stated, fully flushed now.

Ia chimed in, "Yia. That's such a pretty name! How come you don't use it?" A few other fellows nodded their heads in agreement. Ia, whose name sounded like mine, except where mine has the "Y" to soften the tone, her name led with a stronger "I," much like her character. She was a wholesome woman, mature and intelligent. She was a balance of Hmong and American. She knew who she was and where she came from and was ambitious and modest. She used her name proudly the way she held herself.

I wasn't sure what to say. No one had ever asked why I didn't use my Hmong name. Many people were relieved to use *Vicky* with a face like mine. For most people, Asian faces often come with names that are difficult to pronounce. "I don't know. It's a hard name to pronounce when you first hear it. Teachers and substitute teachers could never say it. They either said 'I-ya' or just spell it out, 'Y-I-A?' So, I used a nickname instead. I went through different nicknames like Jamie, Heather, Barbara in elementary school, and then in seventh grade looked through a baby book and came upon Vicky, so I have used it ever since."

They took in my explanation with empathy, having had similar experiences.

"Do you know what Yia means?" Ia continued to ask me.

"Of course. Frying pan," I said matter-of-factly. "That's why I don't like to use it. Whenever people ask me what it means, I hate saying it means 'frying pan.'"

"Well, yes, but there's another meaning for it. It's in the intonation. Because when you say *'yias,'* it's a frying pan. That intonation is often used for boys. But *'yia'* also means *'yiag yiag'* and is used for girls. Do you know what that means?"

"No, I don't," I admitted. Having grown up speaking Hmonglish at home—a mix of Hmong and English— my grasp of the Hmong language was not as strong as most of these guys.

"*'Yiag yiag'* means strong, supple. Something that is bendable but not breakable. It is sturdy and flexible. That's what your name means." The others in the room nodded in agreement, adding in their own thoughts.

A wave of emotions rose from my chest. My throat swelled and my eyes started to water. I held back the tears. I couldn't say anything but nod.

Ia sensed the emotions welling in me and dropped her voice to a tender and confident reassurance. "It's a beautiful name. You should be proud of it."

Tears escaped my eyes, my lips curled into a painful smile, and I nodded my head again, still at a loss for words.

Julien broke in with a timely joke to relieve the room of the tumescent emotions and converted it into joy, taking the attention off of me. I was grateful for the diverted attention. Julien was a love bear. Standing at five feet eleven with a football player frame, he and his brother, Stephan, were exceptionally tall for Hmong men. They mainly spoke English with us, and French with each other, and once in a while, Hmong with a French accent, which made it a really sweet combination to hear.

That experience taught me I don't need to cover up who I am or add anything to prove my worth. Who I am is enough. I can strip away the excess and simply be myself, perfect with room to evolve. Like the simplicity of squash shoot soup, I don't need anything extra—I'll continue to grow along the way.

Step 3:
Allow the Explosion

Mom picked up one of the squash shoots and expertly snapped a small stem off a bigger one, then peeled off the fuzzy outer skin. Following her lead, I grabbed a stem and determined where to snap it, but it didn't break off the way hers did. Instead, it bent over and juice started to seep out, making it even harder to snap the stem, as if it were protesting the way I was handling it. I had to practically yank it off. It was not happy. The tip had now become soggy, making it difficult for me to peel off the fuzz. I looked over at Mom again to see how she did it. The snapping sound popped from a stem that was clearly pleased to be handled by her, and again the skin happily stripped off.

"How come mine doesn't come off like yours?" I asked, picking up another piece to demonstrate how the stem was behaving in my hands. I got the same result as before: a soggy stem that wouldn't snap off, making me use a bit of force to tear it off.

Mom immediately knew what I was doing wrong. "You're using too much pressure. Do it lightly," she said, picking up another piece to demonstrate. The stem danced in her hands as though it were tickled to be held by her. All the fuzz perked up, and she lightly snapped it at the point where the smaller stem joined with that of a larger leaf. It popped right off, singing into the silence. The fuzzy skin on the edge of the stem waited patiently to be peeled off, happy to be stripped by her hands.

After the demonstration, she put the peeled shoot in the bowl to join the others. The way she tended to it, with confident yet light hands, allowed it to relax and do her bidding. She treated the shoot as if it were a part of her. I was treating mine as something separate, a piece of sustenance that was a pain in the ass to prepare. I saw it as an unnecessary burden whereas Mom treated this preparation as a ritual, creating a space for the shoots to demonstrate their true essence. In her attentive hands, they were alive; and in mine, they protested and hid.

I picked up another shoot and allowed the fuzz to brush across my palm and fingertips. I'd always experienced it as prickly and grating on my skin, something I hated stripping off but knew I had to in order to eat the shoot. Now, as I gave it my full attention, I noticed that the fuzz was not prickly but rather tickly, and felt soft, like dipping my hands in goose feathers. I ran my hand from the start of the stem to the tip and could feel the tendrils wanting to wrap themselves around my fingers. There was a leaf that was slightly larger and darker green than the others.

"Should I keep this leaf, Mom?" I asked, unsure of what to discard.

"That leaf is too old," she said. "Just keep the young ones. Your sister-in-law Khoua Neng likes the older leaves and she'll use them, but me, I like them soft and tender.' Once again, Mom revealed something about herself that I had not known before.

I, lightly but confidently, snapped the young stem from the older leaf, and this time it popped off. I picked at the fuzzy skin and watched it come off the stem all the way down to the tender leaves. Then I peeled another and another. After a few rounds of this, I noticed that when my attention was fully focused on the shoot, it was easier for me to peel the skin. But once I thought I was in the groove and started thinking about other things, my hands would get heavy and the shoot would not obey. I had to bring my attention back and feel it in my hands.

Mom moved swiftly and finished peeling the rest of the stems while I made my way through a few. She kept her attention on me and what I was doing at the same time she focused on snipping the shoots and keeping an eye on the boiling pot of water, making sure all things were in the right place, moving at the right pressure and speed. I felt as if I were one of the ingredients she was moving along, making sure I did my part in a timely manner.

She turned down the heat under the pot because the water was bubbling too hard. She put the squash blossoms in the bowl with the peeled shoots and instructed me to rinse everything. As I rinsed the shoots, Mom put the baby squash on the cutting board and sliced them in half or in quarters, depending on their size, to prepare them for the soup.

As we moved about in the kitchen, I noticed the intimacy of our movements together became easeful, a natural rhythm. We were able to connect through the subtle act of cooking. There wasn't the tumescent tension of walking on eggshells or the volcanic pressure of explosion that we used to experience.

×   ×   ×

If college was freedom, graduation was soaring straight up in the sky. And my imagination had expanded as a result of my five years of college. To top it off, I studied abroad in Chile for six months and during that time traveled to Peru and Argentina. I tasted new cultures, cuisines, people, scenery. And substances.

As a teenager, I was against drinking alcohol and judgmental of those who did. In my first year of college, while the guys at HSU drank beer, some of us girls stuck to wine coolers. By sophomore year, I started feeling angsty, constrained by the "too good, nice girl" box I was still stuck in. I wasn't experiencing the wild college life I had seen on TV or heard about from classmates. I had spent my academic life staying within the lines— school clubs, extracurricular activities, research papers, and work to build my résumé.

One evening, during a night of pizza and card games, I broke out of the box I'd been stuck in. I told the group that if we weren't drinking, I was going home. They were shocked but happy to oblige. Two of the guys over twenty-one went across the street for tequila, Smirnoff, and lime. They came back, and soon we were playing drinking games and taking shots. A lot of shots. The shadow I had suppressed for so long emerged. Each year, I became bolder and tried more things. My last year of college was filled with new experiences, including smoking marijuana and exploring my sexuality. I was finally free.

I graduated and spent six months studying abroad in Chile. It was a rich experience—immersing myself in the heart of the universe, exploring South America, and befriending fellow travelers as we did spontaneous things together.

After returning home in the spring, I worked a temp job doing easy, mindless work with some cool people who became friends while I searched for a job in the Bay Area. With no real responsibilities, we became a party crew.

By then, Leah was eighteen and Mary was twenty-one, both having their own experiences. The three of us were in the age range where we could go clubbing together. One Thursday night we decided to go out with Mary's college friends to the Rage for eighteen-plus Asian Night. We were getting ready to go, doing our makeup, when Mom came into the bathroom to ask where we were going. Her tone did not hide her disapproval. We told her we were going out with some friends. She kept telling us not to go, but we ignored her.

It had been five years since Dad died. I had been away, my younger brother Chong and Mary were both in college now, and Leah was graduating from high school soon. Mom was lonely with no companionship and no one to sit around the house while she sewed or worked in her garden. Her days were awfully quiet and isolated.

Her frustration at being ignored, at having no respect from her daughters, heightened the anger.

My own anger rose to the surface. "Mom, we're only going for a few hours! We'll be back home."

Her insistence morphed into guilting us: "Do you know what people are going to say about you? When people see you, it'll make me lose face. They are going to say it's because you have no father that you girls don't listen. You have no one to discipline you. You're a bunch of bad girls. Don't you have any shame?"

"I don't care what people think, Mom! I'm not going to live my life dictated by what people say about me. I don't care. This is my life." I took the brunt of Mom's anger, so that Mary and Leah didn't have to.

"Right, right, this is your life. Your life is my life, too. What you do will come back to me. Do you hate me so much that you want people to say, 'Look at that old lady whose daughters are bad girls. No one wants her daughters'? Is that what you want?"

"I don't care, Mom. I'll never marry our Hmong people. They're a bunch of old people who still wish this was Laos, who just want to control the girls and have them make babies and cook and clean at home. This is America. I don't care."

Each biting word increased the pressure in the room. Mom's boiling rage matched my own. I had done so well to suppress it all these years by not coming home. Now living back at home felt like it did before I left. This was the reason I left in the first place.

Seeing that her words were not penetrating, she retreated to the living room in defeat, shoulders hunched.

The three of us finished our hair and makeup, and already dressed, we quietly headed for the door to put on our shoes.

Upon seeing us, Mom stood up immediately and advanced toward us. "*Mej tsi txhob moog na has. Tsi nov kuv los?*" Don't you guys dare leave. Didn't you hear me?"

"Mom, we're leaving. We'll be back," I responded in English. At moments like these, my Hmong is no match for her, so I responded in English to throw off the potency of her words.

Leah turned toward the door and opened it. She made it out the door when Mom lunged toward us.

"I said don't go! What kind of daughters are you!" Her voice rose to a level of stern anger I'd never heard before.

The three of us ran toward my red Honda Civic parked on the street. It was nine thirty. The cool night air slapped against my face, contrasting with the heat radiating from my body. Mom's anger pierced through the thick silence of the night.

"Come back here!" she shouted.

I unlocked the car, and we all got in. Mom ran barefoot onto the lawn, rageful and broken.

I drove off without looking back. At that moment, I was consumed by too much hate and anger to feel any sympathy. I just felt relieved to be out of the house, away from her disapproving, disappointed gaze.

We arrived at the club and met up with the rest of Mary's friends in the parking lot to take a few shots before heading in. We had talked about taking Ecstasy that night. Mary and Leah had tried it before but I hadn't. I'd heard all kinds of things about Ecstasy from the blissful-in-love state to the sexual-aroused state to the "too much of it burns holes in your brain" side effects. I heard just enough to put me on the cautious side and opted for not taking any shots and taking only half a pill instead of a full one. Mary and Leah followed suit. Mary's friend split two pills into half pieces and gave each of us a half.

"Just swallow it," Mary instructed.

I put it in my mouth and swallowed.

We were on the dance floor, dancing to the loud booming techno music that permeated the whole building. Sweaty bodies pressed up against one another, faces flaring in and out with the flashing lighting when the ecstatic sensation swept up into my body. My body was covered in tingling sensations. An overwhelming feeling of bliss washed over followed by an ecstatic feeling of love.

Leah looked at me. "You're feeling it, huh?" she said as though she could feel right into my body, and she probably could.

I smiled widely and nodded my head. Leah ran a finger down my arm. Every nerve ending exploded into bright light where she touched. As her fingertip danced across my skin, waves of ecstasy pulsed through me, a symphony of pleasure echoing through every fiber of my being.

I closed my eyes. My body became the rhythm, the beat, the melody, the sweet, pungent, and musky smell of sweat and alcohol. At that moment, there was no separation between self and sound and touch, there was only the euphoric beating of love.

The night came to an end at the club. It was two in the morning. By the time we walked out, I still felt electric and blissful, my chin tight, biting down on my teeth, which Mary had told me would happen. We made our usual after-clubbing stop at Jack in the Box for Sourdough Jacks and seasoned curly fries. At the first bite, my body became salt, meat, grease, cheese, and tomato. It was the best thing I'd eaten. The fries followed suit and exploded into a million flavors on my tongue.

By the time we got home, it was close to three in the morning. I parked the car and we walked toward the door, still energized from the Ecstasy. My body felt as though it were still dancing. Mary unlocked the door and walked in. The lamp in the living room was still on.

Out of nowhere, as quick as a panther, Mom pounced on Mary, grabbed her by the arm. "*Nam tsuv tum!*" There is an insult in Hmong that when an elder says it to you, there is no hope for you. It translates to "tiger bite," meaning you were stupid enough to approach a tiger and get bitten.

Mom raised her hand and brought it down hard on Mary's thighs. The first hit landed on her, then registering what was happening, Mary pulled away from Mom but was still in her grasp.

I lunged toward Mom, "Stop it!" I yanked her arm away from Mary and stood in front of her. "If you're going to hit anyone, hit me!"

Mom grabbed my wrist hard with one hand and with the other swung it toward my butt and yelled in Hmong, "What kind of daughters do I have that never listen!" She swung with all the force that was in her tiny body. Once. Twice. Three times. I stood there and let her hit me. Then she stopped. And broke down. A wail, so deeply painful, erupted from her lips and pierced my heart.

The room split open.

"Don't you know how worried I am! I don't know if you girls are dead or alive. You daughters who have no heart to consider what it is like for me and how I feel!"

In the twenty-four years of my life, I've seen her wail from death, from grief, but never anything like this.

"Don't you know that you have no more father and it's just me. What do I do with you girls? What do I do with this life when no one is here with me to raise you, to discipline you? You don't respect me at all. *Saib tsis taug kuv le.*" You can't stand the look of me at all.

I had no words.

She let go of my wrist.

All the rage that was in the room crumbled into a sorrow so deep it felt as though it was the burden of all mothers. Of all daughters. Of all women. My body became the ache. The grief. The loneliness. I understood for the first time the pain she held inside. I felt how lonely she had been. How scared. What strength it had taken to be alone and still keep going. She always had to just keep going. And I hadn't made it easy.

Mom was sobbing in deep gulps. I started to cry. Mary and Leah started to cry from where they were standing. We were four women sharing one pain. The pain that we collectively felt and had been holding since Dad died. We stood there in the dimly lit living room. The shadows on the wall—silent witnesses to this ancient and timeless ritual of women erupting in pain together.

I don't remember how long we stood there. Mom finally collected herself. Her voice soft, almost a whisper, all the anguish drained out of her. None of us knew what to do or say to reconcile this moment. "It's late. Go to bed," she finally said.

We moved in silence. Shoes off. Makeup off. Brushed our teeth. Washed our faces. My eyes were puffy from crying. Contacts out. Glasses on.

Mary and Leah shared a room and went off to theirs. I went into Mom's room. Her body already under the covers. I crawled to the side by the wall. Pulled the blanket over me. Put my glasses on the windowsill.

It must have been the comedown effects of the Ecstasy, but as I lay there, a wave of grief washed over me, and I started to cry. Silently at first. The waves grew bigger and bigger. A tsunami rolling through me that I could not outrun. My body shook from the crashing of grief against my heart. Mom turned toward me.

"Don't cry. Don't cry." I felt a hand on my shoulder. The sobbing came deeper, pulled from my gut. My eyes squeezed tight. Tears continued to cascade. I drew my legs in. Curled into a ball. My back to Mom.

A traffic jam of words lodged in my throat. A single sentence formed in my mind, blaring at me like a neon sign. The internal voice in my head repeated those words like a broken record again and again and again. I could not get it out past what felt like a thick lump of opium lodged in my throat. A hand was squeezing my heart so tight I thought it would burst.

I cried for minutes. Mom's soft, strong, earthy hands that have known courage and fear, life and death, on my shaking shoulder. Her hand was like a lifeline, dripping her own courage into my body, her own certainty. It reached inside my throat and pulled out the opium to free my voice of all the words that had longed to pour out.

"I'm sorry . . . I'm sorry . . . I'm sorry . . ." It was a universal apology from deep in the bowels. I was saying it to Mom. To me. To anyone who would listen. To no one.

I'm sorry for being like this.
I'm sorry that I'm not enough.
I'm sorry that I was born a girl.
I'm sorry that this is our life.
I'm sorry that I couldn't be better.
I'm sorry that I hurt you.
I'm sorry that Dad is dead.
I'm sorry that he isn't here.
I'm sorry that I couldn't do anything about it.
I'm sorry that I had that dream.
I'm sorry I couldn't stop it.
I'm sorry.
I'm sorry.

"I just want you to be proud of me." I did not have the words in Hmong, but Mom understood.

I cried again, this time the cries of the little girl from third grade in her white-and-yellow sunshine dress who stood by the side of the auditorium stage waiting for her name to be called so she could walk across the stage to get her graduation certificate, but her name never came because they had forgotten her. She was the last one standing by herself while the rest of her classmates were all on center stage. The principal walked over and asked for her name. Asked her to repeat it a few times because they couldn't pronounce it. They went back to the mic and repeated her name. The little girl who walked shyly across the stage, who looked out into the crowd and did not see the faces of her mother or siblings because there was a family event that day so her mother was busy cooking and tending to the guests. She walked toward the principal and received a handshake, but no certificate because they had forgotten her.

I cried for the girl who was not allowed to go to her non-Hmong friend's house because her mother warned her that if anything went missing in the house, they would blame her. The little girl who was taught by her mother that she must remain invisible to be safe in the world.

I cried for the teenager who was compared to her nieces who were better at sewing than she was, who were better at cooking than she was, who were more disciplined than she was, who were more helpful with the chores around the house than she was. She was told by her mother that she was never good enough. Not good enough to be a daughter, not good enough to be a daughter-in-law. Who couldn't cook a single meal for her father to eat.

"I just want you to be proud of me." Those words repeated themselves out of my mouth in between gulps of air.

"I'm sorry. I'm sorry. I'm sorry." "*Kuv tsis yog ib tug ntxhais es ua tau tej yaam tsua koj. Kuv xaav ua kuam koj zoo sab xwb na.*" I am not a daughter who could provide you with anything. I just want you to be happy.

"*Tsis yog le ko. Tsis txhob has le ko.*" It's not like that. Don't talk like that. Mom started to cry. In English, "I am proud of you."

The words took over the space between us and enveloped us inside its warmth. The heavy waves of sobbing subsided into the exhausted afterglow of tenderness. I turned onto my back. Our arms slightly touching each other.

She continued in Hmong, "The reason I'm so hard on you is because I don't want others to look down on you. I don't want them to say you are undisciplined, bad children because you have no father. It is much harder now without the protection of a father. You are open to scrutiny. Others will watch you. They watch what you do, who you become. I am so proud of my daughters. I have good daughters. But you have to be careful. You have to watch yourself."

"But why do we have to care about what people think? They will always say something negative. I don't like that we Hmong people are like this. It is so hypocritical.

No one is perfect. Old people are always looking for things to criticize. We just have to live our lives, Mom, and do what makes us happy. We have freedom here."

"The old people know the lineage, the culture, the ways. They don't say these things just for the sake of saying them. They have wisdom. They are old, and you may not agree with them, but you still have to respect them. *Yug yuav tsum taw saib yug tug kheej.*" You must look after your life. A phrase that means your life is important enough that you have to take care of it, look after it.

"I miss Dad," I said into the darkness. Fresh hot tears streamed down the side of my face. "We don't have a father." There. I allowed myself to say it. I hated those words when Mom used them in anger, to hold them as a weapon to control me. But in that open space, I finally accepted, acknowledged his death. Because of his addiction, Dad was hardly around and present in our lives. He was a shadow in the background. But at that moment, he became my father. A father who was no longer with us. I cried for the seventeen-year-old girl who had shut down and braced herself against those words five years ago.

"I miss him, too." Mom's words were a salve on my heart.

We lay there in the dark, for the first time having found a tender spot with each other.

The sun slowly made its way toward the horizon, breaking the night sky into the deep indigo dye reminiscent of Mom's hand-dipped hemp fabric. The predawn light gently washed away the darkness, leaving the silhouette of a new blueprint binding mother and daughter.

"Let's go to sleep."

Step 4:
Approval Reveals Hidden Gifts

The boiling water with the lemongrass was ready. At Mom's request, I put the baby squash pieces in the pot first to give them more time to cook. After they were placed in the pot, I took the bowl over to the sink to wash the small pile of dishes and put them in the dishwasher to dry. I took out a few bowls and spoons and set the table.

Without checking on the readiness of the baby squash, Mom directed me to put the shoots in the pot and add some salt, but not too much. I wasn't sure what was too little or too much, so after I added salt, I asked her to taste it. After she did, she added a bit more. We let the soup cook for a few more minutes.

"You want the squash to be tender but not completely broken apart," she said. I wasn't sure exactly what that meant, so I kept my attention on the pot, stirring the soup periodically and pulling out a shoot to test it for tenderness. Every few minutes I'd ask Mom if it was ready, to which she would respond, "Is it soft yet?"

"I'm not sure."

Mom walked over to test the squash. Once she was satisfied with the tenderness of the squash and shoots, she added the blossoms for the last few minutes of cooking.

The blossoms wilted and added a pop of orange-yellow color. The sweet, nutty aroma with a hint of lemongrass filled the room.

"It's ready. Set the table."

I put a bowl of rice, the squash shoot soup, and Thai bird's eye pepper dip on the table and we sat down to eat. I spooned some rice into my bowl, then added the squash shoot soup with a few pieces of the baby squash and some of the chili pepper. The smell of the blossoms steamed in front of my face.

If you could smell the color green, this is what it would smell like: a subtle, earthy, late-summer smell that comes as the fall moisture descends and nudges the heat particles into the soil. I took a spoonful of rice and squash shoot and took a bite. The taste of the soup was grassy, sweet, and nutty; nourishing. It was hearty and warm and at the same time light and delicate. The leaves of the shoot teased the tip of my tongue with soft fuzz. Then, the earthy taste of the baby stems left a thick wet kiss at the back of my mouth on their way down. My body exhaled after that first bite. The nutrients soaked into my veins, and I could feel myself become one with the scene. There was nothing else but me, that bowl of warm rice and squash shoot soup, and Mom.

I imagined she was having the same experience I was. We ate in silence for the first few minutes as I reflected on the time we'd spent cooking. Instead of criticizing me for doing it wrong, she'd patiently shown me how to make sure I got it right. As I eased into her instructions and allowed myself to be directed by her, she focused her attention on what I was doing, moving me from one task to the next. The more receptive I became, the more her gifts revealed themselves to me.

When I was younger and we were in the kitchen together, I hated being there. I had always felt it was beneath me to learn something I deemed inferior to academics and sports. She would constantly tell me I was doing something wrong. We clashed and exhausted each other with our power struggle. Today's experience was the opposite of that. I opened the lens of understanding and saw that throughout her life Mom had always in some way been following her own path. As a result, she clashed with us kids who were raised in America, as we tried to align ourselves with the rhythm of the country we called home: school, career, marriage, kids; work hard on weekdays, then relax on weekends.

No wonder we couldn't hear each other—I had to silence her to pursue the American dream, with its relentless push for intelligence, success, and glory, while her dream was quieter, deeper, stripped of excess, and grounded in family and the rhythm of nature. Neither was wrong, but we couldn't hear each other. To me, she fell short of my civilized, educated standards, and I felt ashamed of her seemingly illogical ways. To her, I wasn't enough—not obedient enough, not domestic enough, not hard-working enough. Despite my constant striving, it wasn't in the realm of the feminine. She was disappointed by my acquisitive, masculine-driven ambitions. We simply couldn't see each other.

Through cooking together, I came to realize it wasn't she who needed to learn English to guide me or understand the value of education to recognize my hard work. She already knew those things. She wanted me to have a good education and become the best version of myself, but she also wanted me to stay connected to my roots and grow from there.

It wasn't she who had to give me anything or acknowledge me for me to feel my worth. I had to climb down from my high horse to truly feel, see, and understand her. I had made Mom an immigrant in the same way America had made me one. It was I who needed to value myself and find the self-confidence to appreciate her.

I didn't need to adopt her ways or settle into a life of family and gardening. I just needed to see her—to be open, to appreciate her, to engage with her, and to receive the gifts she had to offer. When I stopped trying to make her see things my way and allowed myself to simply be with her, she began to reveal her gifts to me.

There was a strength and order to how she moved in the kitchen, in the world, that I had not seen until I was willing to be taught by her. There was an elegance and simplicity to her movements, which were rooted in a language of nature. What I once saw as nagging and complaining, I began to understand as her deep attunement to how things needed to be to align with nature. There were no words in our modern vocabulary to communicate her world and her wisdom.

I slowly came to understand that it was on me to build a bridge between us and communicate those gifts to others. To describe her world. To show her wisdom. To reveal the nature of her essence. To fortify her soft power.

I am her translator. But I am not here to translate English. I am here to translate Hmong.

Ntxawm Xyooj, Yer Xiong

Sometimes I'm exhausted speaking English. There are times when I find myself pausing in the middle of a thought and feel the stone-cold weight of English on my tongue. My brain feels like a shriveled-up prune, and my forehead is full of lines from thinking so much that even Botox couldn't make it smooth again. I'm physically drained from trying to explain, explain, and explain some more things that should be simple and intuitive, or from navigating through my mental dictionary to find the right words—words that will help someone understand exactly what I mean. I feel as if I've spent the day teaching someone how to breathe, and in the end it still feels as if nothing has been said. Nothing is known.

Sometimes my ears long to hear my native tongue. My body craves the soft harmonious melodies of our language. I often stay up late to watch Hmong channels on YouTube or listen to our poetry songs. I surrender to the words taking me deep into the mountains of my ancestors. The yearning of my soul to return home finds temporary relief. I understand why Mom spends her evenings on YouTube.

When I'm with Mom speaking a language that I rarely use, that is more foreign on my lips than English, my mind and body exhale. When I see her, I initially panic. I struggle to find the right Hmong words, so I use English to complete my sentences, wanting her to be in my world. I look at her expectantly, waiting for her to respond.

She understands about a quarter of what I say, but she nods as if she knows, and perhaps she does know. She never asks me to explain anything. She never asks me to find the Hmong words to communicate what I'm saying. She just knows.

Being with her, I feel English and Hmong bouncing off each other in my brain, fighting for space, for air. Hmong, which is used to bending but not breaking, knows its own value and waits patiently until, after a few hours, English starts to relax and let go, trusting that it will be understood in this foreign land. After I've been with Mom for a day, I finally breathe freely as Hmong takes over. My command of the language gets stronger and more confident, the correct words flowing from my lips like a well-tuned instrument playing a familiar melody. The sharp edges of my voice soften, and my heart warms to the gentle whispers that breach the protective walls I've constructed. Immersed in the metaphors and poetic verses of my mother tongue, I hone my senses to grasp Mom's every word, awakening to a world of vibrant colors, textures, and riddles.

I find myself hungry for knowledge, to understand phrases I've never heard before. Mom scatters words and their meanings on the fertile ground of my mind, putting down roots to tie me to home. She fills my bowl with stories of our homeland, of her childhood, and the games she used to play. She teaches me the dishes her mother and sisters taught her, and I feel the flow of our lineage transferring from her lips to my hands. She nourishes me with food she knows I love, like minced smoked beef, while peppering me with its history.

In Laos, beef was something Mom ate once every two or three years, when they performed a ritual called *nyuj dlaab*, in which a cow is sacrificed so the ancestors in the spirit world will have food to eat. There were three reasons this ritual would occur: If someone in the family was very sick, if a shaman doing a fortune telling saw that an ancestor was hungry and calling for the family to send a cow, or if the family did it voluntarily to honor and provide for those who had passed. All the family members in the village gathered to help with the ritual, and then the beef was divided among them. Because beef was such a rare commodity, every part of the cow was used, including the blood, the intestines, and the brain.

Once Mom's family received their share, she would help to prepare the beef for smoking by cutting it into one-inch-thick strips, salting it, and then leaving it to marinate overnight. The following day, they would light a big firepit. Then Mom and her sisters would tie a string to one end of each strip and hang them on a branch over the fire to smoke slowly for a few hours until the meat was dry. This method of preserving beef made it possible for the meat to last weeks without refrigeration.

Mom told me of the many dishes she would make with it—from a soup with mustard greens and ginger to a stew with Thai eggplant and herbs. Sometimes she would fry it with greens, or she might simply eat a piece with her bowl of rice mixed with water. And then there was my favorite way to eat it: minced smoked beef pounded in a mortar with ginger, Thai bird's eye chili peppers, and cilantro.

As she recounted these stories, I became immersed in an ancient world deeply rooted in the earth. I began to understand the trust she held and the secrets she possessed about the earth, her deep connection with the moon as she intricately wove its cycles into the planting and harvesting of vegetables.

In the same way her mom showed her how to make family recipes, Mom showed me how to make minced smoked beef by having me there alongside her.

How to Make Minced Smoked Beef

Yield: Feminine Power

Cook time: Until you are filled up

Ingredients:
Depletion
Vajra pride
Sovereignty

Step 1:
Be More You

Mom opened the refrigerator door and removed a piece of the smoked beef she got from our cousins the previous weekend. They had a family ritual to honor their ancestors. Since it was just the two of us for lunch, she only prepped one piece. She took out a cutting board and set it on the counter. I watched her move around the familiar territory of the kitchen with ease to retrieve her carbon steel Hmong knife from the drawer and stand in front of the cutting board. With the flat spine of the knife, she pounded the beef to soften it, starting at one end and moving to the other. The thudding of the knife making contact with the beef sounded like a knock at the door.

I pulled out my iPhone, turned on the camera app, and zoomed in on the beef and her hands. Her hands worked easily with each other; one hand turning the beef around, the other pounding with the knife. I zoom back out to capture her full frame. Her eyes cast down in concentration covered by lids that now droop down low.

She laughed. "Why are you focusing that on me?"

"I just want to capture how you make it," I replied matter-of-factly.

"It's not worth taking," she tried to brush me off to no avail, so she gave in, keeping her eyes down.

Her face had changed over the last few years. It felt like overnight she went from a fuller frame and strong backbone with a head of wavy black hair to thin, petite, almost fragile. Her gray hair peeked out at shoulder length from under her turban. The lines and age spots on her face told of the decades she'd spent under the smile of the sun. Her little chipmunk cheeks took over the sides of her face. Everything about her body, her skin, had given in to gravity. Mom was getting older. Each time I visited her, the months, the years showed on her body. But her spirit was still stubborn, feisty, and strong as ever. Mom's black shirt, with abstract floral patterns featuring small orange circles inside larger white circles, flowed with brown branches weaving through the flowers.

She flipped the knife over to the blade and began mincing the beef, sending little crumbs randomly flying into the air as they escaped the cutting board.

I put my phone down and asked her in Hmonglish, "Mom, did you see on the news a few months ago about Sunisa Lee? The Hmong girl that was on the news who won the gold medal in gymnastics at the Olympics."

"Who?"

There was no way to say *gold medal*, *gymnastics*, and *Olympics* in Hmong, so I had to describe it, "The Hmong Lee girl who competed and swung on sticks and danced on a wide stick."

"Oh, yes! It was all over the Hmong news for weeks. It was all they talked about."

"Yes! She was really good, Mom. She won the highest award."

"Yes, they said she's really good."

"Mom, the news is all over the world. It's not just here in America. It's amazing that we Hmong can become big and important like that, right, Mom?"

"That's right. Hmong people from France and Thailand all heard about it. People will see her and say that we Hmong can do that, too."

"Since she won, there's been more coverage in the news about Hmong people. She's the first Asian who won something like that—not only Asian, but she's Hmong."

"Yes, it's a very good thing."

"Mom, America and the world will know who we are."

"Yes, they will know who we are. That is a good thing for us." She sounded proud. In her lifetime America will know who we are.

Mom finished mincing the beef and used the knife to scoop it into the mortar.

I knew she had heard the news because it was all over the Hmong news on YouTube. I was curious to know what she thought about it, how she felt about it. Did she understand the impact this had on our people? She was not political, but she was opinionated. She didn't know what was taught in school. She didn't know the history of America or the history of the country she was born in; she was not aware of worldly news nor did she need to be. She only knew of the states and countries where Hmong people live But she knew that when one Hmong person was spoken of badly in the news, it spoke badly of all Hmong people, and when something positive was spoken of, it reflected on all Hmong people. In my younger years, she would always lecture me: "What you do and how people see you isn't just about you, it reflects on your sisters, your family. The world will look at you and say Hmong people are like that." That was a lot of pressure to live up to. I would always rebel, tell her I didn't give a shit about what people thought, and continue doing what I was doing. I was starting to understand her wise words.

The year 2021 was the beginning of a huge coming out for us Hmong people, starting with Sunisa Lee blowing up the stage at the Tokyo 2020 Olympics with the gold medal in the individual all-around gymnastics. The news clip of her family and friends erupting in cheers as her score was announced for her gold medal–winning dance routine filled the hearts of every Hmong family. America was proud that she brought home the gold. Asians were proud of her for being the first Asian to win the gold. Hmong people were simply proud. Hmong parents saw new possibilities, and Hmong girls found a role model who looked like them.

The power of that wave carried into the following year when in June 2022, Chef Yia Vang, of no relation to me, from Minnesota appeared on Netflix's show *Iron Chef: Quest for an Iron Legend.* He showcased classic Hmong/Laotian dishes, bringing our cuisine to an international audience. Even though he didn't win, he opened the door for the world to know what Hmong food is. He immediately followed his appearance with many more TV shows.

The following month Gia Vang made her debut as a weekend news anchor and reporter for the NBC Bay Area (KNTV) in San Francisco. She had previously been successful as the anchor for the Minneapolis morning show, *KARE 11 Sunrise.*

In November of that same year, Sheng Thao, related to us through marriage, became the first Hmong American mayor of a major metropolitan city, Oakland, California.

The wave continued, carrying my sister Mai and her husband and his side of the family to New Orleans in January 2023 to cheer on his niece Payengxa Lor, the first Hmong woman to compete in the Miss Universe beauty pageant as Miss Universe Laos. She made history in many areas by being the first Miss Universe Laos to reach the top sixteen finalists in the competition. Being the first Hmong woman to represent Laos, she took the stage in full Hmong regalia, wearing pieces of clothing that represented the different cultures in Laos and wearing four *qheej*, Hmong musical instruments, behind her. This was significant not only because she was on the international stage, but because she was representing a country that, half a century ago, sought to persecute us. There is still much work to be done in the reconciliation between Hmong and Laos with violent acts still happening deep in the mountains, but this was an important step in raising global awareness.

America and the world are becoming aware of us.

We had always been a quiet people. We stayed in the background, knowing the dangers that could happen if we drew attention to ourselves. Don't brag about being good at something or you'll be exploited the way our people were exploited with opium. The way we were recruited in frontline guerrilla warfare and abandoned for extermination afterward. The way we hosted Laotians in our village only to be arrested and gunned down. And because we stayed quiet, America did not know us for a long time. That is not to say that the Hmong hadn't been represented in the media before, bringing out our gifts and voices. Kao Kalia Yang was the first Hmong writer to tell our story. That is not to say that, for decades after the Secret War, there weren't Hmong and Americans who lobbied in Washington, D.C., for Hmong soldiers who fought for the CIA to be recognized as veterans and receive veteran benefits.

In 2000, President Bill Clinton signed the Hmong Veterans' Naturalization Act, providing Hmong veterans who had fought alongside American forces in Laos with the opportunity to apply for US citizenship. It allowed about forty-five thousand Hmong veterans and their loved ones to waive the English language requirement and permitted an interpreter for the test. This was a small victory for the Hmong in America, and especially for those who had spent the last two decades lobbying for the recognition of the Hmong people's role in the war.

There are two ways to be heard: through destruction or through creation. When you destroy, you are left with rubble. When you create, you establish something that will eventually make the old obsolete.

A creative wave of talent swept through the Hmong community, turning on the lights from one individual to the next like a power grid coming online after a long blackout of fear and silence.

For more than four decades, we have been evolving through our creativity and gifts, enabling us to be heard. In the mid-1970s, Hmong women began telling our stories by sewing story cloths in Thai refugee camps, depicting graphic scenes of our lives and the war in Laos. We hosted Hmong New Year in cities where we lived to showcase our food and culture. We were recognized as sustainable and regenerative farmers, enriching local farmers markets with organic and new varieties of produce.

We are becoming more of who we are, out loud. No longer behind closed doors. No longer quietly hiding in the bushes. Our voices are breaking free. The opium our parents placed in our throats to quiet us and prevent us from giving our location away to the enemies, is cracking open as the seeds of wisdom and value wake up within our bodies. Our hands, once invisible, are breaking through glass ceilings, winning Olympic gold medals, showcasing our food on frontline stages. Our silent voices are now singing our songs. We are rising to tell our stories. To fight for others who are not being heard. We are teaching a taker society how to come back to the earth. To listen to her whispers. We are transforming the pain and grief of our parents and grandparents into gifts that will make us known in the world—not just as refugees of war, but as creative geniuses rising to the top while staying rooted at the bottom. We are becoming writers, actors, singers, hip-hop dancers, comedians, race car drivers, musicians, artists, fashion designers and more on local, national, and international levels.

We are given conditions in this life not to get free of, but to be free inside of.

America is starting to know who we are.

Step 2:
Know Who You Are

Mom went to the fridge and took out a piece of ginger. "These are Hmong ginger. They are bigger than American ginger and better, because they don't have so much fiber. They are also more fragrant and contain more juice. You can find these at the Hmong or Asian market. I'll give you some to take home." I had no idea there was more than one kind of ginger.

With the same Hmong knife she used on the beef, Mom scraped the skin off the ginger. She again used the flat part of the knife to pound each piece from one end to the other, just as she had the meat. The juicy, fleshy part of the ginger came right off and collected into ginger pulp, leaving the fibers intact at the other end. She threw the fiber away and gathered the ginger in one hand, squeezing the juice into the sink. She put the ginger into the mortar. "You don't need all that liquid," she said, as if she had heard my question.

My camera continued to focus on her hands. Her face. Her relaxed concentration as she created a dish her mother used to make for her. Other than the pounding of steel on ginger, it was quiet in the house. Cher and Sister-in-law Cher were out with friends, and the kids were upstairs either playing video games or doing schoolwork.

"Yia, go to my cabinet and get me a packet of *tshuaj mob laug*." I turned off the camera and put my phone down. I headed to her bedroom to fetch her "old-age medicinal tea." I opened the cabinet and scanned her Hmong herbs and American pills until my eyes landed on the gold envelope. I opened it and pulled out a single packet. I put the envelope away, and a picture frame toward the back caught my attention. Mom's framed American citizen certificate with a picture of a younger her and the name Yer Xiong written in print. I hadn't seen this certificate in ages. I reached out to touch the name.

Can you imagine being given the wrong name? Being called by a different name. Given a different identity. All because of a careless mistake. Because America didn't take the time to understand her name. Because America couldn't hear the soft, steady strength of *Ntxawm*. Because America did not see her as a woman, only as an immigrant to bring into its borders to fulfill its duty as a "good" nation after violently tearing her home apart.

Because America did not know who she was, Mom came to America as May Xiong.

I, myself, did not know Mom's Hmong name until I was in high school. For as long as I could remember she was May. May Xiong. That was how I spelled her name on the monthly income report for general assistance. That was what I announced to teachers at parent conferences and what I told the front desk attendant at appointments. May Xiong.

I didn't know Mom's name until she became an American citizen. She was always *Nam*, Mom. A woman's name was rarely used in our culture once she married. She was given titles that noted her position, her status, her value, her wisdom.

Once Mom married Dad, she was no longer Ntxawm. She became roles and titles.

She became *Nyaab Tsaav Kuam*, Daughter-in-law Chang Kua.

She became *Tij Dlaab Tsaav Kuam*, Sister-in-law Chang Kua.

Tais Hluag, Younger Sister

Nam Tais Tsaav Kuam, Aunt on Mother's Side Chang Kua

Puj Tsaav Kuam, Aunt on Father's Side Chang Kua

Nam Hlub, Older Sister-in-law

Nam Ntxawm, Younger Sister-in-law

Puj, Grandmother to her daughter's kids

Tais, Grandmother to her son's kids

Puj Koob, Great-Grandmother

Her mother was the last person to call her Ntxawm. *Mi naib* Ntxawm, darling Ntxawm. Her mother loved her so much that after Mom and Dad were married, she called Dad by Mom's name, "*miv vauv* Ntxawm," darling son-in-law Ntxawm, instead of the customary "*vauv*."

In America, Mom was May. She was May for seventeen years until she became an American citizen.

On August 6, 1997, Mom came back from the naturalization ceremony in Sacramento with her certificate in hand. She was nicely dressed in a floral-print skirt and matching blouse with a polyester blazer.

"Look," she said proudly. "*Kuv ua tau xaam xaj Ameka*." I am an American citizen. Proud, not because she was now an actual citizen, but because she was able to do it. Because with her limited English, she passed the oral, reading, and writing test on the first try.

Mom passed her citizenship test through sheer determination and memorization. She committed the

Pledge of Allegiance to memory, but didn't understand its meaning. Diligently memorized the names of dead presidents she had no connection to. Learned the Declaration of Independence was adopted on July 4, 1776. Practiced over and over annunciating the name "John Hancock." But she questioned why people fought over a country that wasn't theirs to begin with. "If you shared land, and if more people worked in the same field, everyone would have more to eat," she would say when I quizzed her. I had no response for her.

She handed me the thick, textured paper. At the top, the bold header proclaimed, "United States of America." Beneath this, the words "Certificate of Naturalization" stood out. Between them was the emblem of the US eagle, its wings outstretched. To the left was her birthday, height, marital status, and country of former nationality. Below that was her photo. Full, soft, supple face. Dressed in her white blouse with purple flowers.

Next to that was Mom's name proudly signed by her Hmong hand: Yer Xiong.

"Mom, you changed your name?"

"Yes. They said you can change your name when you become a citizen. I wanted my real name on it. So, I changed it to make it right."

"Wait, then why has your name been May this whole time?"

"I don't know. When we filled out our paperwork to come to America, they made a mistake. They must have given me Mai's name and spelled it M-A-Y."

"What's 'Yer' in Hmong then?"

"Ntxawm," she announced with confidence.

"Ntxawm," I repeated. Her name rolled off my tongue for the first time. It was a fitting name for Mom. Ntxawm. *Ntxhais ntxawm*, youngest daughter. She didn't seem fazed that I didn't know her name. But I was shocked. It never occurred to me to ask about her Hmong name. She was always either Mom or May. I never gave her an identity other than Mom, who was critical, or May, who I had to translate for.

"You guys never corrected them?" I pressed, angered by the situation.

"We didn't know anything at the time. We didn't know what they were saying or what they were writing down. They just asked you questions, someone translated it to you, you answered, and they translated it back. We didn't understand anything. Didn't know what was happening. We just did what they told us."

America made a mistake that changed her name from Yer to May. For a long time, Mom didn't know that was the name they gave her. She didn't read English. No one did. America handed them our paperwork, documents as valuable as silver bars, so Dad kept them together.

When we settled in Minneapolis, Mom attended English classes. She learned to spell M-A-Y X-I-O-N-G. She practiced and practiced with her newly American hands, writing slowly and meticulously with a pencil. The letters were as awkward to meet her as she was with them. Her first written name, May Xiong, still resides in a notebook alongside our flight tickets and documents, tucked inside a red plastic bag in her closet, where she keeps everything. These hands, the American hands, were crude and clumsy with the feel of pen and paper compared to her Hmong hands; swift and smooth with needle and thread. These Hmong hands that filled yards of fabric with imprints of who she is.

She learned to say, "May Xiong."

She learned to say, "My name is May Xiong."

It didn't matter to Mom that America called her May. She knew who she was. The people who mattered to her, her family and relatives and friends, they knew who she was. They knew her character, her skills, her patience, and her beautiful needlework. They knew she was quick to learn English and spelled words correctly. They knew she was a hard worker and showed up early at every family event. They knew she was innovative and generous with the prices she charged for sewing traditional Hmong clothes for them. They knew she was a good driver and could take them from place to place.

It didn't matter to Mom that America called her May. In her heart, she was Ntxawm, *mi naib* Ntxawm.

I used to bow my head in embarrassment every time an American mispronounced my name. I wanted to run and hide. I changed my name to Jamie. Barbara. Heather. Vicky. So I could feel American. So I didn't have to correct my teachers, substitute teachers, bank tellers, baristas, strangers that Y-I-A is Yia. I'd tell them, "It's like 'yeah,'" to make it easier in their mouth. I didn't correct them to soften their throat to sound 'yh' instead of a hard 'ye.' I was not that confident. Instead, I looked down, ashamed to be Hmong.

But no, not Mom. She knew who she was. She knew she's the youngest daughter, daughter-in-law, sister-in-law, little sister, aunt, niece, mother, grandmother. Hmong strangers called her *Tais*, Aunt. Wise. Elder. Woman who has experienced life. Tasted every morsel of grief and continued to create love for her children. Woman who you should listen to because the lines on her face and dirt under her fingernails can tell you about the sound of the moon.

On August 6, 1997, Mom became a citizen of America, and the first thing she wanted America to know is that her name is Yer Xiong. Ntxawm Xyooj. She is proud to be Ntxawm Xyooj, proud for America to know her name. Proud to be an American citizen with her Hmong name.

America had her renounce allegiance and fidelity to any foreign prince, state, or sovereignty, but it cannot make her renounce her homeland in her heart. America had her swear to defend the Constitution and its laws against all enemies, foreign and domestic, without knowing that Ntxawm Xyooj had been doing that long before she set foot on its soil. America had her swear to bear arms on its behalf, to perform noncombatant service in the armed forces when required by law but never once publicly recognized or apologized for bombing her soil. America asked that she perform work of national importance under civilian direction when required by law, to which she has and is performing the greatest work there is to do: to remind America that we cannot cut ourselves off from nature because nature is the source of all power and nourishment. Mom recited the Pledge of Allegiance to the American flag, a flag that didn't represent her, to which she has been loyal and devoted in defending before she became May Xiong.

On August 6, 1997, America accepted her as a citizen. They asked her why she wanted to become an American citizen. They asked her for the colors of the flag. They asked her where the president lives. But not once did they bother to inquire about her journey to this country or the sacrifices she had made for America.

They did not ask her, "Who are you?"

They did not ask her, "What can we do for you?"

America does not know her.

In the stew of yellow and brown faces on the streets of America, you may see an old Asian immigrant, a slow driver on the highway, an Asian lady to push past on the street. I see a dazzling flash of light as it bounces off steel.

America will know Ntxawm Xyooj.

Step 3:
Power It from Below

Mom took a small handful of cilantro from the fridge, then opened the freezer and took out two small Thai bird's eye chili peppers. She ran the peppers under the water for a second, just to thaw them slightly, and squeezed the flesh out of the skin into the mortar. "I don't like the skin. It's better without it," she said. That was the first time I'd seen her do that with peppers, and something I wanted to try for myself. She rinsed the cilantro, chopped it up, and put it in the mortar.

Once all her ingredients were in, Mom took the pestle and pounded everything together so that the juices mixed with the beef. The healing zing of ginger and the earthy, rich smell of cilantro filled the air.

I opened the golden packet and emptied the contents into her mug. Brought it over to the water dispenser and filled it with hot water. Took a spoon from the drawer and stirred the contents in the mug. I placed it close to her. Picked up my phone and videoed her again.

"Do you use fish sauce?" I asked her.

"I don't use it because I don't like it, but it really depends on whether someone likes it or not. The beef is already salty, so you don't need to add salt to it." She continued to pound for a minute more, then tasted a piece of beef. Satisfied with the flavor, she kept pounding for another minute to soften it some more.

Once satisfied, she scooped the contents of the mortar into a small bowl. My mouth watered just looking at it. I could already taste the ginger. I set the table with a bowl of rice and two empty bowls and spoons. Mom spooned the beef stew on the stove into a bowl and set it on the table. "I brought this home from the event," she said, referring to the cousins' family ritual the previous weekend. The beef stew looked succulent and tender with a mix of tendon, tender meat, pieces of ginger, and scallion.

I brought Mom's medicinal tea to the table and sat down on my usual seat to Mom's right, with Mom at the head of the table. I filled the bottom of my bowl with beef, added a layer of rice to cover the meat, and pressed it down to make a nice compact dish, exactly as I had done as a kid. This was my favorite way to eat it. Sometimes, I would add scrambled eggs on top of the rice. It became a nice, two-layer bowl of beef and rice. I took my spoon and scooped up a generous portion of beef and rice. I put it in my mouth. The burst of salt from the smoked beef along with the ginger, cilantro, and pepper mixed with the warm, sweet nuttiness of the rice took me right back to my childhood, to happy and carefree times when I would run around with my nieces playing house or Chinese jump rope.

I wondered if Mom had the same experience with her food, if it took her back to happy childhood memories. At that moment, it was just me and Mom and the minced smoked beef and our memories. Niya and Senpai ran over to beg for food.

"No, go away!" Mom looked down at the two dogs and batted them away with her hand. They continued to sit there waiting for any morsel to drop.

"What are you doing tomorrow after I leave? Are you going anywhere?"

"No, there is nowhere to go. After you leave, I'll just go back to laying around. Every day is the same, just laying around. When you're not here, there's nothing to do." Mom threw a piece of beef down to Niya and Senpai, and they quickly dove for it.

"It's okay, Mom. You shouldn't be working so hard anyway. Sit around and rest. You work too much."

We finished the rest of the meal. I cleared the table and did the dishes while Mom put a few things away and took her tea to her room.

The rest of the day was quiet and peaceful. Mom went back to her routine of listening to the Hmong radio station on her iPad in her room, and I went to the living room and opened my laptop to do some work.

Our time together had evolved from heated arguments or stone-cold silence to storytelling and stillness. In the kitchen, we had found our rhythm together. Two women, fertile in our own lives as individuals, yet interdependent, mutually influencing each other. We cannot take ourselves out of control, cannot press our own buttons, and no one pushes my buttons like Mom. A look from her, an utterance, a comment can reduce me to childlike tantrums or elevate me into an inspired artisan.

In the kitchen, I have found different parts of myself. Being with her is a process of discovery that has taken me to the edges of my identity: from rebellious teenager to obedient daughter, to nurturing mother making her medicinal tea, to cocreator in the kitchen. The static identity that Mom has also worn for decades dissolved into teacher, woman, innocence.

Despite the hardships Mom endured while growing up and the losses she experienced, she never complained, nor did she collapse under life's challenges. Instead, she grew stronger. Her trials became memories etched into the lines of her hands and the wrinkles beneath her eyes. She continued to live, not in spite of her past, but because of it. She transformed the most difficult moments into opportunities to acquire new knowledge and wisdom. Her aim was not to distance herself from her past—she had already found liberation within herself, all the while remaining steadfast in honoring her upbringing, our cultural heritage, and imparting valuable lessons about our lineage to us, her children. That was her unique knowledge and her gift to us.

After a weekend of Mom weeding away the beliefs that drained my vitality, she gently sprinkled her favorite flower, Queen of the Night, over my heart; a reminder that beauty thrives in the stillness of the dark. She sent me back out, re-nourished, soft and supple, resilient, capable of bending but not breaking, like the meaning of the name she gave me, Yia, spoken like a whisper in the wind. I returned to the world above, where English guided me while Hmong took its rightful place below, powering and directing from deep inside.

Crossing Over

The first dish every Hmong girl learns to make as soon as she stands taller than the stove is steamed rice, not in a rice cooker or in a one-pot stovetop. For a Hmong woman to know how to *cub mov* with rice that comes out plump, soft, and fluffy is a testament to two things: 1) the quality of daughter-in-law she will be, and 2) the quality of the mother who raised her.

Every mother either takes pride in how obedient, patient, and precise her daughter is, or she feels shame in how lazy, stubborn, and short-tempered she is. A good daughter-in-law is judged by the quality of her food and precision of her sewing skills. I had neither of those. A good mother is judged by how well her daughters do. I did not help in that category.

A Hmong mother's role is to raise her daughter well so that one day she will pass her on to a new family. Once her daughter is married, she no longer belongs to her mother. She belongs to her husband's clan. So, a mother must train her daughter well.

If the daughter-in-law is not to the liking of the new family, they have the choice to send her back, and should that ever happen, it would be a disgrace to the family for having raised an unsuitable daughter-in-law.

My life was about raising me to be that good daughter-in-law, but because I never married, I'm still my mother's daughter. I'm considered an old maid at this point and, according to Hmong standards, no one would want me. But I'm not worried about that.

"You have to start your life and have kids to take care of you in your old age. I'm not going to be around forever. What are you going to do when I'm not around?"

"I'm taking care of myself now, Mom. Don't worry," I told her, avoiding the more intimate conversation.

It was something I didn't want to talk about, but have thought about. One of my nieces once asked me if I've thought about which nephew I wanted to "raise and support."

"What do you mean 'raise and support'?"

"Well, you don't have any children of your own. So, you have to start thinking about which nephew you'll support so that when you're old, he'll take care of you. Otherwise when you're old and pass, it'll be hard to get the care you'll need or the proper funeral."

"Oh, wow. I have no idea," was my disturbed response.

The purpose of the Hmong familial system is to have a home, to have a life, and to have children to care for you. Mom would tell me that the reason you want to marry your own kind is so your kids will be Hmong.

They will take care of you, and when you pass, they'll know the proper rituals to perform. "You have to know the name and location of your birthplace," she lectured me, "so that when it is time, your children can tell the soul guider where to guide your soul to retrieve your shirt. This is the most important thing for us Hmong. If you marry an American, they won't know how to give you a proper Hmong burial so that you can get back to your ancestors. They won't know the rituals to continue every year to honor you, to ensure that you have a house and that you have money and food burned for you in the spirit world."

Because I am no one's daughter-in-law, my relationship with Mom was able to transform from mother–daughter to woman–woman. How we got there was a long journey.

Growing up with five sisters, three of whom were older and two younger, I was able to avoid many of the duties of a good Hmong daughter. At family events, I didn't join the women who were preparing and cooking the food for the day's feast. Instead, I played with the children or washed the dishes, and eventually promoted myself to washing green onions and cilantro.

In high school, when Cha went away for college and I was the oldest girl in the house, Mom declared that it was time for me to learn to *cub mov*, steam rice. Needless to say, shortly after I learned, I handed that duty to Mary and busied myself with sports, academics, and a job after school. Soon enough the lesson Mom had taught disappeared from my mind.

Determined to start the training to make me a good wife that day, Mom burst into my room while I was reading a romance novel. She stood there, her curvy yet strong five-foot-three-inch frame demanding attention. Her long black hair was pulled back in a bun on top of her head, revealing a tan, full face with rosy cheeks and brown, piercing eyes.

"Yia, you have to learn how to *cub mov*. How are you going to find a husband if you can't make rice?" she said in Hmong, sounding impatient.

"I don't *plan* to marry a Hmong man," I bit back, matching her agitation with my own for interrupting my fantasy.

"That's right, you'll live off of Big Macs," she sassed right back. "I'll teach you how to make it. Go to the kitchen!" she commanded.

Mom was not one to ask me what I wanted to do. Having raised nine children, she'd learned that if she wanted anything done, she needed to give directives, not options.

Knowing that I couldn't ignore her, I stuck my bookmark to save my place in the book, and stomped past her and toward the kitchen with Mom close behind me.

How to Steam Rice the Hmong Way

Yield: Life

Cook time: Until you let go

Ingredients:
Death
Honor
Service

Step 1.
Choose Love

As soon as we reached the kitchen, Mom started her instructions. "Get the big bowl from the cupboard and fill it with rice."

I opened the lower cupboard where all the big stainless steel and plastic bowls were stored and pulled out a stainless steel one. "How many cups?" I asked.

"How many cups?" she repeated, confused by the question.

"Yes, Mom, how many cups do you want?"

"Just fill the bowl halfway," she said. Mom was not deterred by the impatient irritation in my voice.

I used a cup to scoop rice into the bowl and showed it to her.

"Too much."

But, Mom, that was halfway, I thought. But I didn't dare say anything. I poured some back into the bin and showed her the bowl again. This time she nodded.

"Now wash the rice," she further instructed.

I took the bowl to the sink and ran some cold water through it, splashing my hand in the bowl and twirling the rice around.

"No, not like that. Wash it." She walked over to stand beside me. "Like this." She dipped both hands into the bowl, scooped up a handful of rice and brushed her right hand over her left as the rice fell back in the bowl. She did this a few more times. The water turned milky white.

"Now drain the rice, put in fresh water, and do it again." Mom, poised and ready to criticize, moved over so I could stand in front of the sink.

I did as I was told. Once the bowl filled up with water, I imitated her actions.

"Not so hard. You'll break the rice. Don't rub it. Just brush one hand over the other."

Again, I followed, this time brushing, not rubbing. I did it a few times as the water turned milky again, but this time a lighter color.

"How many times do I do this?" I asked her, ready to be done.

"Just keep doing it until the water is clear."

I proceeded to drain the water, fill the bowl, and wash the rice again, brushing one hand over the other. This time I felt the individual grains, cool and gritty to the touch, tickling my palms as they brushed against one another. Water ran between my fingers, sliding down into the bowl.

After a few more rounds the water remained clear.

Mom told me to stop washing and fill the bowl with water all the way to the top. Once I'd done this, we left the rice to soak overnight on the counter and carried on with the rest of the evening, with me back to my book in my room and Mom to her sewing in the living room.

Despite her sharpness and critical eye, I was lucky to have gone this long without learning to *cub mov*. Most Hmong girls my age were the cooks. They were the first to wake up to *cub mov* and make breakfast for their parents. I was considered spoiled and *tau zoo nyob*, meaning someone who gets to lounge around doing nothing. To Mom, if I wasn't cooking for her and Dad, that meant I didn't love them. To me, I was in America and this was no longer the old country. I had school and more important things to do and just because I wasn't waking up at five in the morning to cook for them didn't mean I didn't love them.

× × ×

June 22, 2022

It was a typical summer's day at The Land. I walked out of the lodge after lunch, following the dehydrated dirt trail through the meadow. The air was buzzing with heat. Molecules collided in the air, making contact with my skin, and immediately creating sweat on my neck and forehead. A lump of saltwater formed at my chest.

My phone rang. My phone was set to silent but the emergency bypass was on for family members only. I took it out of my back pocket. It was Chong.

"Hey, Chong."

"Hey, Yia." He paused. "Mom's at the hospital."

I stopped in my tracks. My mouth suddenly became very dry. "Oh."

"This morning Mom coughed up a lot of blood. Cher took her to the hospital."

The lump of saltwater dripped toward my navel.

"They're waiting for the doctors to run some tests."

"Dammit. Okay. She told me a few days ago that she was coughing up blood. I told her to go to the doctor but she wouldn't go and said it was only a little and it stopped. Damn."

"Yeah, it started a few days ago. We'll know more when the doctor comes back with the test."

"Okay, I'm on my way home."

I hung up the phone and texted my two best friends, Rachael and Rachel. "Go," they told me. I walked faster down the slight slope. The plum trees to my left were bright green against the backdrop of dry yellow grass.

I looked down at my phone. A text from Courtney. "I'm getting ready. We can leave in twenty minutes."

"Okay," I responded. That was how fast our network of connection worked. As soon as one of us needed something, one of the girls was there to handle the rest. I would normally tell them I'm good to go on my own. This time, I didn't.

I arrived at my shared two-bedroom house and went into my bedroom. I grabbed my carry-on Tumi suitcase from the closet and packed enough clothes for three days and all my toiletries.

Within fifteen minutes, Courtney walked in to help me finish up and we got in the car and drove off the property.

We entered the no cell service zone of Highway 128 through the mountain. After driving this route for five years, I had it down to a science. I had the markers for exactly where I should be at certain times. I was often the driver, not the passenger, so my scenery was fixed on the gray asphalt and curves.

Today, however, my gaze welcomed the expanse of nature. We reached the first plateau of the mountain, where the road dropped off hundreds of feet below, revealing a sprawling valley. Lush hills covered the expanse with green trees. The clear blue sky stretched into infinity above. I rolled down the window for fresh air. The rushing wind shattered the silence. Despite the tranquil scenery, fear gripped my mind. I looked up at the soft, pale blue sky but found no answers. The trees closed in around us, casting shadows over the road. Moments of sunlight pierced the spaces between the trees and electric poles. The air cooled slightly as the trees breathed oxygen into the atmosphere. Courtney kept to a steady speed as we started to round curves along the mountain.

My mind kept replaying the conversation with Mom a few days earlier. I should have told Cher to take her to the doctor. I should have forced Mom to go. I should have had Mai talk to Mom to convince her. I shoulda . . . shoulda . . . shoulda. . . . Mom was stubborn not as, but beyond, a mule. I felt angry and guilty but also help-less. The issue with her lungs had gone on for years with the doctors constantly telling us there was nothing they could do. Because she was ninety-four, they didn't think she was operable. Here I was, armed with the language in a country with the most advanced technologies in health and science, and I couldn't do anything for Mom's health. They couldn't do anything for her.

I struck up a conversation with Courtney to keep my mind from burning with paralyzing thoughts. Sunlight broke through the trees once in a while and shone a honey light on her dark complexion and black, curly, slightly afro hair. She'd been growing it out to an almost mohawk look. Courtney kept her eyes on the road, her voice soft, too soft most of the time, and I had to lean over and ask "what?" every time she spoke.

Forty-five minutes later, we were off Highway 128 and turned right to the cute little town of Cloverdale to fuel up at the main gas station. Courtney walked into the Starbucks for a coffee, her petite frame dancing in and out of visibility like a ninja flying over a rooftop. I walk into the Mini Mart for more water bottles and a bag of Doritos Nacho Cheese. Whenever I go home, I always buy a bag of Doritos or Flamin' Hot Cheetos. They're more for comfort than for snacking. They're the chips I grew up with.

Back on the road, Courtney put on some neo soul music from her Spotify playlist. I opened the bag of chips and allowed the overly salted fake cheese chemicals to cake in my teeth. My mind drifted into the warm, rich, and smooth voice of Lianne La Havas. We drove for another two hours and twenty minutes through Santa Rosa, Vallejo, Vacaville, Davis, and Sacramento.

Once in front of Mom's house, we grabbed our bags, walked to the door, and pushed the doorbell.

"Roof, roof, roof." Niya. "Roof, roof, roof." Senpai.

The door opened. "Hi, Aunty Yia." Ethan's frizzy curly hair was untamed around his head in a full-on afro like a puffed-up owl, and his small beady eyes smiled at me from behind his glasses. He moved to the side to let us in.

"This is my friend Courtney. Court, this is my nephew Ethan."

"Hi." His eyes diverted to the floor.

"Hi, Ethan."

Niya and Senpai, seeing that we weren't intruders, led us in, hurrying into the living room. Niya noticed I stopped following her. She came back toward me, barking.

"That's the bang bang dog," Courtney says, not as a question but a statement.

"Yep, that's her," I confirmed. My niece Nikki had taught Niya a famous trick. All my friends knew her for her trick. Just for fun, I demonstrated it to Courtney.

"Niya, Niya! Sit!" She sat on her hind legs and looked at me. I pointed my right index finger toward her, my thumb held up, imitating a pistol. "Bang bang!" Niya rolled over onto her back and played dead. I left her there for a few seconds. "Up!" She rolled over and got back up. "Good girl!"

Courtney and I laughed. Every time I came home I would capture a video of Niya doing this trick and send it to my friends. They loved her. I told them she's a little ghetto Sacramento dog. I didn't know how Nikki got her to perform that trick, but it won people over every time.

Mom, hearing all the commotion, walked out of her room.

"Hi, Mom!" I put my arms around her. She looked thinner and tired. She let me hug her. I broke away and introduced her to Courtney.

We were both glad to see each other but tended toward an under-expression of our emotions. I walked into her room to put my suitcase away. I showed Courtney to the side room where she would be staying. It was my sister-in-law's craft room. It became a guest room once you put the inflated bed in and it had a door for privacy.

Mom and I didn't talk about the incident. It felt as though I was coming home for a normal visit. She was right back on her feet in the kitchen. She asked if we'd eaten. She went through the refrigerator and pulled out some smoked beef. There was a box of KFC fried chicken on the counter. As Mom moved through the kitchen to prepare dinner, Sister-in-law Cher joined to put the salad together. Courtney and I sat on the couch and played with Niya and Senpai. They were very happy with the attention.

Once dinner was ready, we sat down to purple sticky rice, minced smoked beef, fried chicken, salad with ranch dressing, and Thai chili pepper with fish sauce. The irony was not lost on Courtney and me. She was from Louisiana, and fried chicken was home food for her. It was a coincidence that Cher had picked some up. We enjoyed the fusion dinner with Cher, Sister-in-law Cher, and Courtney getting to know one another. Mom mainly ate in silence. The kids grabbed their plates and went back to their computers.

After dinner Mom got up from the table and headed to her bedroom. Cher called for Ethan and Kaylie to do the dishes and clean up. Courtney and I went into the guest room to set up the bed.

After I got Courtney settled, I joined Mom in her room. She was doing her usual, listening to folk stories on a Hmong channel on YouTube. I sat on the bed next to her in my usual spot. It's where I sleep when I'm home. I opened up my laptop to do some work. We both did our own thing in silence. We drank in each other's company, our energy syncing up with one another.

Mom was the first to talk. "Yia, what happened this morning really scared me. I woke up this morning. It was so early. I was coughing and coughing. I went into the bathroom. I coughed so hard. My chest was bubbly. I thought I was going to die. I coughed and all this blood came out. My chest was boiling. I couldn't breathe. I couldn't get any air. I fell to the floor. I threw up in the toilet. There was more blood. I thought I was going to die. I tried to scream. My chest was filled with liquid. I couldn't scream for Cher. The coughing finally stopped. I yelled for Cher. I was so weak, I couldn't get up. Cher and Daughter-in-law came. They called the ambulance. Breathing was so hard. Yia, I thought I was going to die. This made me scared."

The shadows on the wall leaned in to eavesdrop.

I listened, feeling her pain, her fear. I didn't know what to say or how to console her. I wasn't used to her expressing these emotions. I wasn't used to her being in this place. The strong, stubborn, self-assured mom was suddenly raw and armorless. "Mom, we are grateful that nothing happened."

We sat there propped up against her pillows, our bodies inches from touching each other. I couldn't shake the image of her crouched over the blood-filled toilet. The wet, bubbly feeling of thick liquid congested in her chest, preventing her from breathing. The gasping for air only to drown in her own blood.

"Mom, I wish we took you to the hospital sooner when you first started coughing blood." I don't know if these words were for soothing her or easing my own guilt.

"I don't know. No one knows these things." Now she was trying to soothe both of us.

"What did the doctor say?" she asked, referring to her test results.

"I'm not sure, Mom. I'll go talk to Cher."

I went up the stairs to Cher's study and asked him more about what the doctor said.

"They said she has some lumps that are larger than they should be. They don't know what it is. She has to do a pulmonary scan, a scan for her thyroid and one for her heart. They will call us to schedule them."

"Let's call them in two days to check on it. I want to make sure she actually gets seen. Her appointments will get lost in the system. This happens all the time. If we don't call back every day, they're just going to ignore it. I'm happy to call them," I told Cher, knowing that he's not as persistent as I would be. One time I called Mom's doctor's office for some results so often, they told Cher I wasn't allowed to call them again.

"Did they say how large the lumps are?"

"I'll give you the printout and you can see." He went to his room and came back with the printout of Mom's tests.

I scanned the sheets.

CT CHEST WITH CONTRAST

** HISTORY **
94 years old, Interstitial lung disease

** FINDINGS **:

HEART AND GREAT VESSELS:
Heart is enlarged.

4.0 cm ascending aortic aneurysm.

LYMPH NODES:
*Multiple enlarged and mild calcified mediastinal
and hilar lymph nodes measuring up to 1.7 cm
could be related to prior granulomatous infection or
sarcoidosis.*

*Cluster of enlarged noncalcified pericardial lymph
nodes measuring up to 1.4 cm and a 1.1 cm
perigastric lymph node with punctate calcification
also present.*

OTHER MEDIASTINUM:
*There are multiple enlarged pericardial lymph nodes
measuring up to 1.4 cm.*

LUNGS:
*There is narrowing of lower lobe airways. There
is complete collapse of right middle lobe. There is a
2.4 x 1.7 cm opacity in the right infrahilar region
may be obstructing mass or consolidation. There is*

*spiculated nodular opacity right upper lobe measures
21 mm on coronal plane (601:58) with pleural
retraction. Suspicious. Multiple area of nodularity
and interstitial thickening also present. Consider
granulomatous infection versus neoplastic process.
Patchy airspace process or atelectasis is also present
along the left major fissure.*

Complete collapse of right middle lobe.

*2.4 x 1.7 cm opacity in right infrahilar
region may be focal consolidation or obstructing
mass.*

4 cm ascending thoracic aortic aneurysm.

Multiple thyroid nodules measuring up to 2.2 cm.

*This finding will be reviewed by an expert
committee, which will coordinate further follow-up
(#PUL5a).*

I had no idea what most of these meant. The word
suspicious caught my attention, along with the number of
times enlarged lymph nodes appeared.

"Can I keep this for now?" I asked Cher.

"Yes, go ahead." Cher started to say something,
paused, then decided to continue. "The doctor said
apparently Mom is supposed to get a CT scan of her
lungs every six months."

"Wait, what?" I was shocked.

"The doctor looked at Mom's chart from the biopsy she did two years ago. She's supposed to get scans every six months to monitor her lungs."

"Did we know that?" My shock quickly turned to anger.

"No. Mom's primary doctor never mentioned it."

"Fuck!" Anger turned to rage as the calculations came in on how this could have been prevented. "Fuck! We need to get her better care. Those primary care doctors don't do anything. She's not getting good care. She's been asking for a new doctor. Mom mentioned you were going to enroll her in Kaiser."

"Yeah, but they're full. They won't take any new Medi-Cal patients."

The medical system in the United States made no sense. You pay tens of thousands of dollars over your lifetime for shit care when you need it. And if you're an immigrant on the low end of the economic ladder, you might as well be performing your own surgery.

Cher continued before I could spew my opinion on the medical system. "But we can't move Mom right now. If we move her now before her appointments are scheduled, that's going to screw it up. The new primary will need to be established before she can get the appointments, and that will take even longer. So, let's wait for those appointments to get scheduled, then we'll move her."

Cher was right. I let it go.

"Okay. Fine. You're right. Thanks, Cher." I went back downstairs, shaking off the anger. I sat with Courtney while she worked. I googled the medical terms: *collapsed lungs, lung diseases, ascending thoracic aortic aneurysm, right sizes for thyroid nodules*. It was all informational. Nothing answered the question of what caused the bleeding and how to fix it.

I took pictures of the results and sent them to Mary, the nurse in the family. After a few minutes she wrote, "Yeah, it says some of the lumps are bigger than normal but nothing is conclusive. They need to do more tests." None of us had been willing to voice what we were all wondering.

I wanted an answer. Any answer. I wanted an answer to the unasked question.

I texted my college friend Martha about what happened in the morning. I sent her the test results. "Ah, Yia, I'm so sorry to hear that . . . this looks serious . . . yeah, some of these are bigger than normal . . . let me know if there's anything else I can do . . . sending your family prayers."

I felt helpless. There was absolutely nothing I could do. It could be months before any of her appointments came through. I closed my laptop and said good night to Courtney.

I walked into Mom's room and put my laptop on the bed. Walked back out into the adjacent bathroom. *What did the doctor say?* I was not ready to answer her question.

I wiped my face with a Yes to Cucumber makeup remover towelette. Brushed my teeth. Washed my face and moisturized. I took out my contact lenses and put on glasses. I walked back into her room and propped myself on the bed. I still wasn't ready but I was very clean.

"Mom, the results say you have some lumps in your lungs. They don't know what it is. The lumps are big. They want to do more tests." I stayed as factual and calm as I could.

"Lumps that are big?"

"Yes."

"Will they have to cut me open to fix it? I don't want to do that." Explaining medical issues to Mom is like talking to a four-year-old. At that moment, Mom did feel like a four-year-old. Her thinning gray hair dropped down to her shoulders. Her collar bones protruded from beneath her skin, creating delicate shadows that added to her vulnerable state, highlighting her fragility and the emotional weight she carried.

"I don't think so. But we don't know."

"I am old. I am not the same woman as in my youth. This body is old." But Mom was not that old. Biologically, she is in her seventies. On paper she is ninety-four. Her body had worked the life of four people.

Even so, I couldn't deny that over the years, I'd felt her light diminish. Grief clinging to her like a heavy shroud. Depression filling the silence between gardening and cooking and cleaning the house like a thick fog of opium smoke.

The room was swollen with desolation. No more words were needed. To puncture the membrane of uncertainty, Mom hit play on her YouTube video. I slid my index finger back and forth on the laptop trackpad and typed in my password. Ironically, the password contained the word "life."

We continued into the night. Mom dozed off to the sound of a woman's voice telling a Hmong folktale. I nodded awake to a line of "kkkkkkk" across my screen. I closed my laptop. Put away Mom's iPad. Turned off the light, and laid down beside Mom. I stared at the grief lingering in the darkness. The words "What if this is it?" invaded my mind before sleep took over.

Courtney and I stayed with Mom for another two days. As late afternoon rolled in, we packed for the trip home. Mom filled two plastic bags with cooked corn to take back to my friends, a raw frozen chicken, and a jar of her homemade pepper with cooked cow skin. We were full from a big lunch of squash shoot soup, boiled corn, and pork stew, and ready to return to Northern California.

Mom walked Courtney and me outside. I gave her a hug. "Bye, Mom. Don't work too hard. You need to rest. Call me if you need anything."

"Drive safe. Call me when you get home." She hugged me back.

Courtney and I got in the car and drove back north, feeling satiated.

Even in Mom's condition, where the unknown of her health would be a reason for her to shut herself off from life, she continued to pour care and love on us— not just the both of us, but the community of people with whom I lived. She woke up early to make rice and made sure we were fed the whole time. I tried my best to cook alongside her, telling her to "sit and I'll take over," but she continued to linger. She didn't think of herself and her illness; she thought of others and how she could love them through food. She chose to love and let that empower her.

Step 2.
Choose the Body

Mom barged into my room and woke me up at six o'clock to continue the preparation for steaming rice. Mary and Leah were still asleep on their side of the shared full-size bed. "Yia, wake up! It's already late! Get up and go *cub mov.*"

I shook myself awake. Oh, God, it's early! My eyes were thick with exhaustion from staying up late the night before to read. Mom left the room. I closed my eyes and rolled back to bed.

Before I could doze off, Mom came back in and yelled at me again. This time she waited until I got out of bed. I pulled back the fuzzy blue blanket. In a groggy state, I made my way to the bathroom to wash up.

I finally appeared in the kitchen with Mom already making her *kua taub hau,* broth with kabocha squash. She told me to get out the bamboo steamer and pot and instructed me on filling the pot with water and the steamer with rice.

I filled the pot to where there was already a watermark. The steamer was cone-shaped, like the kind of straw hat Asians in movies wear while working in the rice fields. I drained the soaked rice and poured it into the steamer, covered it with the lid, and set it over the pot. The steamer caught the rim of the pot about a quarter of the way in. There was already a second pot on the stove that was filled with the boiling water we needed for soaking the rice again after it was cooked.

"How long does rice steam for?" I asked her. "How many minutes?" I was ready to set a timer and go sit down to watch some Saturday morning shows.

"Thaum cov mov tuaj tes muab phau lug rau dlej kub." When the rice arrives, take it out to soak in the boiling water. Mom's response was cloaked in cryptic wisdom.

When the rice arrives? I had no idea what that meant. Hadn't the rice been there the whole time? Where was it arriving from?

"How do you know when the rice *tuaj*?"

"Saib teb paub xwb mo." Just watch and you will know. Her words were a testament to her intuitive gift.

I ceased my line of questioning, realizing Mom wasn't inclined to provide a clear, step-by-step explanation. My fleeting hope of catching a moment of TV evaporated as Mom promptly assigned me the task of washing the dishes

With a reluctant sigh, I resigned myself to the chore at hand.

Mom's intuitive nature is one of her gifts. She lives according to her senses, her body alert to the environment around her. To Mom, there are no cups, quarts, or liters. There are no tablespoons or teaspoons, grams or ounces. She cooks with her senses. Mom learned from watching her mother and sisters. She grew up observing and imitating them, tasting the food they made, doing it precisely the way they did it. Mom's measuring tools are her senses, and they tell her the exact quantity of an ingredient that is required as well as the exact length of time something needs to cook. Her nose knows the smell of a dish when it's done, or how much time it needs. Her tongue is her cookbook. When Mom tastes food, all her senses are there to evaluate it.

In high school I was not so familiar with my intuition. I did not have the environment to be able to slow down and tune in to nature, to learn the songs of birds and coloration of plants. My environment was enclosed in walls to learn history that was not my history, math that I would never use, science that dismissed anything that couldn't be proven. It was all based on logic and reasoning and appearance. It was all head based and facts. Then back at home, I was expected to sense when food is cooked and plants are ready to harvest and to be creative with needlework on clothes that I would only wear once a year. The messages were conflicting between the intuition of the body and the rational intelligence of the mind.

×   ×   ×

October 22, 1997

I was seventeen years old and a senior in high school. For three days, the hospital lobby was filled with cousins, aunts, uncles, in-laws. Some faces I recognized, many I did not. Cousin after cousin came in to pay their respects to Dad, announcing themselves and telling him to wake up and come back to us. He was in a coma. There was a thick tube coming out of his mouth attached to the ventilator that was keeping him alive. He had septic pneumonia. His organs had failed. His liver, lungs, kidneys, none of them were working. The IV drip that was flowing through his veins had nowhere to release. His body was unnaturally swollen like a balloon—chest, hands, feet, face, lips. He was no longer the slim, strong father I knew but a swollen shadow of death. For years after he died, whenever I closed my eyes, that was the dominant image I had of him.

The doctors came into the lobby filled with thirty-plus family members. They told us they had done everything they could and there was nothing more they could do. They gave us two options. We could continue to keep him on the ventilator to see if he comes out of his coma, or we could take him off of it. But if he did come out, he would be a vegetable. They left us with those options.

My half-brothers and elders gathered together. What do we do? Do we keep him on the ventilator to sustain his life? Or do we take him off the ventilator and let nature takes its course? It was a few more hours before Mai and her husband landed at San Francisco International Airport and then drove two hours to San Joaquin General Hospital in Stockton. Mom asked that we wait for Mai to arrive before any decision was made. But the elders disagreed. The doctors wanted us to decide soon. We couldn't wait that long.

The room was thick with grief, confusion, and anger. I felt as though I were drowning in a storm of emotions. Buoyed about with no anchor. Everything was a blur to me then, and still a blur to me now. My voice locked in the thicket of emotions. What do you do when the life of a loved one is in your hands?

There was a shuffle in the crowd. Someone informed me we had to move. My immediate family was ushered into a conference room. Long tables were arranged in an oval in the center, with chairs lining the perimeter. Everyone took a seat.

An elder began to speak. I can't remember what was said. I presumed the words were about Dad, about life and death, about the difficult decision that lay before us. Perhaps about love and family. Eventually, he presented the situation: We had to decide whether to maintain life support or remove it. Opinions varied, so it was agreed that each of Dad's sons and daughters would have the opportunity to voice their feelings.

I can't remember the exact words spoken, but I remember the division. Some of the family wanted to keep him on the ventilator; they clung to hope. What if Dad emerged from the coma? Why couldn't we wait, given the technology available to sustain his life? Others pointed out that Dad was suffering, and we needed to consider the quality of life he might have—if any at all. What if he never awoke?

I remember we were voting on Dad's life. I remember accusations flew about who truly loved Dad and who was letting go. I remember there was a loud rip in the room—we were standing on the edge of two tectonic plates torn apart by an impossible decision. Grief infected the family like a virus.

There's a Hmong proverb that the father anchors the family lineage. Without him, there is no stability. Our foundation had already begun to crumble.

The elders intervened before more hurtful words could spread through the room. They acknowledged the difficulty of the situation and urged us not to let it divide us. They affirmed that all of Dad's children should have a say, emphasizing that each opinion was valid, including those of the youngest among us.

In the haze of that conference room, the only vivid thing I remembered was the dream I had a few days before Dad was hospitalized.

× × ×

I was in the house we were living in. I came out of the bedroom into the living room. Unlike our real house, this dream house had a fireplace. A small stack of wood was burning, smoke wafting from the chimney. Khoua Neng knelt beside the fireplace. Before him lay a bowl with uncooked rice grains and a whole raw egg in the center—the traditional setup for calling the ancestors. He lit three joss incense sticks, chanted softly, waved the incense in three swift motions, and placed them into the rice bowl. The room filled with smoke.

He turned to me and said in Hmong, "They said that this time, when Dad goes, he's not coming back."

I froze, his words hit me like a ton of bricks. The shadows on the wall stepped into the room. Everything, including Khoua Neng, faded into darkness. The words sank into my heart, unleashing an intense ache followed by a fiery burst. I couldn't breathe. The ache rushed into my eyes; tears cascaded down my face. Gasping for air, I awoke to tears flooding my pillow, my heart aching. My eyes searched the darkness, drowning in tears. Realizing it was a dream, I reached for the table lamp. Click, click—a snap. The bulb blew out. Cha slept soundly beside me.

A voice in my head urged, "Go to Mom and Dad's room" It guided me out of bed. I stumbled in the darkness, feeling my way to the door, tears still pouring down my face. I found the knob and opened it and made my way to their room. As soon as I was in their room, my legs gave out and I collapsed on a box of clothes by the door, sobbing deeply.

Mom woke up to my crying and reached for the light. "Yia, what's wrong?"

She woke Dad up. They were both looking at me in the brightly lit room. I couldn't speak. I couldn't stop crying. The words echoed loudly in my head, "This time, when Dad goes, he's not coming back."

"What's happened?" Mom pressed, more sternly. "Did you have a nightmare?"

Finally calming, I managed between sobs, "I had a dream . . . Khoua Neng . . . He said that this time, when Dad goes, he's not coming back." I broke down again.

"It's nothing," Dad reassured me. "Just a bad dream."

"What happened in the dream?" Mom asked for more information.

I recounted the dream for her, what I saw, what I heard, what Khoua Neng told me.

After hearing my words, she said, "It's okay. It's only a dream. It doesn't mean anything."

But I knew that wasn't true. I knew this was what adults did with us kids. They don't want us to worry, so they tell us it's nothing.

"Go back to bed. It's just a dream," Mom repeated. I wanted her to say more, to tell me it's not true. I wanted her to say they will do something about it. That they will call a *txiv neeg*, shaman, to do a ceremony to protect Dad. But I didn't know how to ask for such things. "It's just a dream." I felt insignificant.

After a few minutes of letting me cry, she urged me again to go back to bed. My tears ceased, and I felt calmer. I turned off the light and closed their door, and navigated back to bed in the dark. Cha still slept. The cold, wet pillow reminded me that what I saw and heard in the dream was real.

×   ×   ×

It was my turn to speak in the conference room. I couldn't look up at the faces. I can't remember what I said out loud. But I remember thinking that Dad was in a lot of pain. I remember thinking we have to do what's best for him. We have to let him go. But I can't remember how much of that I actually said or was able to say. I don't remember if the words were just lodged in my throat or if I managed to get it out in between sobs.

There was so much running through my mind. I wanted to tell them about my dream, but I was not so brave. I couldn't sift through the thicket of feelings to find the Hmong words to tell them about the dream. I wasn't even sure if it was significant in this situation. What help would it do now? And at the same time, I felt guilty that I dreamed about it. Maybe it was because of my dream that this was happening? Did I cause this? Could I have prevented this? Could I have insisted that Mom and Dad call our shaman to do a ceremony to retrieve and protect his soul? Was I given the dream to prevent this and had I failed? If I told them about it now, would they be angry that I didn't say it before? Would they blame me for not preventing this from happening? Why didn't Mom and Dad listen to me? Why must the elders always freakin' dismiss us children, saying it's nothing? Was it because I was a girl that they didn't care to listen to me? Why the fuck didn't they listen to me! Why the fuck did I have the dream? Why the fuck didn't I say anything before?

Everyone had spoken.

The votes were cast.

We're pulling the plug.

Every particle in the room was swollen with grief. The shadows on the wall slid into the background.

The aftershocks of the meeting would divide our family for years to come. No one could have predicted what happens to a family with no father, no lineage anchor.

Mom told them to wait for Mai and her husband to arrive before we let him go. We informed the doctors.

Hours later, they finally arrived. Mai immediately embraced Mom, offering comfort. Mom broke down in her eldest daughter's arms. I had never seen Mom so fragile, so engulfed in grief. The strong, exacting mother I knew lost her composure, becoming a mere lump of sorrow. She appeared incredibly vulnerable, as if a feather might shatter her.

×　×　×

October 23, 1997

In the early morning hours, Dad's fourteen sons and daughters gathered around the body I had called *Iv*, Dad, for seventeen years. He was no longer slender, strong, stubborn with a commanding voice. This body looked nothing like our father.

The nurse asked us to stand back while she prepared him. She had done this many times before.

She took out the IV, the morphine drip.

Turned off the ventilator.

Extracted the tube from his mouth.

She stepped back.

Beep, beep. Beep, beep. The heart monitor skipped.

We stepped closer, surrounding him.

His chest rose one last time

and deflated like a balloon.

Beeeeeeeeeepppppppp.

Six thirty a.m.

The room erupted into painful wails from Mom, my half-brothers, and their wives, in traditional Hmong mourning. Us younger ones cried, our arms entwined, clinging to one another. There was no space between wailing and sobbing.

I looked out at the tear-stricken faces matching my own. My brothers Tang and Chong and my little sisters Mary and Leah. My heart broke further.

They didn't know this was going to happen.

But I knew.

I knew that this time, when he went, he wasn't coming back. I wanted nothing more than to escape the weight of that knowing, that responsibility.

And I did.

I didn't know how to process this pain and the flood of emotions that came so I severed the connection to my body. What followed were years of numbness buoyed about by the world of appearances and ideas of who I should be, and decades of trying to find my way back to my body.

Step 3.
Choose Life

I kept my eyes on the steamer, looking for an announcement of the rice's arrival. After a long enough time, a cloud of steam started to shoot out from the steamer and evaporate into the air. Sometime after that, Mom announced, "Now it's arrived."

She instructed me to pour the rice from the steamer into the big bowl she had put in the sink. I took two pot holders, folded them over the edges of the bamboo steamer, and picked it up from the bottom. A rush of steam followed suit. I carefully took the steamer over to the counter and set it down. I took off the lid, and sweet, cloudy steam danced into the air. Taking the steamer by the edge, I lifted it up and quickly tipped all the rice into the bowl. The V-shaped rice plopped into the bowl and crumbled into clumps. Hot steam rushed to my face, burning my lips, cheeks, and eyes. I stepped back in surprise.

"It's hot," she told me, seeing my reflex. Obviously.

She then instructed me to take the wooden spoon and spread the rice out a bit more, and I did as told, this time putting some distance between myself and the attack of the steam. I set the handle down and walked over to the stove with pot holders in hand. Carefully picked up the second pot of boiling water that had been waiting. I brought it over to the counter.

"How much water do I pour in, Mom?"

She walked over to stand next to me and watch me. "Cover the rice."

I picked it up and poured the hot water into the rice, watching it crumble into a puddle. I kept pouring the water up to the top of the rice.

"That's good," she said matter-of-factly. "Not so much that the rice will be soggy and not so little that it'll be hard."

Those instructions didn't mean anything to me, but I didn't question her. I set the pot down with some water left in it. Having been on a long journey to arrive at this moment, the grains quickly drank the water.

Next, Mom told me to gently stir the rice to make sure all the lumps are loosened. I did so patiently.

Mom told me that the waiting, the patience, and the timing are most important in rice-making. If the rice soaks too long, it will become mushy, and if it doesn't soak long enough, it'll be hard. Once again, there is no timer. Everything is done with the eyes, taste, senses.

You had to let go to the present moment instead of trying to figure out the process.

She instructed me to fill the steamer pot with the water again so that it wouldn't dry out in the second steam.

Midway through soaking, once half the water had been soaked up, Mom told me to turn the rice over so that the top rice could get more water and the bottom rice wouldn't get over soaked.

With the wooden spoon, I turned the rice over so that the top rice got a chance to drink. It's important to turn it gently and not stir it, or it will break. This process requires soft, confident hands. Once the rice had been flipped, we let it sit again.

When the rice had enough to drink, meaning that all the water was gone, she told me to use a small bowl to scoop the rice back into the bamboo steamer and cover it up. Again, I did as told. I lifted the bowl from the sink onto the counter so that I could lean the bamboo steamer against the sink. I carefully scooped in the rice. I could feel Mom's eyes on me, judging and criticizing my every move as though I were at a dance tryout.

I was putting the lid on when Mom's voice scolded impatiently, "There's still rice in the bowl! Scoop *all* the rice out. You're wasting so much rice!"

Goodness, you would have thought I'd thrown out a whole buffet tray of rice! There was only a handful of rice scattered on the side of the bowl. But I didn't argue. Annoyed, I picked up the wooden spoon, gathered all the grains together, and then scooped every last grain into the steamer.

"That's how you do it. You don't want your mother-in-law to say you waste food."

"Geez, Mom, I'm not married!"

She ignored the comment and proceeded to tell me to put the steamer back on the pot and turn the stove back on. Despite my resistance to steaming rice and making it unpleasurable for her, Mom just kept going. She wasn't fazed by my protest. She had one goal and one goal only, to ensure that I would be a good daughter-in-law. She was determined to guide me there.

I wanted to ask her, "How do you know when the rice is cooked, and how long does it steam for?" but I didn't ask. Instead, I collected the bowl, pot, and utensils and started washing them.

×　×　×

June 27, 2022

I immersed myself in the stream of life, yet Mom's health loomed over me. The words that haunted my nights now pursued me through the daylight hours. "What if this is it?" I suppressed the question, but it weighed on my chest, draining my energy and casting a shadow on my spirit.

Three days after the visit, I called in all the help I knew. I texted Sofia to ask Alejandro, a shaman from Mexico, for a healing session for Mom. We'd been working with him and his wife, Karla, for three years. They'd become very good family friends. Sofia spoke Spanish fluently, having lived in Spain for a few years before I met her.

She immediately responded, and asked for Mom's name and a photo. I told her the situation and to focus on her lungs.

I texted Rev. Jo, one of the few Aramaic scholars of the Bible and a practitioner at the Agape International Spiritual Center run by Reverend Michael Beckwith, to put in a request to her prayer group. She was on it.

I submitted Mom's name to the Tibetan Buddhist group I studied with, for healing mantras.

The following day, Sofia gave me the report from Alejandro. "He said yesterday when he first started it looked bad. Today it looks better. He will keep working. He saw what you said about her lungs and arteries. There were some black clouds over them. He did a cleansing. Seems like it's moving now. She should be feeling better."

His words lifted some weight off my chest. I called Mom to check on her.

"Hi, Mom. How are you?" I said in English.

"I feel much better today," she responded in Hmong. She sounded lighter, even chirpy. She continued, "Yia, if getting better means I have to get new lungs, then I will do that."

It took a few seconds to register her words. "Mom, you do?!" Alejandro's cleansing was really working its magic. For years she had not wanted to go to a doctor for fear that they would take out her organs.

"Yes, if that's what it takes." She felt certain of herself.

"That's really good, Mom. We will get you tested. They will tell us what we need to do." This opened the conversation to bring up Alejandro.

"Mom, I've been working with a shaman from Mexico. I asked him to do a healing session for you. He did it yesterday. How did you feel yesterday?"

"Oh, you did? I felt good yesterday. I had more energy. I didn't feel tired."

"That's good, Mom. Yeah, he said you would feel better." And then after a short pause, I continued. "Mom, he said that there were some black clouds over your lungs and heart. He did a cleansing of them."

"Oh, wow, is that what he saw? That's what he said? Okay, I felt better yesterday. Tell him thank you very much. I'm really touched that he did that. Maybe you can ask him why I threw up blood? Why was my body shaking? Ask him why my chest had so much blood and it came so suddenly."

I had never encountered this with Mom before. Not only were we talking about her health, she was letting me into her fears and questions about what happened. She wanted to know as much as I wanted to know. It was something that I hadn't considered before. I thought that I was alone in trying to figure out what was happening with her. But here she was, letting me know she was just as worried and wanted to find a solution.

I assured her I would inquire and relay his insights. We discussed a few other topics before ending our call.

Later that night, sitting in bed, I texted Sofia and gave her the update on Mom to pass on to Alejandro. I relayed Mom's questions for him.

After a few minutes she texted: "He said he feels some desire to stop living. There's some feeling of pain from her past. He says she's in the middle of an abyss.

She's deciding if she wants to continue on this plane or not."

"On our call today, she said if living meant getting new lungs, she's willing to do that. She's never said anything like that before," I texted.

She responded: "He says she wants to live if she says she wants new lungs, but she must let go of the pain and the drowning. Or the feeling that is drowning her. There's something pulling her down. Things from her past. She has to choose to let that go and decide if she wants to live. Tell her tomorrow and see what she says."

"Yes, I'll talk to her. Tell Alejandro she was really receptive and appreciated that someone was looking at it. She said she felt better since yesterday and has more energy."

"So beautiful. She needs some love." Another text came through. One that I had been avoiding. "Alejandro just said we have to clean you too, liberate you from guilt."

Damn, how did he know that? "LOL okay, okay. I definitely felt that *a lot* today."

"Whole family healing! What did you feel?"

"Just a lot of guilt all around. Guilt that I haven't been able to help with her health. She told me she coughed up blood and I didn't make her go see a doctor . . . I'm just not ready to let her go yet . . . I feel like I just finally am starting to get to know her and there is still so much more to learn from her and her life and her story . . . My heart just keeps saying 'I just found you.' I felt that a lot today."

"Oh Yia . . . Alejandro said it's a good moment to be with her now to love her and tell her all these things . . . Does she know you feel this way?"

"I haven't said these things to her." And how could I? I could barely express my feelings in English, let alone say them in Hmong. Emotional expressions in Hmong were not something I grew up with. There were two feelings I knew how to express—anger and sadness. Love was from another planet.

"Oh, you must tell her."

"There are a lot of Hmong words I wouldn't be able to say."

"You can piece it together, no?"

I scanned through my Hmong vocabulary, the Hmong love movies I'd seen:

Kuv thov txim, I'm sorry.

Kuv hlub koj, I love you.

Ntsug peb nyob, Stay with us.

Tsis txhob moog, Don't leave.

"Yeah, I can."

"Now is the time to tell her what's on your heart . . . She's dying to know you . . . to feel you . . . It's so vulnerable and so beautiful. All the things you feel, you must tell her . . . She's like, 'I may as well go, no one loves me.' and you're like, 'She can't go, I haven't finished loving her.' OMG there's so much love between you two it's so intense."

My chest cracked open into a deep ache, making it hard for me to breathe. Blood spilled through my pores. The dam behind my eyelids broke. The phone blurred.

She continued, "You are what she's been looking for and this is what you've been looking for . . . You have to tell her . . . It's better than any love story you will find in the movies."

"Yeah . . . all true," I managed to text in between sobbing. My body continued to thaw, life pumping back into my veins. I took my first deep inhale in days. "Wow, I needed that."

"That's right . . . You needed to cry."

"Yeah . . . Thanks, sister."

The following afternoon, I called Mom. After a few minutes of our usual greeting, I told Mom what Alejandro had said. "Mom, he said the issue with your lungs and heart is because you are holding on to grief and sadness from the past." I pause for a response.

"Is that what he said? He saw that?" Mom's tone changed from curiosity to somber. "Yes, I have much grief. There is so much grief."

"Mom, he said your grief is weighing you down. He said there is a big hole there. You have to choose if you want to live or not, Mom. You have to choose to let go of the grief. To be here." My voice started to shake.

"When I am by myself, these thoughts just come in. Thoughts of wanting to leave this world. Of not wanting to be here. I can't help it. That's why I keep myself so busy. If I stop, I start to think about leaving."

I broke down, tears streaming down my face. I gave up trying to keep my voice steady. "Mom, you have to stop thinking about wanting to leave. I still want you to stay."

She started crying. "It's not that I even want to. When I stop working, they just come in. When I'm alone these thoughts are here. There is so much grief in my heart."

"Mom, I'm sorry I haven't known how to love you. I want to learn how to love you. I want you to live your days out with us. I know you have grief and I'm sorry. I haven't been able to make you happy. *Kuv hlub koj.*" Saying all these in Hmong was not as foreign as I had thought it would be. The words flowed, surprising me. It felt so right and so good to finally say them. It was as if this pocket of love had been waiting for me to ripen so that it could naturally flow out of me.

"Yia, this is why I want to know that you are taken care of. This is why I want you to get married, so that when I'm not here, you are taken care of." These were the words, the feelings underneath all those years of pressuring me to find a husband and start my life. It was so that she would know I was loved and cared for when she was gone.

"Mom, I have a great life. I'm happy with my friends. I'm happy doing what I'm doing with my life."

"I'm glad you have a good life. I'm glad you are happy." That was the first time she acknowledged my life.

"Mom, he says you can have new lungs, but you have to decide if you want to live. You have to choose it and let go of the grief."

We didn't come to a joyous resolution, but we both said what was there to be said. We opened a new spot in our relationship. I couldn't choose for Mom. It was not my place to make that decision for her. All I could do was tell her what was in my heart. When we hung up the phone, though my heart felt lighter and Mom and I had found a connection we'd never found before, the question pressed on.

What if this is it?

A week later, I was in my online Tibetan Buddhism class where the teacher was taking us through a Bardo Jangcho ceremony. A *bardo* is the period between death and rebirth. The ceremony was a way to assist those spirits that haven't crossed over to go through this cycle into the afterlife so that they may be reincarnated. During this ceremony, the teacher also gave blessings for those who are terminally ill. He spoke about our job in being with loved ones who are ill. "Our role is to serve them through this transition. We can't hold on to them if they want to leave. It is not for us to decide. It is their karma."

It struck to my core. I heard him. It gave me a deeper understanding of my relationship with Mom. I couldn't pull her. I couldn't want more for her than she wanted for herself. It would be a disservice to place my desire above hers. It was so contrary to what we are taught: to fight for someone, to convince them to live, to hold on to them when they want to go. I was here to serve Mom's desire, whatever that was. Not to place mine on her.

The following day, Marcus, my half-Sri Lankan, half-Swedish friend of ten years, texted me. His father passed away a year earlier. We had a beautiful conversation about his experience with his dad.

"One of the most powerful things I did with my dad was I started talking to him about dying."

"Oh, wow. How was that?"

"It's the most intimacy I have ever had with him. I was the only person who would talk to him about this huge experience of dying. I got to see him as a man, apart from my father, and really get to know and love him. We had such a good time together toward the end."

"That's a powerful experience. What did you even ask? How did you begin the conversation?"

"The first question I asked was: 'Do you feel scared of dying? Is there anything you'd like to do before you die?'"

"What did he say?"

"He told me he didn't feel scared, that he felt ready. That he felt very tired from all he did in his life and was at peace with it. It was the most present I ever felt him."

"Were you ready for him to go?"

"I was, which was big for me. This was a man I spent my life adoring and also not truly knowing. Before he died, we completed our karma. And then we got to spend this really lovely time together, in these questions and this conversation about death. It was like a bonus with him, and they were some of the most special moments of my life."

"I think I still must reconcile with myself whether I'm ready for her to go. Part of me is, because she would be relieved of her grief, and part of me feels like I just found her. There's still so much about her I don't know. She's also all I have left of my culture."

"I felt all those things, I understand."

Our conversation opened my mind to the other side of death. Not the fear of death, but the living *with* death.

It's something our society doesn't discuss. It gave me the possibility of having intimacy with Mom and death.

Later that evening, my friend Nicole texted me to see how my heart was doing. I told her about what I heard in the Tibetan Buddhism class.

"That's funny, I thought of you when he said that," she wrote back.

"I don't know, Nic. I don't want to lose her. I feel like I've just found her. I still have so much to learn from her. We are just beginning."

"Honey, you found each other. That's more than most people will ever have in this lifetime."

She was right. I knew she was right. I cried, whether it was at the possibility of losing her or at the relief of having found her, they were one and the same.

"Completing your karma is to serve her desire."

"But how do I do that?"

"You know how. By being her guide."

My rational mind wasn't sure how to do that, but my intuitive sense knew what she meant.

That night I went to bed, turned off the light, and searched in the dark. The question was not there. In its place was an image of Mom and I talking about life and death. Death *is* life. It was not meant to be feared or wished away, but to know and become intimate with. In its place was a blank canvas in a jeweled room waiting to be filled with Mom's words.

× × ×

July 8, 2022

"Hi, Mom. How are you?" I sat underneath the grandmother oak tree in the field of our property. The shade provided solace from the scorching summer heat.

"*Mi naib*," darling daughter, she began in Hmong, "I want to live. I hope there is nothing wrong with my lungs. I want to live with everyone. I want to stay here with you all!"

×   ×   ×

August 25, 2022

It was the peak of the workday, the air buzzing with creativity as my friends and I talked through an event coming up the following week, when the ringing of my phone broke through the flow of ideas. Cher. I excused myself to pick it up.

"Hey, Cher." My hand gripped the iPhone, a sense of foreboding creeping up my spine. My pulse quickened, anticipation mingling with dread.

"Hey, Yia. Just got back from Mom's doctor."

My heart lurched.

"Okay . . ."

"We got the results back. The lumps are benign! They are not cancerous."

For a moment, time seemed to freeze as I absorbed his words. Relief flooded through me in a dizzying rush.

"Oh, thank God."

"Yeah, he said it's nothing. We just need to keep an eye on it and get her lungs scanned every six months or so. But she's okay."

I exhaled, the weight of worry lifting off my shoulders.

"That's so great! How's Mom?"

"She's doing great. I told her there was nothing, and she just needs to keep doing her breathing exercises for her lungs. But she's in good spirits."

"That's great to hear."

A wave of gratitude washed over me, the tension in my muscles slowly releasing.

"Okay, that's all. Just wanted to share that."

"Thanks, Cher."

Relief flooded through me, mingling with gratitude and a newfound sense of closeness with Mom.

Step 4.
Guide Each Other Home

While I waited for the rice to steam the second time, I put away dishes and wiped down the countertops. I scrambled some eggs for breakfast, and Mom tended to her chicken soup and kabocha squash broth. I set the table with plates and spoons, napkins and hot pepper, all the while keeping my eye on the rice.

Eventually a second wave of steam shot out of the steamer. The sweet aroma of rice filled the house. At some point, Mom told me the rice was ready. I still don't understand how she knows.

I removed the steamer from the pot, and she told me to pour rice into a clean bowl. As I tipped the steamer, a mountain of rice plopped down into the bowl. Each grain looked proud, plump, pearly white. This time the grains held on to each other on the way down, forming lumps, but you could easily see each separate grain. Mom told me to fluff the rice to let the steam out, then scoop some into a smaller bowl for the table. The rest goes into the rice cooker to keep warm for the rest of the day.

I brought the smaller bowl to the table, scooped out chicken soup into two bowls, the kabocha squash broth into two bowls, the scrambled eggs onto two platters and arranged them on the table for our family-style breakfast. The proud rice was the centerpiece, bringing all the other dishes together.

I did a quick round of the house, telling everyone to come and *"noj mov!"* which literally translates to eat rice!

I sat down at the table, scooping rice and eggs onto my plate. Rice with any dish creates a symphony of flavors, sometimes blending them in perfect harmony, other times highlighting the contrast. I took a spoonful of rice and eggs, blew on it lightly, and put it in my mouth. The lump of rice was warm, soft; each grain danced in my mouth as I chewed, slightly sweet and delicate, but earthy, plump, and moist, mixed with the salty, dry thickness of eggs. As I swallowed Mom's instructions, I realized that this was the taste of her love.

A few years ago, a chef friend of mine from Africa looked at my palm. He tended to avoid people's palms, he told me, because they speak to him and he doesn't want to know. But he was drawn to my hands that night and couldn't help turning my palms up to look at them.

After a few seconds of studying them, he asked for the first letter of Mom's name.

"Y," I responded, curious.

He looked at it for a few more seconds. "You and your mom have been together for many lives. You've been in different roles with each other, but you're always together."

I resonated with what he said. "You know, I believe that."

True relationships happen in the invisible. In this lifetime, she's my mother, and I'm her daughter, but it's also so much more than that. We often get stuck in the idea of a physical relationship and never break out of that to discover who the other truly is, to find each other. The work of any relationship is to break through the form to know all the different facets of yourself and the other person, to understand who you are in relationship to them and what is required from you to bring love to the relationship.

I always wanted Mom to be a certain kind of mom who would ease the pain, guilt, shame, and lack of value I had, and by doing that, I couldn't see her. But now I have so much more. I was given the gift to be her guide, to be there for her as she birthed into this phase of her life.

True relationship is guiding each other home. It's becoming love to serve the relationship, and drawing out the best from the other.

I didn't appreciate Mom's teachings when I was young, but now I've come to understand her intuitive method of transferring knowledge from one woman to another. I used to be annoyed when she answered my questions with, "If you watch, you will know." But I now realize that she was training me on more than just cooking, cleaning, and sewing to be a good daughter-in-law. She was guiding me to have access to all my senses. To open up to my own intuitive nature as a woman and tether me to the lineage that I come from. She was trying to guide me home.

This wasn't an overt kind of training. Not even a conscious one. But it is the intuitive ways of the feminine; like a mother tree that ensures the trees around her thrive so she sends them energy and nutrients through the roots.

On a trip home, I asked Mom to teach me how to *cub mov* again. This time, I watched everything she did, allowing myself to be guided by my senses. I wanted to learn how to steam rice not to be a good daughter or daughter-in-law, but to connect with the roots of where I came from. As convenient as it was to scoop some rice into a cooker and press a button, I wanted to learn the way Mom learned, the way it has been in our lineage for centuries. I may never have a daughter of my own to pass it on to, but I want the world to remember what it's like to feel the tiny grains of rice in your hands when you rinse them. I want people to smell the sweet aroma of the earth and taste the plump, soft, chewy texture of life. I want people to remember there was a time when all there was, was this moment—enveloped by the scent of love and the magic of dancing white clouds in the kitchen.

Coming Home

At the end of the year, during November and December, there is a flurry of New Year rituals, *noj peb caug,* every weekend at our cousins' houses. Sometimes there might be two a day on Saturday and Sunday as each family takes down, cleans, and makes a new altar for their ancestors as a shaman or soul-caller in the family performs the *hu nplig*, a ritual to call the souls of all the family members back home, invite them for a meal, and burn joss paper money for them in the spirit world. It is a time for all the children to come home and join in the festivities. Married sons bring their wives and children; married daughters sometimes come back home with their husbands to help. It's not mandatory for the married daughters to be there, but it is mandatory for the boys, because they are the carriers of the lineage.

Traditionally, chicken lemongrass soup was made from chickens freshly killed and plucked in the back-yard and served with rice and tofu made a day or two in advance. The preparation and festivities, the intricacy of the ritual and attention to detail, the way certain things had to be prepared in advance, and the roles everyone knew they played, created a well-orchestrated symphony.

As a kid, I didn't know what these rituals were for, but I sensed that they were important, and I was happy that my cousins came over and we got to run around the house and play together. After that, we got to eat an egg symbolizing the return of our soul to our body, and for three days we couldn't spend money, so that we would be wealthy in the new year.

As a young teenager, I was indifferent to the rituals. The noise was loud; there were a lot of people, and dishes to wash over and over again. I took on the role of babysitter and usually played with the little kids in the bedroom to avoid holding the chickens to be killed and plucked. I left that for my sisters and sisters-in-law while I waited for the event to be over and wondered how long it would take Mom to notice I wasn't doing anything and yell at me to wash the dishes.

In high school, I grew to hate these occasions. I could no longer get away with not participating in the killing and plucking of the chickens. I was grossed out by it and would happily have handed over the task to a cousin and washed some dishes. But I hung in there, mainly so I wouldn't get yelled at by Mom or embarrass her and make her lose face, *poob ntsej muag*.

While I didn't realize it at the time, and as much as I hated being forced to participate so that I wouldn't bring shame on my parents, this ritual was also the string that tethered me to that fragment of tradition. It helped me find my way back to where I belonged.

Mom called me a few days before to ask me to come home for the ritual. I wanted to invite my friend Amanda, who I thought would appreciate it, so I asked Mom if that would be okay and she told me to let Cher and Sister-in-law Cher know. They too welcomed Amanda and insisted that she stay at the house, not in a hotel. Hmong hospitality means welcoming even strangers and making them feel at home. You treat every guest as you would a son or daughter, offering them whatever you have to give.

On the weekend of the ritual, Amanda and I made the four-hour drive to Elk Grove from Mendocino County. During the drive, I couldn't stop thinking about finally getting to eat Mom's food again after two years of the COVID-19 pandemic when, because of her lung issues, we had thought it best not to gather in person for Christmas and had met over Zoom instead.

I could already taste the fresh tofu Mom would prepare two days before the ceremony. It was a lengthy process that required patience, so she only made it once a year for this special occasion. One year, when I was a high school sophomore, she had attempted to prepare me for becoming a daughter-in-law by having me make the tofu with her. I never made it again, opting instead for the convenience of store-bought tofu. But after realizing that it wasn't as good as homemade, I didn't use tofu again except when I was feeding vegetarian friends.

Upon arrival, we were greeted by my niece Kaylie along with Niya and Senpai whose barking went from fierce protection to excitement once they recognized me.

We put our bags in Mom's room, and I called out to her but received no answer. "She's probably in the backyard," I told Amanda, and Kaylie confirmed that, of course, I was correct.

We walked through the living room and kitchen to the sliding glass door that opens to the backyard. I called out to her again, but found only Cher who was chopping up fresh salmon.

"Hey, Cher, this is my friend Amanda," I introduced them. "Did you guys go fishing this morning?"

"Yes, we did! Caught two salmon. It's the end of the season, though, so they aren't that great."

"Where's Mom?" I asked him.

"She's in the garage," he replied as he continued to chop and wrap the salmon in plastic bags and vacuum-sealed them.

Sure enough, that's where we found her putting away some greens and other produce she had brought back from Khoua Neng's farm in Lodi.

"Hi, Mom!" I introduced her to Amanda. Mom didn't say much, not because she didn't want to know Amanda but because she wasn't confident in her English.

I took Amanda around the garden, pointing out Mom's herbs and my sister-in-law's flowers, guava trees, dragon fruit trees, and other plants. Mom and Sister-in-law Cher each had their own areas and tended to their own plantings with love and pride. On the left side, along the fence, were Mom's traditional and medicinal herbs. On the right and through the center were my sister-in-law's flowers and fruit trees. The two have found a way to coexist.

When it was time to prepare for dinner, I invited Amanda to help and learn from Mom. We made my favorite squash shoot soup, sautéed mustard greens, broiled Hmong pork sausage, and chicken lemongrass soup. Mom would instruct Amanda on how to peel the fuzzy layer from the squash shoots, then leave Amanda to follow her instructions while she herself went to work on something else.

Once the food was ready, we set the table, transferred everything to serving dishes, and I went around the house to call everyone to *noj mov.* My attempts to reproduce her food during the past two years had never done it justice. Now it tasted even better than I remembered.

As we ate, I briefed Amanda on the next day's ritual. Mom caught on and started to tell us how *noj peb caug* was celebrated in Laos. She started speaking in Hmong as though Amanda understood, and I would have to wait for her to pause so that I could translate.

"Back in Laos, *noj peb caug* was very different from how it is in this country. In Laos we would wake up way before the sun rose, before the rooster crowed, to be the first ones to go down to the river to gather water for the day. Everyone would compete to see who got there first to receive the blessings for the new year. It is said that if you arrive first, you will have a fruitful year and good luck. Your dad was *nquag nquag!* He would be the first one up and be ready to go to the river before anyone else was awake. He would be down by the river before any of the other families. Your father was a hard worker. He never complained about working hard.

"Once he came back with water from the river, he fed the animals. In Laos, we did animal calls to call the animals home. There was a different call for each animal."

At this point, she made a sound for each animal: cow, chicken, pig, horse. Amanda and I were fascinated. She asked us if we did any calling for our animals on The Land, and we told her we didn't. She said she should teach us these callings, and then she went over them again. Amanda repeated the callings and brought out her phone to record them. Mom was laughing and enjoying herself. I'd never before seen her so talkative and open among people who were not Hmong.

"After feeding the animals," she continued, "your dad would prepare the joss paper and fold paper money bars and other items for the altar." I explained to Amanda this was spiritual money that would be burned for the ancestors during the ritual tomorrow. They were sheets of natural fiber paper that were folded into the shape of a bar imitating ancient Chinese silver bars. As Mom continued her story, my sister-in-law had started to fold the paper money bars with Kaylie in the living room. I pointed them out to Amanda to show her what Mom was talking about. I asked Kaylie and Sister-in-law Cher to save a few so that after dinner we could teach Amanda how to fold them.

Dinner came to an end, and Amanda and I cleared the table. My nephew Ethan was assigned dishwashing duty while Amanda and I joined my sister-in-law and Kaylie in folding the last few money bars. Kaylie showed Amanda how to do it while my older nephew

Scott's son, Levi, who was two and had developed a crush on Amanda, was showing her his collection of dinosaurs. Amanda went to work like a natural, watching Kaylie fold and following what she did.

The paper was about five inches by seven inches, all gold with a one-inch-wide orange trim along the edges. It was very much like origami; one edge folding over the other then another and another and then you get a magically shaped object, in this case, a three-dimensional silver bar in the shape of a boat. Sister-in-law explained to Amanda that when these money bars are burned, they resemble gold bars in the spirit world. This is money for our ancestors so that they have something to live off of and can buy clothes and livestock in the spirit world. The spirit world is the same as the living world where our ancestors had land and livestock and farmed, where all our lineage families lived together in one village.

When the evening wound down and everyone had gone to their rooms, I got Amanda settled on the air mattress bed in the guest room, and I slept with Mom in her room. Tomorrow was going to be a big day.

Mom must have awakened around five in the morning to put away the previous night's dishes and make her morning herbal tea. I had set my alarm for six. I wanted to sleep longer but knew there was much to do. By the time I got to the kitchen, Mom already had two pots of water on the stove. I showered, dressed, and went to check on Amanda, who was awake and texting.

It wasn't long before Cher and Sister-in-law Cher appeared from upstairs. Tang and Sister-in-law Tang arrived shortly after that. Everyone knew what their role was and settled into their routines.

The weight of being a Hmong man in America lay heavy with the duties of culture, family, and traditions at odds with Western notions of wealth, achievement, and status. To be a Hmong American man meant straddling the wild bucking bronco of both worlds with the expectation of doing it with grace and poise. It was a high standard to achieve for any person.

I watched my brothers grapple with this delicate balance. They have excelled—becoming homeowners, nurturing bright and wonderful children, and faithfully participating in family traditions. While they may stumble over the precise recitation of Hmong chants, riddles, and proverbs, nevertheless, they understand the significance and can pass it on to their sons.

At the surface level, I see our men don their American personas like tight wetsuits, striving to be good citizens. However, it was during family events, such as celebrations or healing rituals, that I witnessed them step into their power and function like symphony conductors. When they worked together, it felt like being immersed in something ancient and mystical. Every nuance of their actions was instinctive, and they moved together with the rhythm of a flowing river. The *"lug paaj huam,"* flower poetry chants they recited at meal tables, resembled the call and response of Shakespearean rap. Throughout my childhood, I watched their choreographed movements at family rituals with fascination.

Tang headed to the garage to find Cher, who was making a different kind of traditional spirit money with a natural fiber paper that would later be burned as an offering to the ancestors. This type of spirit money resembles actual paper money in the spirit world. He piled four pieces of paper on top of one another and set them on a block of wood. In his left hand he held a steel stencil cutter in the shape of a C and in his right hand was a hammer. Cher then hit the stencil with the hammer twice. The stencil penetrated the sheets, making a cut through the papers. The cuts form a pattern that, when you pull the paper apart, become long thin strips that remind me of snowflakes. I'd grown up watching this New Year's ritual, and I loved the sound the stencil made when steel touched steel and made contact with the wood block below. The block showed the wear and tear of thousands of cuts made over the years. As I watched Cher's motions, I saw Dad's hands in his, confident and heavy with the lineage he is now tasked to pass on to Scott.

Tang traded places with Cher, who told him how many pieces of joss money he'd already made and how many more were left to do. Tang took the tools and started on the next piece. In ten or twelve years, he will be passing this job on to Liam, his four-year-old son.

Cher went out to the backyard, grabbed a live chicken, and carried it into the house. He stood in front of the altar with the chicken tucked under his left arm and addressed the ancestors.

"Great-grandfathers and great-grandmothers, Dad, and Uncle Xeng, today we celebrate a new year. I will be cleaning your house now so that you have a clean house to live in for the year. You may go outside to enjoy the day while I clean the house. I have a chicken here for you and I will let you know when to come back in for the *noj peb caug* feast."

Cher handed the chicken over to Sister-in-law Cher to take it back out to its cage in the backyard. A little later this chicken would be sacrificed and used for their meal. He then took down the items on the altar: three shot glasses of water, the little mound of uncooked rice grains, the rice bowl of incense, and the bull's horns. He took down the pieces of joss paper that hung on each of the three sides of the wooden slate that was held to the wall as the altar base, then took down the top joss paper, the sides, and the wall piece. Once all the joss paper was taken down, all that was left was a piece of wood shelf. He wiped down the naked wood on the wall. By itself it just looked like a twelve-by-twelve-inch shelf held up by two metal brackets that are normally hidden by the joss paper so that the shelf appears to be floating.

Amanda and I stood there and watched. I asked Cher and Sister-in-law Cher about the altar, and they responded in English so that Amanda would understand. In all the years I halfheartedly watched this ritual, I'd never asked about it. I watched it now as if for the first time. I don't recall Dad or brother telling the ancestors that he was cleaning their house. I don't remember the meticulous way the altar was taken down and rebuilt.

They told us that the altar is our ancestors' home. Just like in real life, every year at the New Year, we clean the house by taking out all the old joss paper, rice, and joss sticks and replenish them for the new year. It's fascinating how we really treat life in the spirit world the same as we do in the real world. There is no separation between the two. They said that the money Tang was now making and the paper bars we folded last night would be burned later as an offering so that they have money to buy animals and food in the spirit world.

Sister-in-law Cher explained that every person has three souls. One soul is next to you, the second is farther away but still close by, and the third ventures farther away, although whether she meant in terms of time or distance I'm not certain. This was much like the ancient Greek mythological belief that each person has a daemon outside their body that often guides and protects them.

"When you're sick," she continued, "it's because the soul farthest out probably got lost and didn't come back, so a soul-calling or a more serious ceremony with a shaman is performed to find your missing soul and bring it back."

She continued telling us that each soul, when born, has a story to live out. That story is written on your "paper" like a spirit contract, and when your contract ends, it is time for your soul to return home to the spirit world. Amanda listened intently with curiosity and acceptance.

Chong and Sister-in-law Chong arrived without their two kids, Maddie and Adam, who were sick with a cold. Throughout the day, we would be moving from Cher's house to Tang's, and finally to Chong's, repeating the same ritual at each brother's home and concluding with the final meal at Chong's.

While Cher was working on the altar and Tang on making the paper money, my sisters-in-law took out two big pots and filled them with water to prepare for the next part of the ritual. One pot was for boiling eggs and the other would be for boiling three chickens once they were sacrificed, plucked, and cleaned.

The kitchen became alive with activities. Mom was preparing the soul-calling ritual for Cher and his family. She filled a stainless steel bowl about three quarters with raw rice, put a dozen raw eggs on top of the rice, and put three joss sticks in the center. The eggs represented the souls of the family. During the ritual, when the souls return home, they are captured into the eggs, which would later be boiled and handed to each person to eat. She instructed me to light the joss sticks and carry the bowl to the front door. I set down the bowl and Mom brought out two chickens that had been kept in their little cage in the garage. Normally she would hold one of the chickens in her arm while she performed the ritual chant, but as she grew older, holding the chicken became more challenging, so she left both of them in the cage by the front door. She opened the door wide enough to stand at the threshold. Amanda and I stood outside, me with my phone in hand to record the ritual. Mom looked at my phone and laughed nervously, shaking her head and covering her mouth the way Hmong women do when they laugh.

"What are you doing? Don't record me. I'm not good at this."

"Of course you are, Mom! And anyway, it's just for me to remember this day."

"Don't show it to anyone. It's not good," she kept insisting, and I continued to reassure her that I wouldn't and that she was great. Mom is very modest, but she is actually proud of her skills. The next day, when I was back home with my friends, I called to tell her how much they appreciated the soul eggs she had boiled and packed for them, and she asked me if I had shown them the video of her chant. To which my response was, "Hey, you didn't want me to show anyone!"

She laughed at that and said, "Yes, yes, you can show them, but tell them I'm not good at it." That's how Mom is: modest and proud.

Mom took a moment to center herself and cleared her throat a few times. In her right hand were the split bullhorn used as a divination tool. Her body began to sway as she began to chant.

Today is a good day,
Tonight is a good night.
I call now, I don't call the illness, the sickness,
Not calling death.
I call now, I will call Cher and the whole family.
One whole year, twelve months have ended
It is the time of the New Year festival,
The night of festival has come
I will call Cher and the whole family to get up
Get up
I have chickens, eggs, incense, paper waiting
  for you
Get up!

I was able to catch a few words and phrases, but the words were in ancient metaphors that I didn't understand.

She told the souls there is chicken and money and food waiting for them. She called out to them, whether they are in the mountains or in the woods or the river, to get up and come home. Come home to this house with a fence and roof and food, where there is a mother and father and chickens to greet them. Get up and come home. She told the souls not to go into the mountains, not to go into the river, not to get distracted and wander off, but to stay on the road and follow the rooster and the chicken and come back home.

Almost each time Mom said get up and come home, the chickens in the cage fluttered around as if they could sense the souls nearby, or perhaps their own souls were out there looking for our family's souls and guiding them home. Once in a while Mom hit the flat end of the split bullhorn on the door frame while she continued to chant. Toward the end, her words became more stern, as though giving the souls a command: Wherever you are, get up right now and come home.

After about eight minutes, she bent over and dropped the bullhorn on the floor. The horns split and landed with one round side up and one flat side up. She continued her chant but the tone changed. Now it sounded like she was negotiating with the souls. She picked up the horn again and dropped it on the floor. She did this over and over until she got both flat sides facing down three times, the sign that the souls were home. She picked up both pieces of the horns and stopped her chanting, completing the ritual.

Amanda and I went back inside, and Mom told me to take the bowl of eggs into the kitchen to boil them, along with a few more, to make sure there were enough for everyone. These eggs now contained the souls of the family members and, once boiled, they would be handed out to eat, symbolizing that the soul was back in your body. She directed Chong to take the chickens she used at the front door out back to be sacrificed.

As I waited for the water to boil for the eggs, I glanced out the window and noticed my brothers had already started the sacrifice. Traditionally, this task fell to women, but my younger sisters-in-law preferred not to perform the neck slicing. Instead, my brothers handled the killing, while the women took over plucking and cleaning the birds.

A large, clear plastic tarp, roughly five feet square, lay on the ground. Positioned on the tarp were a soup bowl to collect the blood, a medium-sized sharp knife, and a large, empty stainless steel bowl for the chickens once they were dead. Adjacent to the tarp sat an empty bucket.

My brothers worked fast. Tang picked up one of the chickens, held its wings and feet together, and extended its neck. Cher put his thumb in the chicken's mouth under the tongue. With his right hand, he picked up the knife and, with one firm cut, sliced into the chicken's throat. Blood dripped into the bowl beneath while the chicken bucked and shook with all the strength left in its body. Tang held firm as I said a silent prayer of gratitude to the bird for trading its life for ours. In less than a minute, the chicken went limp and Tang put it down on a clean area of the plastic tarp. They continued with the other chickens.

Once they'd finished, they took the small bowl of blood and the knife back into the house and left the rest for the women to do. As the women situated themselves to prepare for the plucking, Mom used a sauce pot to scoop the boiling water from the huge pot that was on top of a propane tank into the empty bucket. She added some cold water from the garden hose so that the temperature was hot enough to loosen the chicken's feathers without scorching the skin. Mom took a chicken by the feet and dipped it in the bucket, then pulled it out and plucked some feathers to make sure they came off easily. Then she turned it the other way, holding it by the head and dipping its feet and legs into the bucket. Finally, she handed it over to Sister-in-law Tang, who started plucking it with quick, steady hands, being careful not to burn herself. Mom prepared the second chicken and handed it to me when it was ready, then worked on the third chicken.

I asked Amanda if she wanted to pluck the chicken. She nodded with curiosity. I went and grabbed a ground-level stool nearby and placed it across from me for her to sit. I showed her how to peel the skin off the feet first and how to snap off the nails. The feet and head are the hardest parts, so you peel them first when the chicken is still steaming from the hot water. Within minutes Amanda got into the groove of plucking the feathers. She worked quietly with Sister-in-law Tang and Mom while I watched.

Amanda told me how meditative it was to pluck the chicken. She was present and focused on the task in front of her, feeling the wet feathers, the skin, picking at the follicles. This was not a store-bought chicken from Whole Foods. This was a freshly killed chicken who had fulfilled its life purpose by guiding human souls back home and whose soul was now in the spirit world. Once it was boiled, it would bring us a message, letting us know if everyone's soul had made it home and if there were any bad omens or sickness coming in the new year.

Once all the main feathers were plucked, we needed to squeeze out any bits that were stuck in the follicles. I handed the chicken to Mom. She dipped the chicken in hot water again to rinse off the feathers and loosen the follicles. She handed it back to us. By this time Mom and Sister-in-law Tang were already done with their chickens. Sister-in-law Tang went back inside while Mom was slicing up both their chickens and cleaning the inside.

We put the chicken in a bowl of clean water to pick out any loose baby hair. We fussed around with the chicken for a while longer and then checked with Mom to be sure it was done. Once she approved, we left the chicken in the bowl for her to slice, gut, and clean the cavity.

Mom completed cleaning the chickens and took them inside. She instructed me to wrap up the feathers and guts in the tarp and throw it in the trash bin by the side of the house. I poured out the water into the garden for the plants. When we went back inside, I realized that in my haste to show Amanda the chicken sacrifice, I had forgotten all about the eggs. The pot was gone and there was already a big bowl of hard-boiled eggs.

"Oh, gosh, the eggs," I said out loud to no one in particular.

"I did them already," said Sister-in-law Chong.

"Sorry, I forgot about them."

"Don't worry. I saw the pot of boiling water and figured you forgot, so I did them."

Relieved that the eggs were done, and a little embarrassed that I had left them unattended, I thanked her, although no thanks were required. All Hmong women grew up with the same teachings, skills, and customs. A dish, a chore, an activity could easily be handed off from one woman to the next. We all have internalized the instruction manual for how to be a good Hmong daughter-in-law.

Once she'd finished cleaning the chickens, Mom put them in a big pot of boiling water and asked one of the sisters-in-law to watch over them while she continued with the ritual.

The next part of the ritual was to sweep away all the bad, negative spirits in the house. These are spirits that cause bad luck, cause you to be ill, to forget yourself. There were special bamboo branches with leaves used specifically for this purpose. Mom started to chant and, with a sweeping motion of the branch, moved through the house room by room, from the kitchen and living room up the stairs, through the three bedrooms and closets, the bathroom and TV room, then she came back down the stairs to sweep her room and bathroom and then out the front door. Sister-in-law Cher followed behind her with a broom and dustpan, sweeping up the bad energy and spirits into the dustpan. Once outside, Mom cast away the spirits. She left the bamboo branch outside leaning against a side wall, and Sister-in-law Cher also left the broom and dustpan. After three days, at the closing of the ceremony, they would burn the bamboo branch with some paper money and release the spirits.

When I was younger, I watched a Hmong movie made in Thailand in which a character was doing this, sweeping away evil spirits while another actor, who played the spirit, was running around the one-room house, ducking and jumping over the branch as it came toward him, trying to escape being touched. When the branch touched him, it would burn him. I remember thinking how silly the movie was. But that scene was actually helpful in visualizing what was happening in this moment.

I went back inside while Mom and Sister-in-law Cher finished up. Cher had put the altar back together, covering all three sides of the wooden platform with fresh joss paper. Each side of the paper had a big gold square in the center. The wall above the altar was covered with the same decorated piece of joss paper. There were chicken feathers glued to the left, middle, and right of the altar. The three cups of water were refreshed and put back up along with the bowl of raw rice with an egg sitting on top, and a clear mug filled with rice grains and three joss incense sticks. The incense is used to guide the spirits home. He lit them and the room filled with a sweet aroma. All the great-grandfathers and great-grandmothers and Dad and Uncle now had a new, cleaned and freshened home, and it was time to call them to the feast.

Cher set up a side table in front of the altar. Around the table were six empty chairs plus one for him. On the table was a bowl of cooked rice with six spoons around it. A bowl with fresh chicken lemongrass soup was placed next to the rice bowl. In front of Cher was an empty plate. He sat down and started the invitation, telling Dad, Uncle, and our grandparents and great-grandparents that we have prepared a feast for them to celebrate the new year. As he spoke, he took a small spoonful of rice and put it on the plate, followed by a little chicken broth. Then he shredded a bit of chicken and added it to the plate. For about ten minutes he continued inviting different relatives to the feast, asking them for their blessings for the new year, creating a mound of rice, chicken, and broth.

Amanda and I watched him, trying not to be obtrusive and make him self-conscious. A part of me was jealous that I was not allowed to learn these words, and a part of me also knew that I have my own part of the lineage to carry. In Hmong rituals, everything is always seeking the masculine and feminine, and in these rituals, the two come together to create an experience for everyone to be inside of.

As we watched Cher, his words were lost on me, but I understood their importance. I gave Amanda a general overview of what he was doing, and she nodded in understanding. When he came to the end of the ritual, he took the paper money he and Tang made earlier and put it into a pan on the floor next to the table to burn for Dad and the ancestors. This would be their money to buy clothes, food, and livestock for the year. Cher chanted the offering of money while the paper burned and evaporated into the spirit world. That completed the meal and offering for the ancestors. Cher took the plate of food into the kitchen and dumped the pan of ashes into the trash. Sister-in-law Cher helped put the empty chairs away, cleared and wiped the table, and put it back in its place by the couch in the living room.

The two chickens that Mom had used for the soul-calling ritual were now cooked and ready for the second part of the ceremony, the offering. Mom stacked a few hard-boiled eggs into a stainless steel bowl. She spooned some rice into a mound on top of the eggs to the side. She laid both chickens on top of the eggs, with the neck lowered down and head faced up, and feet sticking out the other end of the bowl. She lit three joss sticks, and put them in the bowl wedged between the eggs to hold them up. She grabbed her split horns.

She instructed me to carry the bowl over to a table that had been set up by the front door. She stood in front of the door and began the offering chant to the souls. The earlier chant had been calling the souls back home, telling them there was a warm meal with chicken and rice to eat, a warm bed for them to sleep in, and a mother and father, brothers and sisters to love them. Now Mom was offering the souls the chicken and rice to eat. The chanting took about ten minutes. Mom swayed back and forth saying the chant and coughing every once in a while. She looked deep in thought, entranced by the words coming out of her. Once she finished chanting, she instructed me to pick up the bowl again and take it to the kitchen.

Mom told me to give each person an egg. Eating the egg returns your soul to your body. I passed them around and took one for myself.

For most of my life I viewed the egg as just an egg, and for the last few years, I hadn't even been there to eat the egg at all. This year was significant. It was a year of coming home to myself, of reclaiming the parts I cut off, of trekking through the woods of my mind, navigating land mines, and finding ways to escape without triggering them. I learned to slow down and feel my way through the intricate labyrinth of a dark forest without stepping on buried explosives. When I did, I found ways to forgive myself, have compassion, and keep moving forward.

Mom was getting ready to read the chicken feet and tongue, so I brought Amanda over. Mom looked at the feet of both chickens. They were all curled up tight. She said those were good signs that everyone's soul is back home. Then she opened one of the chickens' mouths and pulled out the tongue. She cleaned it of any meat and revealed that the tongue was bent forward toward her. Then she pulled out the tongue of the second chicken and did the same thing. The tongue was also bent toward her. Both of these were signs that the year would be good without any trouble or illnesses in the family. She put the tongue back into the bowl with the chicken. Mom pulled out a plastic bag and slid one chicken in to take to Chong's house later to chop and cook for the feast. She instructed me to wrap up the other chicken with aluminum foil and put it in the refrigerator. This one would be used for a meal tomorrow. Normally, the chickens would get chopped up and put back into the pot to cook with tofu, but since we were cooking the final meal at Chong's place, we'd take it there to do it.

Each son has an altar for the ancestors, and Mom does all the soul-calling ceremonies. Dad used to be the person who did the soul-calling ceremony for each male household. After Dad died, my half-brothers did the ceremony for their own homes and for my brothers. Cher, Tang, and Chong hadn't learned the chants. Eventually Cher learned how to do the preparation and the altar chant and feast chant but not the soul-calling chant. The soul-calling chant was more complicated with words and riddles that we didn't know how to translate.

Tang and Sister-in-law Tang went home to start preparing for the ceremony at their house. Chong and Sister-in-law Chong soon followed. Meanwhile, the rest of us cleaned up the dishes and tidied up the kitchen before leaving.

At Tang's house, we repeated the same preparations we had just done at Cher's. Mom prepared the chickens to start the soul-calling ceremony at the door. Tang finished cleaning the altar, and Sister-in-law Tang put up the water for boiling the three chickens that would be sacrificed. When it came time for Tang to set up the table and chairs and invite Dad and our ancestors to eat the meal, Cher went over what to say and how to say it with both him and Chong. They joked about recording the words and just playing a tape while making the mound of rice, chicken, and broth. They laughed and continued repeating as Cher gave them the chant. The invocation involves much more sophisticated language than we are used to; *old language* is what we young ones call it, but for the elders it's simply Hmong.

Each ceremony brought me to a deeper understanding of the ritual. I began to flow through each one, anticipating and available for the next move. Even Amanda found herself at ease, going outside to watch the chicken-killing without me and getting close enough to take some pictures of the things that fascinated her. She went from observing to understanding to being part of the scene.

By the time we ended the ceremony at Chong's house, it was almost two in the afternoon—eight hours of ceremony with no break or food except toasted pita and decaf Nespresso earlier at Cher's house, and our soul eggs in between. By the end of the ceremony at Chong's house, I suddenly realized how hungry I was.

We finally sat down for lunch to celebrate the closing of the year and the beginning of the new year. It was a casual Hmonglish meal with rice, chicken soup with fresh tofu, barbecue ribs, sushi, noodles, and tossed salad. It was served buffet style. Amanda and I stood in line and helped ourselves, and I explained each dish that needed explaining to her. We sat at the communal table. She was at ease, enjoying the food and listening to conversations that were a combination of English and Hmong.

Mom sat to my left, telling me about the tofu and how Sister-in-law Chong had cut the pieces too big. They should have been smaller, she said, so that they cooked more thoroughly with the chicken and tasted softer and smoother. To my untrained tongue the tofu tasted just fine, but after she mentioned it, I bit into a piece and could taste what she was talking about. I kept that tip in mind and told Mom that maybe Sister-in-law Chong would do it right the next time.

I looked around the table at my brothers, their wives, and the children, all joyfully famished after a full day of preparations, ceremonies, cooking, and cleaning. Four generations of the Vang family at the table. *Each soul is home.*

Everything felt natural. We were following a design laid out thousands of years ago, connecting one generation to the next. The same blueprint that has guided the lives of Hmong families wherever they were in the world. In this singular, pitch-perfect moment, we were more than just a gathering of family; we were the living echo of an ancient tradition, connected by an invisible thread woven by Yer's unwavering devotion—a thread that anchored our souls and assured us that, no matter where life led us, we would always find our way back home.

Today is a good day,
Tonight is a good night.
I call now to the souls that have lost their way
To get up,
And come home.

Love,
Yiag Vaaj

ACKNOWLEDGMENTS

As a teenager, I dreamed of being a writer but feared I lacked the command of English to pursue it. I chose a different path, but the words kept waiting at my door until I was ready to let them in. I wouldn't have had the courage to do so without the following people.

To my ride-or-die sisters: Nicole Daedone, Rachael Hemsi, Rachel Pelletier, and Joanna Van Vleck. Thank you for believing in me until I could believe in myself, for reminding me that I carry something precious inside, worth protecting and sharing. Your unwavering, unconditional love has brought out my best and carried me through my worst. I wouldn't be this woman without each of you.

To everyone in the Eros Sangha: Your encouragement and constant reflections of my gifts kept me moving forward. Thank you for that steady support.

To Courtenay Lapovsky, my publishing manager and friend: Thank you for the pep talks, late-night texts, and the reminders to ask my spirit guides for help when I felt stuck. The space you held for me allowed my best work to flow onto the page.

To my senior editor, Beth Wareham: Thank you for pushing me to reveal more in my writing, for challenging my doubts, and for your relentless enthusiasm and belief in my voice. You brought out the courage in me.

To the team of editors at Soulmaker Press: Ira Silverberg, Ken Wapner, Gabrielle Meyers, and Judy Kern. Thank you for reading early versions of my manuscript, offering guidance, and encouraging me to keep going. You were the first professional eyes to see my writing, and your belief in me made this book possible.

To my brothers and sisters: Cher, Tang, Chong, Mai, Phou, Cha, Mary, Leah—thank you for your support and acceptance of my untraditional life. You are my home.

To my half-brothers, Khoua Neng, Yia Lue, Xong Chao, and my half-sisters, Chao, Yeng, and Bla—you kept Dad alive through your memories and the way you love me.

To my nephew Gung Chou Vang, our family historian—this book owes its richness to your knowledge and dedication to preserving our family's stories. The videos and pictures you provided gave life to these words.

Most of all, to Mom, Ntxawm Xyooj, Yer Xiong: Thank you for teaching me how to be a powerful woman through your silent strength. *Kuv zoo siab tias koj yog kuv nam*. I love you.

ABOUT THE AUTHOR

YIA VANG is the author of *In Yer's Kitchen: Memoir of a Hmong Daughter*. This is her debut book, which intertwines Eros philosophy with reflections on the journey of two women learning to see and honor each other as individuals through food and stories. Her writing explores universal themes of feminine power, identity, and connection distinct to a woman's way of being.

Yia was born in a refugee camp in Thailand after her family escaped persecution in Laos following the Secret War. She grew up pursuing the American dream, only to come full circle and rebegin where her roots are, realizing that is where home starts. Yia graduated with a BS in communication from the University of California, Davis. She dedicates her life to creating conditions for human flourishing. Through personal stories and a deeply subtle, nuanced view of womanhood, she invites readers to expand their ideas of intimacy and lineage.

ABOUT SOULMAKER PRESS

German philosopher Arthur Schopenhauer wrote that the truth comes in three stages: First, it is ridiculed. Second, it is violently opposed. And finally, it becomes self-evident. For those who can hear, truth in those early stages sounds like the whispering of the soul to itself. A relief, a resting place for the derided, the ostracized, the outsider.

Soulmaker Press is a full-service, privately held, international publisher, fostering avenues for writers and readers to explore new ideas in the space where intellect, science, the arts, and the mystical converge. We draw upon the writing and editorial talents of an international team to deliver the highest-quality reading experience, wherever books are sold.

Powered by Eros, in classical mythology the fundamental force in creation, our work is rooted in discovery and art, including works often considered taboo. We take special interest in the shadow, the unconscious, the creative process, and a feminine nonrational system of order. Precisely because it includes both the spirit and soul, the profound and the profane, emotions and the body, Eros offers a deeply needed perspective of unity that the world is sorely lacking. It's the magic that has been missing, and our books on spirituality, health and wellness, women, social reform, memoir, and science are intended to restore its intelligence to our lives.

Soulmaker Press is part of a greater initiative to reintegrate what's been cast out as unlovable. Initiatives include: breakthrough somatic modalities for healing trauma and expanding consciousness; rewilding land; creating programs for shifting prisons to monasteries that reintegrate the soul; prison gardens; and Free Food restaurants in San Francisco and New York City.